D0585243

The Victory Tests

The Victory Tests

England v Australia 1945

Mark Rowe

SPORTS
BOOKS

Published in Great Britain by
SportsBooks Limited
1 Evelyn Court
Malvern Road
Cheltenham
GL50 2JR

Cover designed by Alan Hunns.

A catalogue record for this book is available from
the British Library.

ISBN 9781899807 94 9

Printed and bound in England by TJ International.

Contents

In memory of Allan Duel
Born Banyo, Queensland, 1923
Rear gunner, 460 Squadron Royal Australian Air Force,
Binbrook, Lincolnshire, 1943–4
Killed in flying accident, near Burton upon Trent,
Staffordshire, June 5, 1944

For anyone to kill me he'd have to kill
every single Australian,
every single one of them,
every single one.

Ian Mudie, *They'll Tell You About Me*

Chapter One

Adelaide One

*I am not a specialist in the history of cricket. But its
pages are presumably studded with the names of those
who made centuries rather than of those who made
ducks and were left out of the side.*

EH Carr, *What is History?* (1961)

As Bradman batted on, and on, and *on*, that Monday,
March 2, 1936, Ross Stanford must have known he would
have only one chance. Stanford was waiting to bat at
number six for South Australia against Tasmania. He was
the lowest in the order, and the youngest, of three debut
batsman. South Australia could take the chance because
Tasmania were Australia's weakest state, not even in the
Sheffield Shield; and a week earlier South Australia had
won the shield, thrashing Victoria by an innings, even
though Donald Bradman had only scored one.

Tasmania made 158 all out. In reply Jack Badcock, the
opener, who had scored 325 in that previous win, was
soon out, but by the end of the first day South Australia
the hosts were well ahead, on 222 for two. Bradman,
ominously, was 127 not out. On the second day, Monday
March 2, one of the debutants, 20-year-old Ron Hamence,
turned his overnight 60 not out into 121. When his, the
third, wicket fell at 387, the other new boy, 18-year-old

Brian Leak went in and Stanford became next man, knowing he might have to face the ball after next. He had to wait for more than an hour. Tasmania had no hope of making South Australia bat again, so Stanford – the 18-year-old son of an Adelaide market gardener – would have only this innings to show what he was made of. At 533 the fourth wicket fell, that of Brian Leak. He had made only 19 in a stand of 146, so fast was Bradman scoring. Stanford walked to the middle to join the world's greatest batsman.

One of the many strange things about cricket is the definition of good and bad: what makes a debut good or bad, for example? The more runs or wickets, the better. Yet runs against bowlers as utterly beaten and exhausted as Tasmania's would not count for much. Even a big score, if made slowly or in a dull or fortunate manner, could harm a batsman's standing. Equally a small score, if made stylishly or ended by bad luck, could leave a man with some credit. Stanford, alas, could not have done worse if he had tried. He recalled in old age:

> *When I walked out to bat my knees were wobbling and I had double vision, I was so nervous. And he [Bradman] did the right thing, he knew I was nervous. He was batting when I went in. He had strike and he played about four shots for two, to get me running up and down the wicket, and then he let me have the wicket. I hit it straight to cover and called for a run and there was no hope of a run and he sent me back. I didn't know what I was doing, I didn't think.*

At least Stanford did not run out Don Bradman.

Two runs later, at 552, Bradman was out, caught and bowled, for 369. The applause of the crowd of 1,500 must have contrasted cruelly with the quiet or at best sympathetic reception for the failed teenager. South Australia batted on, to 688, and Tasmania went in again just before the end of the day. They were out again before the end of the third day, the end of the season, losing by a colossal – so colossal it was needlessly humiliating – innings and 349 runs. Stanford was no bowler, so he had no second chance to do anything. If anyone doubts how cruel sport can be, they can see in the Adelaide Oval museum a black and white photograph of the match scoreboard, showing the Don's 369 above Stanford's zero. Black and white, failure and success, were seldom so obvious. Stanford knew it: 'I didn't do any good,' he said.

If at first you don't succeed, try, try again, is an English saying. In Australia in cricket, as in life, if you do not do enough to keep your place, you soon lose it, to someone younger and more promising than yourself, who deserves the chance you once deserved. What happened next to those three young men on debut reflected how well each had done. Hamence had the most successful career, playing three Tests and touring England in 1948 as one of the Invincibles. Leak played a few more times for South Australia. Stanford was not picked the next season, nor the next, nor the next; then war came.

———————

At least for Stanford there were up to six batting places at which to aim – five if you count Bradman. Most teams only wanted one slow left-arm bowler like Reg Ellis, so at any step from club to state to country he could find his path blocked. South Australia was the home of the little leg-spinner Clarrie Grimmett, one of the world's most famous, though he was not picked for the Ashes tour to England in 1938. His fellow state leg-spinner Frank Ward went instead. Any hopeful South Australian slow bowler would have to step into a dead (or rather retired) man's shoes; and Grimmett was still going in his late 40s.

A man with cricket ambitions could move, as Grimmett had. Reg Ellis was one to stay put, despite all his wartime travelling. When aged 91, he was still living in the part of Adelaide in which he grew up, a mile or so from the sea.

> *When I was young I was a fast bowler. I played with the men up the road a little bit, at Morphett Vale at 14, and in between we used to just bowl at the wicket and I used to bowl down these googly balls and the captain a man called Jack Anderson said, 'Why don't you bowl spin?' I said, 'I don't know, I have never thought of it', and from then I bowled spin. We came down here to Port Noarlunga and they opened a new oval just over the other side of the river and brought the Sturt cricket team of which Vic Richardson was captain and we played them and nearly beat them. I got five wickets in that game and he invited me down to Adelaide and I started in the Bs. I played five matches in the B grade and got five wickets in each innings, 25 wickets in five matches, and got posted up to A grade and I played for senior colts then, that was an A grade team of all young fellers. I topped the bowling aggregate that year, that's how I got into the team but by that time there was Grimmett and Ward playing for Sturt, two Test bowlers, and I had no chance of getting into the team without they gave up.*

What competition – two Test bowlers at your local club! Yet cricket in Australia's state capital cities – the same applied in Melbourne, Sydney and Brisbane – thrived because the great men, like Vic Richardson, a Test batsman, took an interest in young talent, as Reg's story shows.

*And Grimmett was captain of the colts team – that's
why I got all the gen there. We had a piece on the pitch
like a two shilling piece, a little shiny piece on the pitch,
over after over trying to hit that on good length. That's
how he got me into bowling on a good length all the
time. I never changed the grip on the ball, I had my
hands around the seam all the time.*

Ellis learned three balls: each depending on where the
hand was facing when letting the ball go. If facing the
batsman it was a leg break for a left hander. Side on was a
top spinner, and out of the top of the hand was a googly.
'The best ball of them all was the top spinner because it
used to gain speed off the pitch. That was my instruction
from Grimmett. He never changed grip either, never ever,
always around the seam. So that the seam hit when it hit
the pitch. It's all in accuracy. The more accurate you are
the better and once you can turn the ball three ways and
you are accurate with it, well, it's got to be good. You got
to set your field accordingly.'

The older, wiser Grimmett taught the slow bowler's
philosophy besides. Whether you did badly, or well,
some would never quite appreciate your skill. There is
a story about arguably the most famous slow ball ever –
the one by Eric Hollies that bowled Bradman for a duck
in his last Test in 1948. Hollies said: 'Look at them. All
cheering for the batsman and not one for the bowler.'
That said, to accept your lot or to be merely patient could
be dangerous. When a batsman went after you, you had
to *think*. Fast, as Reg Ellis said:

*Hard to say, you just did what you thought would stop
them. Bowl fast, slower ball, yorkers to them, depends
how they attack you. Sometimes you got hit around and
sometimes you didn't, but that's all part of the game.*

You did your best. That came easy for an Australian lad, born in the Barossa valley in 1917, whose family moved to Port Noarlunga when he was aged seven. It was an outdoor and beach life, cool in winter, hot and dry in summer. Lads sunbathed in their spare time on the jetty; only later would they know they had given themselves skin cancers.

My father bought a vineyard, a full section, 80 acres. But unfortunately my father was a bad alcoholic and a gambler and we lost the lot. Oh, he used to stay away from home for a fortnight sometimes and we never saw him ... That meant I didn't drink, I made sure I wasn't going to drink in my life and I never have, and I have kept fit all my life. Had a brother, he turned alcoholic too, he was like [Keith] Miller, didn't care a hang.

It was hard for a while; Reg worked pruning vines. He married: 'We had £5 after we paid for everything and we went to Whyalla; ship-building had just started and anybody could get a job at Whyalla.' They lived on the beach in a tent for about nine months, not because of poverty but because the growing town did not have enough houses. 'I worked as a navvy with a shovel from eight to four then with a truck. I had two jobs.'

He was also making his name in cricket. In October 1939, he bowled alongside Grimmett for a South Australia Cricket Association team, captained by Bradman. This early-season tour into the bush was one more way of seeking and bringing on talented youth. Grimmett and Ward were still the state's two slow bowlers that season; Reg Ellis was in line. He had already volunteered for the air force. He thought of becoming a wireless operator; or, when he began training to be a pilot, a fighter pilot. The air force, as it often did, had other ideas.

Chapter Two

Lord's, May 21 1945

The applause of a single human being is of great consequence.
James Boswell, *The Life of Samuel Johnson*

They began to queue outside Lord's at 6 am, and not only Englishmen. Australian soldiers in slouch hats, freed from prison camps weeks or days before, were there 'to cheer on their heroes', so the London *Evening Standard* put it later that day. Australia began the second day of the first Victory Test, Monday, May 21, well placed, on 82 for two in reply to England's 267. Lindsay Hassett, the captain, was not out 27, the nightwatchman and wicket-keeper Stan Sismey not out 11. They were able to wait for the short ball to pull during a mixed spell by the leg-spinner Doug Wright. Hassett gave a chance off Wright, and Bill Edrich at short leg dived full length like a goalkeeper, got his hand to the ball but could not hold it. Hassett and Sismey added 84 until both men rather gave their wickets away. Sismey from some reports had little chance; a short-pitched ball from Edrich kicked badly; Sismey raised his bat in the way, for protection, it seemed, and off the handle went a dolly catch to Wright nearby, at short leg.

Then Hassett, 'well set for a century', according to the *Daily Telegraph*, lost his off stump on 77. He lifted his head to a good length ball from John Stephenson, who had finished the war as a Lt-Colonel with a DSO and a mention in despatches, trying to hit him out of the ground.

That left Australia 171 for four, and gave England a chance of gaining a small lead on first innings. Walking out to join Keith Miller, Australia's most exciting batsman, was Ross Stanford, Australia's last batsman before the all-rounders and bowlers.

Miller found 'a capital partner' in Stanford. The pair were complete masters of the situation, so the *Daily Telegraph* reported. They began quietly, most of their strokes going behind the wicket; and they saw off Walter Robins, who had the spinner's traditional couple of overs before lunch. After lunching at 196 for four, Miller 21 not out, the two air force pilots batted in light rain for ten minutes before Miller appealed successfully. The stop for rain may have helped Australia; on their return Stanford snicked Stephenson but Edrich at second slip could not hold the greasy ball.

By late afternoon the bowlers were tiring. Alf Gover for instance had been at his fastest the evening before when he soon bowled James Workman. He had a spell of half an hour of venom from the pavilion end in the morning, but became slower and looser.

Stanford recalled:

> *One of the great disappointments of my life was to not get 50 in that particular innings, one of the best innings I played, because I hit every ball in the middle of the bat that day, for some reason – stumped on the leg side. Jack, JWA, Stephenson, Lieutenant-Colonel in the Army. Bill Griffith was wicket-keeper; he was later secretary of the MCC.*

It was, the *Telegraph* commented, 'a brilliant bit of stumping on the leg side by Griffith'. Stanford had helped put on 99 in 90 minutes. From 270 for five, another hard-hitting all-rounder, Cec Pepper, added 87 for the sixth wicket with Miller.

Bob Crisp, the former South Africa Test fast bowler, a Second World War decorated tank commander, veteran of Greece, North Africa and Normandy, and now a staff reporter on the *Daily Express*, wrote: 'At 5.30pm the members' bar had run out of beer due I think to the Australian celebration of Miller's hundred.'

Three wickets did fall for nine runs: Pepper was caught behind off Stephenson, Albert Cheetham was out for a duck, giving Wright his first wicket on a long day; and Miller was caught for 105. Some felt that Miller never looked comfortable against Wright and that he gave a very hard chance, to Wright, at short leg off Gover on 33. Miller was in the 90s for three-quarters of an hour before he reached his hundred in three and a half hours. Unusually for Miller he hit only six fours.

The *Telegraph's* verdict was: 'Instead of a carefree aggressive batsman with a partiality for the full blooded drive we had known him to be last year, he showed a restraint hitherto unsuspected yet he was always attractive to watch.'

That left Australia at 366 for eight. For England, already well behind, the worst was yet to come.

In the words of the *Daily Telegraph*: 'Williams received an ovation on coming out to bat and he and Price pleased the crowd hugely in the closing stages by lashing out at the tired bowling. They rubbed it in to the extent of 88 runs in three-quarters of an hour.' While Bob Crisp suggested that Hassett might have declared an hour earlier, to bowl at the English, surely Australia were wiser to show who was boss. Graham Williams hit 11 fours in his 53; Charles Price hit Wright into the pavilion for the only six of the day. The day closed with both men out caught and Australia 455 all out, a lead of 188.

Australia had not won the match, but they had beyond doubt won the first two days. England could at best only hope to save the game on the third and final day, Monday, after the Sunday rest day.

By the Monday, the newspapers were already judging the two sides. It was, as they saw it, not only the fact that Australia made more runs; it was the way they did it. *The Times* complained: 'At the end of the day England's bowling was so enfeebled that RG Williams and CF Price scored runs with an almost impertinent liberty. We expect Australia to bat to the bottom of the batting order but surely not so easily as this.'

The *Daily Telegraph* pointed to the 40-minute break in the early afternoon for a shower. 'The England bowlers were handicapped for a while by the wet ball. But that is not offered as an excuse. In reality the Australians outplayed us.'

The Manchester Guardian agreed. It reckoned England's biggest peacetime cricket problem, 'the dearth of Test match bowlers was fully exposed by the Australian batsmen at Lord's ... the truth is that England has had no opportunity yet to replace Verity and Farnes, both killed in the war or WE Bowes only recently returned from a German prison camp'.

Talking of former prisoners of war, the Australians had picked one, Graham Williams, only back in England for a couple of weeks. Some newspapers picked up the story; some did not, presumably for lack of space – the *Telegraph* in particular printed only a fairly long match report because the type was of magnifying-glass tininess. The *Guardian* reported: 'The crowd welcomed the former prisoner of war Williams by cheering him all the way to the crease and he enjoyed himself.'

That scene stayed in Keith Miller's mind and if anything became more important with age, a story with meaning, one to go over again and again, as some old people do. It was a story that spoke too to people like the Australian cricketer then broadcaster Richie Benaud, who first looked to the older Miller as a hero, then as a teammate, a mentor, and a friend. Benaud told the story, in full, in his own autobiography, *Anything But*, in 1998, and again in his obituary of Miller in the 2005 edition of *Wisden*. Besides the beauty of the story, there was something touching about a man as charismatic and famed as Miller feeling so deeply about someone far less famous entering an arena. Stan Sismey said in 1999:

> *Yes, Keith Miller and I were both agreed on that, and he [Williams] was a tall, thin chap. When he went out at Lord's the crowds rose unanimously and gave him a magnificent reception. It's one of the most emotional things I have ever experienced on a cricket field. Keith and I often talk about that moment.*

The emotion was two fold: the sight of the tall, gaunt man, thinned by years in German captivity; and the emotional response of the crowd, that plainly evoked a lasting response in Miller. He told Benaud: 'It was the most touching thing I have ever seen or heard, almost orchestral in its sound and feeling. Whenever I think of it, tears still come to my eyes.' It became a touchstone of what the Victory Test series, and the war, meant to Miller; it was something never to be bettered, with all that meant, including the bittersweet side that nothing else, no achievement, would ever match that sublime moment.

That 49 by Ross Stanford, though hardly as significant, turned out to be his best score of the Victory series. He did not even play in the next 'Test'. It was not something of which he made a big deal; he volunteered to make way for another returning prisoner of war, the batsman and

RAAF captain Keith Carmody. The Victory Test summer brought out the best in players and watchers alike.

What had happened to make such great occasions possible? What was the journey – not only in miles, from one end of the earth to the other, but in experience – of Ross Stanford, Reg Ellis, and their fellow Australians?

Chapter Three

Lichfield, Staffordshire, Wartime

They were in fact – and they knew it – faced with the virtual certainty of death, probably in one of its least pleasant forms.

Sir Arthur Harris in the foreword to
Guy Gibson's *Enemy Coast Ahead* (1946)

They were an unlikely pair. Corporal Blagg was 'a bowler in the Bassetlaw League', from Shireoaks, a mining part of Nottinghamshire; and Leading Aircraftsman Ross 'played for Central Coast, Gloucester, New South Wales', according to the local newspaper, the *Lichfield Mercury*. Their team was unlikely too. The *Mercury* was not allowed even to print its name, because to say that the airfield – RAF Lichfield – was in the area might aid the enemy. Blagg and Ross were the star all-rounders in a mixed English and Australian team sent from the aerodrome, a couple of miles outside the city, to compete in the midsummer evening Chauntry Cup.

Blagg was one of the hundreds of ground crew, mechanics and others who looked after the aircraft – in Lichfield's case, Wellington bombers, already worn out from front-line missions. Ross may have been a mechanic, a trainee airman or an instructor. RAF Lichfield in air force jargon was 27 OTU – an operational training unit.

It took in mainly Australian pilots, navigators, bomb-aimers, wireless operators and gunners who a few months later left as crews who had learned how to fly a bomber, together. Even before those crews reached a front-line squadron, their life could be dangerous, and short; the nearest village churchyard at Fradley already had rows of the remains of crashed crews.

RAF Lichfield did not enter a team in the 1941 cup, because the base was built only that year. Bomber Command training units had little time to spare in the summer; the pressure went down the ranks, from the top: push crews, during the better weather, on to the front-line squadrons. Crews were dying over Germany as quickly as new ones joined.

RAF Lichfield never slept. As soon as crews learned how to fly by day, they began flying by night. Yet every man needed some rest, as the station commanders understood. The job of putting 11 working men onto the right cricket field, on the right weekday evening, was no different from peacetime. Many of the teams in the cup competition before the war – workplaces such as Cannock Chase Colliery and Burntwood Mental Hospital, and villages three or six miles away – could not spare the time or could not find fuel for the couple of cars to take the players there and back.

The 25-over-a-side Chauntry Cup was much like other midweek evening cricket before or since. A team could get by with four or five, or even fewer, stars. A natural sportsman like Ted Blagg – a Nottingham Forest footballer who was a wartime cricket professional for Longton in the nearby North Staffordshire League – was far too good, almost unfairly so, for the mainly occasional cricketers he faced. In the 1942 final, on Friday, August 7, when RAF Lichfield beat the local rugby club, Blagg and Ross bowled unchanged and batted at three and four.

The scene when Pilot Officer Page accepted the trophy must have been familiar to peacetime cricketers too: the official speakers who always go on too long; the winning players not minding too much, because they still feel the glow of victory, even as the shadow of the pavilion lengthens or goes altogether. As the dusk turned cold on the city's edge, and the three spires of the cathedral in the mid-distance faded – a landmark for many grateful weary fliers – the very English scene may have made the Australians think how far from home they were.

The Lichfield cricket club chairman Councillor John Haworth, giver of the cup, spoke warmly to the visitors. He said that when they started the competition, they had little hope of ever bringing people from Australia to play in it. They did not of course expect Bradman, but the next best thing had come in the form of young Australian fliers. He hoped that when they went home they would remember that match. And they were very sorry that they were unable to present miniature replica cups as they did to all the finalists before the war. (Metal like everything else was short in the war, and had to go on bombers before sports trophies.)

Mr Haworth probably did not know it, but it is fairly likely that Bradman *would* have been there that night, had Bradman not dodged the war so well. He was quite old to be an airman – he was about to turn 34 – but a teammate, South Australia's wicket-keeper Charlie Walker, was only six months younger, and he died over Germany in 1942.

The fact is that many of those who volunteered for the air force, like Bradman, found themselves within a couple of years on their way to Bomber Command in Britain;

15

and many passed through Lichfield. We can speculate whether Bradman would have avoided cricket, preferring to concentrate on his studies; or if the urge to make runs, and the wish to please his hosts, would have been too strong. Certainly Lichfield was a likelier destination than the path Bradman did take: into the army on the PT, physical training, side ('a physical culture expert down in Victoria', sneered Miller later); invalided out with what friendly biographers such as Charles Williams have called 'an acute muscular condition', and onto the front line of Adelaide Stock Exchange. Conveniently Bradman felt well enough after the war to score eight Test centuries and to live to 92.

Not just in Lichfield, but wherever in Britain the Australian airmen went, they made a stir. Their exotic accents were exciting. That they had come halfway around the world, to fight for the Mother Country, was flattering. How did these Australian airmen, who never numbered more than a few thousand, excel so at cricket? Another way of putting it: why was England, with about six times as many people, so unable to beat Australia at cricket? As a South African, writing in the leading mass market newspaper of the era – Bob Crisp in the *Daily Express* – put it bluntly during the first Victory Test: 'There are about 20,000 Australian servicemen in England. Many are returned prisoners of war unfit for violent exercise. From the remaining handful the Australians have fielded a team which completely mastered the English bowling yesterday.' The year 1945 was not the first nor the last time that Englishmen would wonder aloud why they were so weak, or Australia so strong – which were not quite the same things.

It was an easy mistake, to think of the airmen passing through as typical Australians. They were in many ways a moral and physical elite. They were young; some finished their 'tour of operations', typically of 30 missions, before they turned 21. Fighting men had never had such long and expensive training lavished on them – the pilots and navigators, at least. Ross Stanford was typical; he enlisted in his native Adelaide in July 1941, yet did not reach a front-line squadron for two years. In between came basic training in Australia, or Canada, where the pilots gained their 'wings', as sewn on their dark blue uniforms; another ocean crossing by ship; more flying in Britain to get used to European weather, then crewing up at OTU; the first flights at HCU (Heavy Conversion Unit) in the sort of 'heavy', four-engine bomber they would fly missions in; only then the front line, where they might die on their first mission.

They had to be agile and intelligent. While they came from all ranks of society, many were office workers, or garage hands, or farmers' sons; men with something about them. Navigators had to grasp mathematics; wireless operators had to send, and read, Morse code. Pilots had to make quick decisions – the right ones – and sometimes call on bull-like strength to master the cockpit controls. All air crew – even gunners who, you could say, only had to shoot straight and stay awake – had to pass eyesight and hearing tests; and had to have good teeth, even. Toothache in a cold aircraft at 20,000 feet would be unbearable. You did not have to be athletic and handsome to be an Australian airman in wartime England; but many of them were.

Plenty of remarkable airmen died, the same as the unremarkable. For all Bomber Command, including the one in eight Australians who made up that international force, roughly half the airmen died or, if shot down, became prisoners of war. That included the last months of the war when missions became easier. For much of the war, to survive a 'full tour', and return to a training unit as an instructor, was against the odds, even freakish. So it was for Don Charlwood, a navigator who trained at RAF Lichfield in 1942 and returned in 1943 after months of operations. In his memoir *No Moon Tonight* he soon saw that behind a door marked by his fellow navigator-instructors with the nonsense name 'Kelly's Brickyard' was a madhouse:

> *In a room perhaps 15 feet by 12, a cricket match was in progress accompanied by intense barracking. Batting was a diminutive flight lieutenant who wore a DFC. He stood about three feet from a wall bearing a large map of England. Bowling was a man as large as the batsman was small. The ball sped down the short room and was cut neatly among paper and inkwells.*
> *'A four to Campbell,' shouted a man beside us. 'A beautiful square cut. And now Kobelke takes the ball again and goes back for his run.'*
> *The crash of the ball hitting the stove drowned the commentary. Next I heard, 'This broadcast is coming to you from the Brisbane Cricket Ground. Your commentator is none other than the Great O'Shea.'*

Someone then spotted Charlwood had come in with their commanding officer; and they fell silent. They were not the only men who have used their freedom to turn a workplace or schoolroom into a little world of sporting fantasy; and their commanders left these veterans to it, knowing what the men had gone through. As Charlwood noted, the veterans did lunatic pranks, not used yet to life after combat. But they still did their work; and they relished their cricket.

In the 1943 Chauntry Cup, RAF Lichfield crushed civilian and military teams alike. In the first round at the end of June, 'OTU RAF' (still not named in the *Lichfield Mercury* because of self-censorship) made 214 for four, in 20 overs, a competition record. Flight Lieutenant Keith Campbell top-scored with 38 and a man identified by the newspaper only as Stanford made 34. That *might* have been Ross Stanford. The timing fits; if it was him, he would have been a trainee pilot passing through. Blagg then took six wickets as an opposing team of bomb inspectors were all out for 19.

In the second round a fortnight later, Campbell and Stanford did not feature – 'of course you couldn't just get leave when you wanted to so it wasn't easy to select a side', Campbell recalled in 1998. No matter; the unit knocked up 108 for nine and bowled out Civil Defence for 49. The semi-final intriguingly pitched the separate but neighbouring 'MU' (maintenance unit) of aircraft repairers at RAF Lichfield versus the OTU. Wartime newspapers were always short of room; for whatever reason, no match report made it to print. We know only that the Australian-English OTU won, because they contested the final, again against Lichfield Rugby Club. Each finalist played two innings, the first on Tuesday August 3 and the second the following evening. By wartime cathedral city standards, it was some occasion: the band of the South Staffordshire Regiment played the first evening, an American Army band from nearby barracks the next.

On the first night, RAF Lichfield won the toss and took first knock. Campbell ran out another of the main players,

Page the captain, but they made the useful total of 147 for six. The rugby club replied with 99. On the last night, the rugby club batting again made 105, leaving the airmen only 57 to win. Page made 48 out of 68, as the airmen narrowly won and batted out their overs to entertain the crowd. Campbell captained RAF Lichfield the following Wednesday in a challenge game against the 'pick of the rest'. The *Mercury* described Campbell gushingly as batting left-handed 'with his usual zest, neatly cutting, glancing and powerfully driving anything off the wicket'. He was bowled for 34 by one that kept low. The airmen made 97 for seven and the 'pick of the rest' won by six wickets in the last over.

So much for the distractions from life on a training airfield; Keith Campbell had tastes of cricket on a greater stage. He played in a two-day match for the Royal Australian Air Force (RAAF) against the South of England at Hove on July 17 and 18. The RAAF scored 331 (Keith Carmody top scoring with 137) and three without loss; the South, including future names such as Eric Bedser and Trevor Bailey, scored 117 and 215, losing by ten wickets. Campbell batting at four was out for a duck; Keith Miller at three made 23.

Also in that team, and in Campbell's former squadron, was Alex Barras. A West Australian, a left-handed batsman who played for his state a few times before and after the war, he also played for the RAAF against Sir Pelham Warner's XI at Lord's in June 1943. Campbell recalled how in 1942 their squadron had gone to North Africa, to help shore up the faltering Eighth Army:

Alex's crew of five were shot down at night in their Wellington bomber over Tobruk, in July '42. He alone survived the crash and found himself 500-plus miles from the British lines, with desert sands all the way in between. The African coast was then alive with Rommel forces. To avoid capture, Alex courageously decided to walk directly south, into the desert. Some time later he accosted a group of Bedouin Arabs and produced our 'lifeline letter', which we all carried, offering Arabs handsome British government compensation, should they safely return us to Allied lines. Alex, dressed as an Arab, was then to walk 500 miles across the desert to freedom, taking six weeks. His comment was, 'If you think a camel walks quickly, try walking behind one for six weeks.'

For this feat Barras gained the Military Medal, an unusual award for an airman.

Keith Campbell next played for the RAAF at Maidstone on August 14 against a New Zealand Services team, that won by 79 runs on first innings. The New Zealanders scored 177 and 53 for nine; the RAAF made 98 (Ross Stanford top scoring with 28) and 65 for six. Keith Campbell made nought and 10. Keith Campbell's lack of runs, he felt in 1998, was not so much due to lack of ability, but lack of practice: 'I hadn't had a bat in my hand for three and a half years, I didn't even know what a bat felt like.' Cricket clothing, too, was hard to find in a country making weapons not whites. Keith Campbell recalled in these early games that Keith Miller always arrived only with his boots, 'and it was a case of finding a shirt and trousers. The latter were always half mast.'

A century earlier the original Campbell, one of Queensland's first free settlers, had gone inland by bullock-wagon to become a blacksmith in the town of Ipswich. As a teenager Keith Campbell had made the return journey by train to play A-grade cricket as a junior member of Queensland Colts. The idea was to bring on youths (like Reg Ellis in Adelaide) under senior men. Bill Brown was captain and Don Tallon vice-captain, both later members of Bradman's 1948 Invincibles.

In old age Keith Campbell spoke of his wartime cricket with wonder, delighting in what he did experience, rather than wishing he had done better.

> *To be able to soak up a bit of the atmosphere at Lord's. That was something I won't forget. I was a reserve for the Dominions with Learie Constantine and we played an English team and I was 13th man, not even 12th man. With the Dominions side they had people like Constantine and the Bedsers and all the old .... Ames, these people, wonderful names for me.*

And in the last game of 1943 at Lord's, the Royal Air Force scored 105 for nine (Miller taking three for 23) and 41 for three; the RAAF won by three wickets, scoring 164 for eight (Miller 91, wicket-keeper Stan Sismey 34 not out). Keith Campbell recalled his one innings at Lord's:

> *I made a duck, I can tell you. I had the privilege of walking through the Long Room and down through the crowd and out to the middle. Two overs later I was walking back. It's a longer walk back, I found. My rear gunner was sitting at the gate as you go out and when I looked out to get my bearings all he could do was shake his head in disgust. Of course Lord's is a great spot, a small ground, compared to our grounds, so steeped in history; wonderful.*

The authorities sent Campbell home to Australia in September 1943, so his RAAF cricket ended there. The heart of the Australian Victory team of 1945, meanwhile, was already in place, both in terms of personnel and spirit.

Lichfield, Staffordshire, Wartime

Campbell knew that he had failed at Lord's. He chose, as a typical Bomber Command veteran, to cherish what he had done, rather than regret anything. He summed up: 'It was a great feeling to feel the old bat in my hand and get to these grounds you had read about and heard about. Unfortunately I didn't make enough [runs].'

Chapter Four

No Mere Gladiators; the summers of 1943 and 1944

Australia! That word will always sound good to me.
General Montgomery, in *By Bomber to Britain* by
WR McDonald (1944)

No-one would begrudge men so lucky to survive combat as Alex Barras MM and Keith Campbell DFC a day at Lord's. But why allow something as frivolous as cricket in the middle of a world war; and why did the Royal Australian Air Force run a cricket team?

Everyone agreed that cricket was good for the character. But you could say the same about growing vegetables, or fishing, both more useful than cricket. Indeed, you could claim that by playing or watching cricket, you were wasting time. In his post-war memoir the 1930s Surrey captain ERT Holmes said he played a few times in the war but was 'never happy about accepting': 'I felt it was rather like going on a picnic while your home was on fire.' Nor did Wally Hammond, the star attraction, feel quite happy about wartime cricket games: 'There was always a sense of unreality and absent-mindedness about them.'

Yes, cricket was good recreation, for watchers and players. A few hours snatched from reality could refresh people to go to work and war again, except you could have recreation by digging an allotment, or sitting in a pub; as many did.

Much quoted since is a wartime secretary of Lord's, Sir Pelham Warner, from his 1946 history of the ground: '... if Goebbels had been able to broadcast that the War had stopped cricket at Lord's it would have been valuable propaganda for the Germans.' Or, as Warner chose not to put it: playing cricket at Lord's was good British propaganda.

Cricket, then, was part of the British war effort; it set us apart from the Nazis. But what made it the business of the RAAF?

The Australian commanders were only copying everyone else. In civil defence, the police, Army, Royal Navy and Royal Air Force, even Home Guard units, some commanders who were cricket enthusiasts ran their own teams. The nature of war meant that ever more men were not fighting in the front line, but in support units. Ground crew mechanics did their shifts, and airmen risked their lives on missions; who could then call at their local for a pint, or the village green for a game, the same as a civilian. While waiting for orders – the lot of every man in uniform – to have a knockabout was welcome, to take your mind off the fact that in a few days, or hours, you wouldn't necessarily be alive. Norman Corbett was a footballer – good enough to play just before the war in the same Wolverhampton Wanderers reserve team as future England captain Billy Wright – who gave up his factory job to volunteer for air crew. He became a wireless operator in a mixed Australian-English crew at RAF Lichfield in 1943, and went to the Australian bomber 467 Squadron, his time at RAF Waddington near Lincoln briefly overlapping with Ross Stanford. He recalled:

*You would be out on the tarmac in front of a big hangar.
There would be 30 or 40 standing about talking. All of
a sudden someone would produce a football or a cricket
bat and ball and you would have 40 or 50 players
playing games.*

This did not explain *organised* Australian teams.
Norman's story holds a clue. Though his crewmates
gave him the nickname Cobber, and the men of all
nationalities had deep – and lifelong – comradeship,
his Australian squadron was not all-Australian. Some
in command did not mind – to win the war mattered.
Some did mind. Aussie sticking up for Aussie was
partly practical – it kept their countrymen together
in units. Making a fuss helped Australians gain the
higher ranks and medals they deserved. Chaplains and
medics looked after welfare. Partly, putting Aussies
first – the work of press officers and photographers
– was symbolic, so their country had credit for how
hard it was fighting. A cricket team, again, was good
propaganda. Whenever Australians played at Lord's,
they were in effect telling the world that they were
fighting for what Lord's stood for.

In the homeland of cricket, the game was useful
propaganda, and part of the scenery. Hence when the
Brisbane newspaperman WR McDonald visited England
in the spring of 1944 and back home wrote a book about
it – *By Bomber to Britain* – cricket was one of the subjects,
to prove that all was well. As a guest of the Ministry of
Information McDonald met some important people – at
Bomber Command headquarters, Air Chief Marshal Sir
Arthur Harris told him there was no airman better than
an Australian. He sampled the sights of London with a
couple of RAAF 'boys' – the London Philharmonic, the
speakers at Hyde Park Corner, and a curry at an Indian

restaurant off Piccadilly. And the RAAF versus the RAF at Lord's, on May 20:

> *Glorious sunshine – a great crowd … It was a remarkable picture – the rich green of the playing area, the white flannelled players, the big crowd, and overhead the balloons with their wires running to earth to keep off the enemy dive-bombers.*

Though McDonald was overdoing it – London had not seen *dive*-bombers for years, if ever – his hosts at the Ministry of Information would have been pleased with the message. Britain was defiant; Australia was part of the team.

The RAAF in Britain began its *official* cricketing side in the spring of 1943 when it sent a circular to RAF stations asking for first-grade cricketers (the level below states) to give their names and records. Hundreds replied. Going by players' history, invitations to a trial early in May at Dulwich Cricket Club followed.

It's impossible to say when wartime cricket began. Australian soldiers in southern England in case of invasion in the summer of 1940 must have played before they sailed to Egypt. The 1942 season at Lord's ended in mid-September with a match between the RAAF and a Royal Air Force team from one (unnamed) station only. Earlier in the season they had a game on the Nursery ground. The Australians, according to *The Times*, wore (air force) blue rather than 'menacing green' caps. One-sidedly, the Australians made 236, to 59; and took 'amazing acrobatic catches'.

How to make sure that new and unknown teams were fairly equally matched was the added difficulty for wartime organisers of cricket, besides the 22 men catching their trains to the right place. Every organiser, naturally, wanted the best men. (Perhaps the most unlikely invited player was in RAAF 454 Squadron's team in northern Italy at war's end. Harry Davis, a newly-ordained priest, had left Sydney for Rome in 1936. 'Padre Davis' took five wickets in each of two knockout games against other squadrons. Had he picked up the game after all those years? Or had he turned his arm over in the Vatican?)

Australian teams could find themselves as outclassed as anyone else. Take the 'Warwickshire Festival XI' against the RAAF at Edgbaston in August 1943. Eric Hollies took seven wickets in 6.1 overs as the Australians were all out for 115. Only their opening pair, the captain the Rev TD Beyer with 24 and Flight Sergeant P Speakman with 53, made double figures. Then four English county batsmen – Charlie Elliott of Derbyshire, John Langridge of Sussex, former England captain Bob Wyatt and George Heane of Nottinghamshire – thrashed 246 off 31.5 overs. Batting again, the RAAF made 108 for six. True, this was festival cricket, to please spectators; but who liked to chase the ball and be shown up as second best?

There were reasons for the mismatch. As the *Birmingham Post* reported the day after, the Australians 'may have been fatigued' by their journey from the south, arriving late and deprived of meals. Meanwhile three of the best Australians then available – Stan Sismey the wicket-keeper, and batsmen Keith Carmody and Jimmy Workman – were playing for the Dominions against England, at Lord's. Who would not, given the choice? Competition for the best players, biggest crowds, and publicity, applied during war as much as peace.

The 1943 season closed with the RAAF beating the RAF in a low-scoring game at Lord's. Four of the Australians

– Keith Miller, Stan Sismey, Workman and Carmody – would be stalwarts of the 1945 Victory Test team.

––––––––––––

For the 1944 season, the Australian authorities put a team of airmen in the field that represented their country against the best that England could muster – which, almost, meant their very best.

On his 1944 visit to England, the Australian prime minister John Curtin attended Lord's on Saturday, May 27, with the High Commissioner in London, Stanley Bruce. They saw the Rest make 280 for eight and Australia win by one wicket. 'No two teams could have risen to the occasion more nobly,' *The Times* wrote appreciatively.

You suspect that cricket was, for the politicians like everyone else, an understandably human chance for a breather. A fortnight earlier Curtin had told a luncheon in London: 'Lord's is to Australia what it is to this country.' Cricket was part of his argument that 'Australia is a British people, Australia is a British land and seven million Australians are seven million Britishers.' His audience cheered; it was what they wanted to hear. Curtin was spruiking – to use the Australian word; he was promoting his country; its unconquerable spirit. Also there were other leaders of the two countries – Sir Keith Murdoch (journalist father of Rupert), and military commanders Alan Brooke and Sir Thomas Blamey. These men had much more serious business. For them, cricket served a purpose; it showed unity, and that kept England – so Australia hoped – on its side. For only a naïve Australian would say that England was on Australia's side already, and leave it on trust.

On Whit Monday, May 29, Australia played England. *The Times* afterwards rejoiced. 'The players were no mere gladiators but serving soldiers and airmen, the spectators like them were taking a hardly earned holiday … there is cause for gratitude that such a scene could take place, that there could be one such almost carefree day to send everybody back to his particular task in higher and better heart.'

Australia batting first lost their openers for 12; then Sismey and Miller; and when the captain, Carmody, dragged on after hitting the ball before for four, they were 87 for five. Ross Stanford and the all-rounder Clive Calvert took the score after lunch to 173, and Australia were all out in 78 overs for 244. England took 48.5 overs to win by six wickets. The Australians without much or any top-class cricket background in their own country did remarkably well against such a strong England team – whose first four bowlers, Trevor Bailey, Gubby Allen, Bill Edrich and Doug Wright, were past or future Test players. The outstanding batsman for Australia was Ross Stanford, who made 51 each day on his first two games at Lord's. 'I never had nerves, I don't know why,' he recalled in old age.

'How did you do it?' I asked. 'Did you just do it?'

'You do it, you know. You have to concentrate. That was one of the great advantages Sir Donald Bradman had over other players, was great concentration. That's how he was able to make all the runs that he did … and he was fit enough to be able to do it as well.'

Yet could Bradman have done what Stanford was now doing? May 1944 was an unusually quiet month for Stanford on 617 Squadron – the Dambusters. He was seizing the chance to play at Lord's after a winter when, statistically, he should have been dead.

By contrast, Carmody flew five missions in May 1944 – each of two or three hours, as his 455 Squadron of Beaufighters, armed with torpedoes or cannon, swept the French or Dutch coasts in search of enemy ships. From

June 6, D-Day, the long-awaited invasion of Normandy, 455's crews, pilots and navigators, did six-hour shifts, waiting in motor buses, on the runway, for orders to scramble at a moment's notice. On June 7 Carmody did a reconnaissance of the Dutch coast. The next day, navigator Flight Sergeant William Roach reported engine trouble on an afternoon mission over the Frisian islands. Other patrolling aircraft saw the 'plane make a diving turn into the sea from 50 feet and sink. The others circled the scene but did not see survivors. The next issue of *The Cricketer* described Roach as a 29-year-old left-hand opening bat, of Fremantle and Western Australia. The magazine had no way of knowing his fate; nor Carmody's.

On June 13 Carmody was one of a dozen Beaufighters on coast patrol from Gravelines to the Hook of Holland. On attacking armed trawlers, they met flak from shore batteries and the boats; and two German Focke-Wulf 190 fighters. Carmody broadcast he had suffered engine damage and would have to ditch. Again his comrades saw no sign of his aircraft, and posted him missing.

Now in Maytime to the wicket
Out I march with bat and pad;
See the son of grief at cricket
Trying to be glad.
AE Housman, *A Shropshire Lad, XVII*

For a man who was already a hero to so many, Keith Miller was having an oddly quiet war. Having arrived in England in March 1943, he was still, unglamorously, in training. He flew at an advanced flying unit at South Cerney in Gloucestershire, then an OTU at Ouston, near

Newcastle upon Tyne. In October 1944 he went to another OTU, at Cranfield, in Bedfordshire. Some men who arrived around the same time as him were already dead, or would die – such as Clive Calvert, killed in December 1944, aged 22.

This is not to say Miller was shying away from the action; like anyone else, he could only go where the air force sent him. All the time, though, it would have been only natural to want to fly in combat, to measure himself, to do what he and his fellow airmen had come for. Only near the very end of the war, on April 4, 1945, did Miller reach the front line: RAF 169 Squadron, flying Mosquitoes in bomber support, from Great Massingham in Norfolk. On April 23 he flew his first mission – a beginner's, really – a 'spoof patrol', up at 9.45pm and down at 2.05am, part of an attempt to divert the enemy from a larger effort elsewhere. The squadron merely logged his four-hour 20-minute flight as 'uneventful'.

His second and final wartime night mission on May 2 was shorter – three hours and 25 minutes, up at 9.05pm and down at half past midnight – but eventful. A dozen Mosquitoes attacked two aerodromes, Jagel and Westerland on Sylt, at low level, carrying drop tanks filled with napalm gel. Of Miller's six going to Jagel in Schleswig, northern Germany, one did not return: as the log put it: 'An explosion was seen by several crews about five miles west of the airfield which might have been due to an aircraft crashing.' Miller's aircraft was one of three that could not drop both its tanks. He had to bring the one 'hung up' back to base – with the prospect of it dropping at any time, and exploding. 'Otherwise uneventful.'

That gave Miller less than eight combat hours, or less than one-twentieth of the combat experience of a decorated, genuine hero like Ross Stanford. Miller would have known this well; and yet he seldom let on, in anything he said or put his name to in writing later, that he had such a slight, brief experience of combat.

While he did not exaggerate his war, he – shall we say – told enough stories to leave the impression that he had as active a war as anybody. His biographers bought the story. But it was misleading. Two missions, in the last weeks of the war, while the German air force, and Germany, were on their last legs? A man could hardly have done less; and Miller knew it.

Indeed, for a man who put so much of his life into public print as Miller, it's suspicious that he never aired this. That would imply that it ate away at him; because it would have been there, on his conscience, guilt that he did not do as much as others. This would matter to a man like Miller, who wished above all to hold his head high in company. If Miller didn't give a hang, what was he doing in England?

Not that fellow aircrew like Stanford would hold a lack of combat hours against Miller, or anyone. Air force veterans were not like that. They knew it took courage every time you sat in a cockpit. As the details of that last mission prove, Miller did face danger. If the war had gone on a few more weeks, Miller would have had a war record to fit a sporting hero.

The air force saw Reg Ellis' qualities of steadiness and made him an instructor – at RAF Burnaston in Staffordshire. He recalled in 2009 that the air force next wanted to make him an instructor of instructors; instead he crewed up and reached a Lancaster bomber squadron, 463, at RAF Waddington near Lincoln, at the end of February 1945. Ellis' first bombing mission was on March 6. Inside seven weeks he flew eleven missions that added up to 75 hours. The air force had its money's worth. But not from Miller.

The Victory Tests

As the 1945 season began, Miller knew he had everything to prove, to himself and to the world, even if the world did not know; or care.

Chapter Five

Eastbourne, Spring 1945

I would say that a parallel difference between club and county cricket is between the work of a man who does casual sketches of his friends on a scribbling pad during his spare time and that of a professional portrait painter.

John Arlott, *How to Watch Cricket* (1949)

The snowdrops were out at the Saffrons, the Eastbourne cricket ground, as men of the Australian Army cut and rolled the grass, put up nets and practised in glorious April weather. The Australian authorities in England chose the Sussex seaside resort to house thousands of their returning prisoners of war, for those few weeks or months before they could sail home. The place did have an Australian cricket connection. There Archie McClaren's 'eleven Gentlemen of England' beat the otherwise invincible 1921 Australians. The real reason the Australians chose the Sussex seaside was, like most things in life, more mundane. Eastbourne had spare room, many of the townspeople having fled in 1940 in case of German invasion. The Australians took over the seafront Cumberland Hotel. Whereas any returning English PoWs could go home, Australians would be at a loose end – and perhaps tempted into mischief – until they set sail. Sports were a well-known, well-meant way to keep some men out of trouble, though admittedly only a few dozen out of the thousands could hope to ever put on whites.

Not that there were many pairs of whites to go around; the weekly *Eastbourne Gazette* newspaper pictured the men wearing their usual khaki uniforms, except for pads. On Anzac Day, they marched to the cricket ground for inspection; and on the next Saturday, April 28, the Australian Imperial Force (AIF) played its first game, against nearby Bexhill. In keeping with English tradition the players were, as Norman Preston reported in *The Cricketer* magazine, 'chilled to the marrow … and we sympathise with the Australians who were still waiting for their consignment of sweaters from the outfitters'. At least the south coast was not alone; on this first weekend of the season, snow at Grantham prevented play.

Richard Whitington (60) and Lindsay Hassett (54 not out) put on 90. Cec Pepper made one before what the newspaper called 'a sharp fall of snow' stopped play for an hour. The AIF declared on 165 for three, leaving Bexhill an hour. No doubt Hassett and his men wanted to put off the moment they had to leave the pavilion. Bexhill still had enough time for batting: they closed on 39 for nine. The Australians went on to play teams in the region, as far afield as High Wycombe; on VE Day, May 8, they visited Dulwich. There the spinners Pepper (five for 20) and Price (five for 25) knocked the Public School Wanderers over for 59. As thousands of men passed through Eastbourne as the advancing Allies liberated prisoners of war in Germany in April 1945, a game at Cambridge University had to be scratched at short notice.

The basis of the team – AG Cheetham, Whitington and Hassett – were among members of the AIF cricket team in Egypt in 1941. For political reasons, the AIF had returned home in 1942. On that top-level political visit to England in spring 1944 the Australian military agreed to send the three men – plus Cec Pepper and the spinner Charles Price – to England. The party had arrived in England via the Pacific and America in time to play an Essex County Services XII – oddly, at High Wycombe in Buckinghamshire – on Sunday, September 10. The Australian XII found a soft wicket 'too English', according to the *Bucks Free Press*, making only 60 in reply to 162 all out. Their arrival, and the timing of their work with returned prisoners, depended on the war. When the Allies captured Paris in August 1944 it seemed that the war could be over within weeks, including the freeing of prisoners from their camps in Germany. Instead, the reception group had all winter to plan 1945 fixtures to the end of September. The flood of returning men came with the end of the war in Europe. Bomber pilots, including Reg Ellis, flew PoWs home. By the start of June, Eastbourne had repatriated 5,000 and expected to receive only about 500 more.

While the AIF side was short of its five best players during the Victory Tests, what ended the reception group's cricketing summer early was that their work was done. As many of the PoWs had been behind wire since the fall of Greece, or Crete, four years before, they did not want to hang around. By the end of June, the AIF had cancelled the rest of their local games; only the Victory Tests and related games remained.

Chapter Six

Lord's, May 19 and 22 1945

VE Day around London was a funny feeling. People were still suffering from a slight stupefaction at being able to stand in a pub without a Doodle or Rocket interfering with an argument ...
RC Robertson-Glasgow, *46 not out* (1948)

At the beginning of May – the Russians had more or less conquered Berlin and the fall of Nazi Germany was days away – *The Times* looked ahead to the season. It listed likely teams from South Africa, New Zealand and West Indies, or at least in the names of those countries, besides wartime travelling sides such as London Counties and British Empire. The traditional counties were barely or not at all ready to play. The Australian Services, on the lines of the 1919 AIF team, were the premier visitors. *The Times* hoped that English cricket would learn a lesson this time, implying that after 1919 English cricketers were second best to the colonials.

And so they had been: between the wars England won the Ashes three times to Australia's seven. The last time England won the Ashes, 4-1, was in Australia in 1932–3, thanks to what Australians called the unfair tactic of

Bodyline, something that embarrassed English authority wanted to forget.

The Times spoke of 'a great opportunity' for an England side to 'take the field without an inferiority complex'. It looks a strange comment from a country on the brink of triumph in a second world war within living memory. It was not the last time in the summer (let alone since) that an English newspaper would imply that English cricket had an inferiority complex, against Australians.

At this stage, the authorities planned three two-day matches between England and Australia: at Lord's over Whitsun and in August, and Sheffield in June. The official end of the war in Europe prompted Lord's to show more ambition. So did the enormous crowds at the first Test – the Lord's gatemen had to push at the Grace gates to lock out people, as if in some medieval siege. A third Lord's Test, the fourth of the summer, was added for mid-July. And early in July, the authorities upgraded the Lancashire versus Australian services match, originally arranged for Manchester on August 21 and 22, to a three-day, fifth 'Test'.

Newspapers that were accurate to a fault – in other words, not all of them – were careful to write 'Test'. For while there was no question of matches between England and the Australian Services being official Tests – quite apart from Australian qualms over their weak side, both countries still had men dying in the Far East fighting Japan – it was natural to term the first game at Lord's, now a three-dayer, a Victory 'Test'.

The 1919 season had begun six months after the November 1918 Armistice, giving counties time to arrange a normal summer, and the AIF time to arrange fixtures, mainly with first-class counties, from Southampton to Leyton and West Hartlepool. By contrast organisers had no time to change the 1945 season from the assumed wartime one, like 1944's. Simply to open the gates on a match between England and Australia the month after Hitler had celebrated his 56th and last birthday in Berlin was an achievement. It showed how badly people wanted normal cricket. The ailing prime minister of Australia, Curtin – he would be dead in a few weeks – sent a message of good wishes to Marylebone Cricket Club (MCC), hoping that the England and Australia series would never again be interrupted.

For the first Victory Test, England, in first innings batting order, were: Len Hutton, Cyril Washbrook, John Robertson, Walter Hammond (captain), Les Ames, Bill Edrich, Walter Robins, Jack Stephenson, Billy Griffith (wicket-keeper), Doug Wright and Alf Gover. Men who would have walked into the eleven (like Denis Compton) and men who would have had a chance (like Joe Hardstaff junior) were overseas; so were men who had not made enough of a name for themselves yet, but soon would (notably opening bowler Alec Bedser). England did look weakest – both in the eleven and in terms of alternatives – in fast bowlers. This would become a lament of the summer; and for years to come.

The Australian eleven, too, was not quite its best because of disruptions and losses. Australia, in first innings order, were: Dick Whitington, JA (Jimmy) Workman, Lindsay Hassett (captain), Stan Sismey (wicket-keeper – who normally batted much lower), Keith Miller, Ross Stanford, Cec Pepper, Albert Cheetham, RG (Graham) Williams, Charles Price and Reg Ellis. Twelfth man was DR (Robert) Cristofani, who had taken most wickets for the Australians in 1944. They seemed to be in form already: on the Saturday before the Test, May 12, the RAAF bowled a British Empire XI out for 118 at Lord's, Ellis taking eight for 21, and the RAAF batted on beyond victory for 189 for seven.

Of the Australian eleven, the largest group by state of origin was, surprisingly, from South Australia: Whitington, RG Williams, Stanford; and Ellis and Workman, who had not played for their state. Described as 'a stone-waller of the Woodfull type', harking back to the inter-war Australian captain and opening bat, the well-named Workman could claim only to have played for the town of Port Adelaide. Back home he was a grocer's clerk. Of the RAAF men he was the only one from ground crew, not aircrew. This would be his first-class debut.

Whitington, well over six feet, 'has the peculiarity of placing his bat so far aslant that short slip affirmed he could read the name of the maker on it,' Sir Home Gordon wrote in *The Cricketer* after watching the AIF in Sussex in June. 'But directly the ball is delivered he straightens it and his method is particularly attractive.'

Of the two states that traditionally provided the bulk of Australia's Test cricketers, four Victory Test men came from New South Wales – Sismey, Pepper, Cheetham and Price (and Cristofani) – and only two from Victoria: Hassett and Miller.

Cheetham, 'tall, dark, debonair', was a welcome bolstering to the fast bowling. Pepper, the 16-stone all-rounder, was easy to have an opinion about. For Sir Home Gordon he was 'very much like Warwick Armstrong when that wily fellow first visited the country and when he stands in the slips with his hands on his knees his position singularly recalls that of Maurice Tate in the same place. He was O'Reilly's bowling partner in New South Wales and the otherwise likelihood of his becoming a Test Match hero may be arrested because he is the recipient of several league offers and has left the decision to his wife now in Australia.' To his comrades' amusement, he could fall asleep anywhere within three minutes.

The bowlers seemed easy to tell apart. Big Pepper, according to the *Sydney Morning Herald*, had a 'rolling, dancing gait … almost in waltz time', while Williams had an 'elbowy' run-up, whatever that meant, and Ellis was, all agreed, 'quiet and wily'. Just before the Test, the *Daily Sketch* had the bright idea of sending their air correspondent, Victor Lewis, to interview Ellis, a pilot. Ellis was no talker and little came of it except aerial puns and a description of Ellis' 'crab-wise approach to the wicket'.

Most, but not quite all, agreed with Norman Preston that Keith Miller was 'one of the main attractions' as a batsman, though like most observers Preston did not mention Miller's bowling – yet.

Everyone liked Hassett, the short, dapper, pipe-smoking, tennis and golf-playing and cinema-going (given the chance) unofficial ambassador. Sir Home Gordon called him 'one of the half dozen best batsmen now playing': 'Fascinating to watch, few being so light on their feet or with such variety of strokes.' Men admired him as a man too. In his end of career memoir, Edrich called Hassett 'tough, amusing and as dependable as gold'.

Hassett had strained his back while bowling in the nets the previous week – itself perhaps a sign that the Australians felt themselves to be short on bowling – but he tested his back with a game of squash and expected to be fit. Otherwise, the most newsworthy player was the only just arrived Graham Williams. He had played for South Australia as a fast bowler for six years, and had endured nearly four years in captivity after he was shot down during the Libyan campaign.

Such were the Australians to face England again, after seven years. We have Whitington to thank for a view inside the Australian dressing room that first morning of the Test. Talking to the press beforehand he kept quiet about nerves, only saying that he liked the extra bit of time that English wickets gave, compared to fast Australian strips. But as the papers added, this was his first time at Lord's. So was he projecting his nerves onto others when he claimed that nine of the players – that is, everyone except Miller and Hassett – feared making utter fools of themselves? Miller was smiling and nonchalant; the faces of others were 'like stunned mullets'.

It was as great a show as English cricket would ever put on. After wartime safekeeping the paintings in the Long Room were on the walls again. Members, everyone who was anyone in cricket and public life, were there, except maybe the politicians, who in the following week would split their wartime coalition. Flight Sgt FB Moran, the Australians' scorer and bagman, took his place in the scorebox. He kept score not in a scorebook but by typewriter (apart from making a red circle in pencil around a wicket-taking ball), in enough detail to show how each batsman did against each bowler.

The crowds were there, let in from 10am for the 11.30am start. The first in the queue along the high walls, at 8am, was GA King, a retired building surveyor from Battersea. 'I thought it would be like the old days when there were large crowds early in the day and when I frequently waited from six in the morning,' he told the London *Evening Standard*. This start of a Test summer, let alone a new cricketing era, demanded sunshine; yet despite the forecast of a hot day, many sensible men in the queue were wearing their overcoats.

The two captains came out for the toss to the hubbub of spectators on every seat. Hammond won the toss and chose to bat, 'obvious', according to Bruce Harris in that day's *Evening Standard*, because of the rain in the air and a cold wind. As Hutton and Washbrook went out to bat, the crowd let out a roar, 'that was partly for the players and partly for cricket on general principles', as RC Robertson-Glasgow noted in *The Observer*. And partly, he might have added, because the watchers felt cold.

Hutton took a single in the first over from Cheetham, bowling with the breeze from the Nursery End. At the other end, Williams tempted him with a ball outside the off stump, Hutton played indecisively, and Sismey snapped up the catch. Hutton, whose last innings against Australia in August 1938 had lasted 13 hours, was out in five minutes for a single. (On his Yorkshire debut in 1934 the 17-year-old Hutton, like Stanford, was run out for nought by a senior player – Maurice Leyland.)

Pepper was first change, on for Cheetham. A big man, nicknamed the Ox, he walked crookedly in to bowl: 'a slow bowler in the full sense', according to Bruce Harris. Robertson pulled Pepper savagely for four and a two in his first over. The 50 came up with Robertson's late cut off Pepper, after 45 minutes. Ellis came on for Williams. Harris noted that Ellis had 'quite a conclave with Hassett over setting his field'. In his Adelaide home in 2009, Reg Ellis recalled an earlier, private talk:

> *It rained overnight and I remember our captain Lindsay Hassett took me out on to the field, showing me the wicket where it [rain] had got in underneath on the downhill end. Anyhow I said to him, 'cor, that will suit me, won't it'; and he looked at me, 'you aren't going to bowl this end', he said, 'you are the only one I can rely on to keep an accurate length and direction and I am going to set a field for you and you are going to bowl all morning'; which I did. They got the wickets from the other end.*

At that memory, Ellis chuckled.

On the biggest sporting occasion for years, for Australians and English alike, most players may well have felt like Ellis, that once they did what they were there for, it did not feel as bad: 'Oh yes, to start bowling, the first over was the worst, always the worst, after the first it was all right.'

To the last ball of Ellis' first over, Washbrook reached forward for a ball that turned away outside his legs. 'He scarcely lifted his foot yet Sismey stumped him in a flash,' Elton Ede reported in the *Sunday Times*. According to Ede, 'some English batsmen lost their wicket just as they began to collar the bowling'. Washbrook, out for 28, added 53 for the second wicket with Robertson; Robertson added 43 for the third with the sweater-wearing Hammond. Robertson gave a most stylish display, wrote Frank Butler of the *Sunday Express*, 'although he seemed uncomfortable against the slow bowling of Ellis', who had him leg before. Ellis looked so easy to play, Frank Butler said admiringly: 'His powers are steady length and beautiful flight.' Ames and Edrich made the biggest stand of the day, 75 for the fifth wicket. Both men mixed sparkling strokes with what the *Manchester Guardian* disapprovingly termed 'indeterminate jabs'. Ames, who made the day's top score of 57, was dropped before scoring. Sismey let out a premature 'howzat' but let a 'lightning delivery' from Miller slip from his gloves. Ames eventually sent a full toss from Cheetham carefully into Price's waiting hands.

Reviewing the first day for the *Daily Express* – a rest day, Sunday, fell before the second day's play – Bob Crisp wrote: 'The thing that strikes me most about the play was not that the England total was so disappointing but that these English batsmen displayed such fine form in their first real match of the season … a triumph of technique over rustiness accumulated in nearly six years of war.' He praised the batsmen for their willingness to take risks.

In the forthright machine-gun style that the *Express* demanded – that was both cause and effect of being the country's largest-selling daily newspaper – Crisp gave readers his verdicts: 'Hammond – his technique is still the best thing to watch in a day's cricket.' And Edrich: 'Bill's bat looks a bit bigger than most other people's. Perhaps it is.'

Some felt Hammond made mis-hits and never got into his stride. About the only thing that every reporter will notice, and agree on, is their own discomfort. Frank Butler, who had left his overcoat at home, complained: 'Nothing happened out on that luscious green carpet to bring a glow to our chilled blood.'

Butler summed up: 'The batsmen were so obviously out of practice. Credit to the young Australian bowlers and fielders but we must not overlook the fact that the bad timing and lack of confidence in men like Hutton and Hammond made the bowling look quite a bit more dangerous than it really was.'

In the Australian dressing room after the first day, the not out batsmen Sismey and Hassett sat on the players' balcony, according to an unnamed *Sydney Morning Herald* reporter, 'fit, happy and confident'. Discussing the day, Hassett said he didn't deserve praise. 'When the bowlers are on top the captain's job is secure.' Asked how he felt captaining Australia, he grinned all over his lean brown face and answered, 'What do you think?'

Williams was tickled at getting Hammond but insisted that the pitch came to his aid. 'I don't turn the ball on the pitch normally and that one came back inches.' Yet surely he and the other Australian bowlers were no more in practice than the English batsmen? One team had risen to the occasion better than the other.

Lord's, May 19 and 22

As it turned out, this was the only Test of the five where Australia's first innings lasted more overs than England's. Australia scored at more than three and a half runs an over, a quick rate for the occasion. It suggests that the more match-fit Australians took advantage of rusty English bowlers; if so, Australia had shown initiative besides ability. Having seen what the other fellows could do, each side knew what they had to do on the last day, after overnight rain. England had to bat most if not all of the day to draw; Australia had to bowl at least as well as they did on the first day, to win by an innings or leave themselves a short run chase. Whether copying the *Manchester Guardian*, or simply thinking exactly the same, the *Yorkshire Observer* was already bemoaning England's 'biggest peace time cricket problem', namely the 'dearth of Test match bowlers'. The same was true for Australia. It was asking much of any bowlers to take 20 international wickets inside three days, on a still easy-paced wicket.

Hammond inspected the pitch and asked for a light roller. Williams began the third day with a maiden over to Hutton. The pitch was lifeless and the outfield sluggish. Miller replaced Williams and after nearly an hour, at 47, the 'first of the tweakers', Pepper, came on. This prompted the batsmen to do some turf-tapping with their bats.

In his first over, Pepper had a loud leg-before appeal against Washbrook disallowed. Another was turned down in Pepper's second over, 'whereat there was some fond derision off stage', Bruce Harris reported. Then Pepper bowled a ball of beautiful length at Hutton who played back. The ball fizzed off the pitch and bowled him: a googly that kept low.

Ellis came on for Miller. Like Grimmett, he had two fielders close to the bat on each side of the wicket.

Robertson and Washbrook treated the bowlers with extreme respect, much like the first innings three days before. Another leg-before appeal from Pepper; and Washbrook was out. During the ten minutes it took Hammond to get off the mark, Roberston hit a Pepper full toss to midwicket for six. Hammond sneaked a single to short leg off Pepper. England lunched at 114 for two; Hammond and Robertson looked more in command.

Hammond jumped and drove the second ball after lunch, a Pepper full toss, to the sightscreen; and drives went for four on either side off Cheetham. Pepper's one and a half hour spell ended, and Ellis took over. At once Ellis beat the bat as Hammond played forward and was leg before for 33. With three men out and England still behind, Robertson went back into his shell; Ames, too, was pegged down.

Though the bowlers kept chipping in with wickets, England were batting beyond tea with only five wickets down. Bill Edrich and Walter Robins took England's lead to 98 before both men were caught. The last four made seven between them, including Doug Wright run out for one. It was peculiar, if England were trying to save the game. It was almost as if England were trying to give Australia a chance.

———————

Whatever the reason, the game that could so easily have drifted to a draw was open for a thrilling climax – if the Australia batsmen were bold. At 5.50pm Richard Whitington and Keith Miller went in, needing to make 107 by 7pm. Promoting Miller was a sign that Hassett meant business, except that Whitington was out without scoring, leg before, and when Hassett as next man in square cut and Miller started for a second run, Washbrook's low quick return from the boundary, taken by Griffith, ran out Miller for one.

Hassett and Pepper steadied the innings then went for the runs, though they fell behind the clock. With the score at 63, Hassett fell to a running catch by Hammond, who had moved from the captain's usual place in the slips to long off. Hammond's cap came off; extraordinary exertion for 1945.

Australia needed more than two runs a minute, or 44 in the last 20 minutes. Cheetham was soon run out, for backing up too much. Australia wanted 38 in 15 minutes, or maybe five overs; then after another over, 31 in 12. 'The crowd of 16,000 kept up a continuous roar and delighted applause as Pepper began to lash out at nearly everything,' the *Daily Telegraph* reported. At 6.55pm, with at most two overs to go, Australia wanted 13. Eight men ringed the boundary as Stephenson bowled the last over but one.

Off the last ball of that over, Bob Crisp reported in the *Express* the next day, 'Pepper heaved his great shoulders in a vast swipe, connected, and the ball sailed high up on to the stand for one of the biggest sixes seen at Lord's.' The clock in the tower of the ground showed one minute to seven when the umpires indicated there was time for another over – four to tie, five to win. England fielders sportingly ran to their positions. Gover was to bowl, meaning that he and Stephenson bowled all innings – arguably another time-saving gesture by Hammond. Even the quickest change of bowlers would have taken half a minute, and as Gover began his run to start the last over, the hands of the Lord's clock were not quite pointing to seven o'clock.

Price, another batsman promoted as a hitter, missed the first ball. The umpires counted one – Archie Fowler, the former Middlesex slow bowler, used six cardboard counters; Bert Beet, Derbyshire wicket-keeper for 22 years, kept little blue marbles in his right hand. Price sneaked a single off the second. Pepper mishit the next and Wright, running like mad, just failed to get his hands to it; the batsmen took two runs. Three balls left, two to win. Lord's was in pandemonium. Gover took his long walk back to the start of his run to a sustained uproar.

This ball was fast, just on the leg side. Pepper made, according to Crisp, 'another rather wild swipe', which went rather luckily between the wide-spaced field. Hutton and Washbrook rushed after it but the batsmen had time to run two.

Australia had won, thanks largely to Pepper's 54 not out. He had given a chance five minutes from time, with 18 needed. Otherwise, as RC Robertson-Glasgow wrote in *The Observer* the following Sunday; '... already he has shown us that he is in the Australian tradition, a member of the fraternity of confident men who rise to the full height of opportunity and enjoy it as Achilles enjoyed knocking the dust out of the Trojans'. Less romantically, the *Sydney Morning Herald* reported that Pepper was suffering from boils. 'He was so tired when he reached the dressing room that he declared he could not run another run.'

––––––––––––

Probably in its way as good a game of cricket as ever was played, *The Cricketer* reckoned. Everyone could feel happy that Australia gained the day: 'A draw would have been something of an anti-climax and praise in which the Australians were unstinted is due to Hammond and his men for never wasting a second of time.'

In later eras used to one-day international cricket, a target of 107 in 23 overs (or 70 minutes, as was the measure in those days) would be routine. In 1945, not only did watchers regard the rate of more than four runs an over as a 'run chase', for the Australians to risk the chase was daring.

On the other side of the coin, England could feel something had gone wrong. Eight years later, in the fourth Test at Headingley, Australia needed a comparable 177 to win in 115 minutes – and so retain the Ashes. Though the worn fifth-day pitch was taking spin, the batsmen did try, including Hassett, who went in first. However, England bowled only 33 overs, and some of those in a defensive way. Miller called it 'one of the greatest time-wasting efforts in cricket history'. In May 1945 Hammond could have wasted time far less obviously than Hutton did in 1953, and denied Australia a win, because in May 1945 the batsmen were straining to reach the target even in the overs they had.

A month later in the weekly column he wrote – or to be more exact, put his name to – Hammond revealed how he had done even more to give Australia their chance. He said that at 5.15pm on the third day he asked Edrich and Robins, who were playing comfortably, to hit out. 'I am quite confident that Robins and Edrich could have batted easily another half hour but that would have meant a drawn game … but they [the public] cannot hope for such cricket in official Test matches. There is then too much at stake.' Hammond had given the public what they wanted: exciting cricket to the very end, thanks to the Australian batsmen taking the chance offered.

To some, this was shocking, unnatural even, like children's shouts on a Sunday sabbath-observing street. Hence Hammond explained himself in print. He was, however, implying that these unofficial Tests were the exception. When national pride was again the wager, the usual slow, proper Test cricket, no chances given (or taken), would return.

Not that Hammond's men found any loss easy to take. 'Every man in the English team felt the challenge of that first defeat and swore by all his gods to reverse matters,' Edrich wrote a couple of years later in his autobiography *Cricket Heritage*. He wrote how he learned with dismay 'the first sharp lesson that we have not got a real Test match quality attack'.

First Test, Lord's, May 19, 21 and 22

England won the toss.

England first innings

L Hutton	ct Sismey	b Williams	1
C Washbrook	st Sismey	b Ellis	28
JDB Robertson	lbw	b Ellis	53
*WR Hammond		b Williams	29
†LEG Ames	ct Price	b Cheetham	57
WJ Edrich		b Miller	45
RWV Robins		b Cheetham	5
JWA Stephenson	ct Sismey	b Price	31
†SC Griffith	ct Sismey	b Cheetham	9
DVP Wright		b Price	0
AR Gover	not out		0
Extras (1 bye, 6 leg byes, 1 no ball, 1 wide)			9
Total (all out, 100.1 overs)			267

Fall of wickets: 1-1, 2-54, 3-97, 4-130, 5-205, 6-213, 7-233, 8-267, 9-267, 10-267

Bowling

Cheetham	13.1	1	49	3
Williams	19	2	56	2
Pepper	19	2	59	0
Ellis	31	8	59	2
Miller	9	2	11	1
Price	9	1	24	2

Australian Services first innings

RS Whitington	ct Griffith	b Wright	36
JA Workman		b Gover	1
*AL Hassett		b Stephenson	77

Lord's, May 19 and 22

†SG Sismey	ct Wright	b Edrich	37
KR Miller	ct Ames	b Stephenson	105
RM Stanford	st Griffith	b Stephenson	49
CG Pepper	ct Griffith	b Stephenson	40
AG Cheetham	ct Hammond	b Wright	0
RG Williams	ct Griffith	b Wright	53
CFT Price	ct Robertson	b Stephenson	35
RS Ellis	not out		1
Extras (9 b, 10 lb, 2 nb)			21
Total (all out, 125.3 overs)			455

Fall of wickets: 1-11, 2-52, 3-136, 4-171, 5-270, 6-357, 7-358, 8-366, 9-454, 10-455

Bowling

Gover	25	3	90	1
Stephenson	36	4	116	5
Edrich	17	2	61	1
Wright	37.3	9	122	3
Robins	10	0	45	0

England second innings

L Hutton		b Pepper	21
C Washbrook	lbw	b Pepper	32
JDB Robertson	ct Sismey	b Cheetham	84
*WR Hammond	lbw	b Ellis	33
LEG Ames		b Ellis	7
WJ Edrich	ct Workman	b Price	50
RWV Robins	ct Hassett	b Pepper	33
JWA Stephenson		b Price	
†SC Griffith	not out		4
DVP Wright	run out		1
AR Gover	st Sismey	b Pepper	1
Extras (18 b, 8 lb, 1 nb)			27
Total (all out, 115.4 overs)			294

Fall of wickets: 1-52, 2-75, 3-149, 4-175, 5-218, 6-286, 7-286, 8-289, 9-292, 10-294

Bowling

Cheetham	17	2	44	1
Williams	21	7	47	0
Pepper	32.4	7	80	4
Ellis	17	3	33	2

Miller	9	1	23	0
Price	19	3	40	2

Australian Services second innings

RS Whitington	lbw	b Stephenson	0
KR Miller	run out		1
*AL Hassett	ct Hammond	b Gover	37
CG Pepper	not out		54
AG Cheetham	run out		0
CFT Price	not out		10

Workman, †Sismey, Stanford, Williams and Ellis did not bat.
Extras (4 b, 1 lb)   5
Total (four wickets, 22.4 overs)   107
Fall of wickets: 1-9, 2-11, 3-63, 4-76

Bowling

Gover	11.4	1	51	1
Stephenson	11	0	51	1

Australian Services won by six wickets. Close of play day one: Australian Services 82-2 (Hassett 27 not out, Sismey 11 not out). Day two close Australian Services 455 all out.

Chapter Seven

The Teams

Cricket is like war in one respect – both sides make mistakes and the side that makes the least mistakes is usually the winner.

WJ O'Reilly, *Cricket Conquest: The Story of the 1948 Test Tour* (1949)

It is a consolation to some historians that with time comes perspective, and the history they write can become fuller and wiser. In truth, perspective can just as easily mislead. While we may hail Hutton and Miller now, knowing what they achieved after 1945, at the time most would have agreed who was the greatest man in either Victory Test team: the England captain Walter Hammond. All agreed he was great – *very great*, an admiring Sir Pelham Warner wrote, in italics, in his 1946 history of Lord's. By his rare use of italics it was as if Warner, himself a former captain of England, wanted to rank Hammond yet higher; beyond everyone else. Warner wrote: 'Success does not spoil him in the least. On the contrary, as his fame grows, the more modest he becomes, and he is understanding and sympathetic to those who have failed ... Everything he does is graceful, with a tremendous sense of power. There is majesty about his batting, he makes the most difficult catches look easy, and his bowling action is perfect in rhythm, swing and delivery.'

Even such praise, we now know – and, it is only fair to admit, with hindsight – gave clues to the disappointing end to Hammond's career. Like other ageing captains since, Hammond seldom if at all bowled himself any more. He captained the first English tour after the war, to Australia in 1946–7, without personal or team success. One of the party, the wicket-keeper Godfrey Evans, in his end of career autobiography aptly titled *The Gloves Are Off*, wrote of Hammond: 'He was unpopular with some members of the side, not perhaps without reason, because he appeared to arrange things for his own convenience. If he took a particular view he considered automatically that it must be the right one, and rarely asked anyone, no matter who he was, for advice. He hardly ever gave any praise.' Evans admitted that he was at the time young and uncritical. As Evans wrote, he was proud to play under Hammond and had yet to learn that Hammond's field placings were not perfect. (Evans incidentally had no chance of playing in the Victory Tests; he was in charge of a British Army 'motor pool' in Frankfurt.)

Other younger players must have felt equally proud, and in awe, of their captain. Even if any had doubts, they did not dare voice them. They did as their elders in the workplace told them. When Len Hutton reached his first hundred in that timeless Test at the Oval in 1938, he thought about batting faster. Hammond sensed it, and would have none of it. The number three bat and fellow Yorkshireman, Maurice Leyland, told Hutton: 'The skipper wants you to go steady.' Hutton did as he was told. In his end of career autobiography, Hutton called Hammond '*the* greatest of all batsman of my time' – note that isolating italic again. Evans, too, described Hammond as great, and called him the 'inevitable choice' as captain as late as 1946–7. In 1945 Hammond was as secure in his position – provided, as always, he did enough to keep his place – as any England captain of modern times.

That did not mean that Hammond was necessarily wise to bat on. True, the peculiar and less regimented list of wartime cricket fixtures probably gave Hammond, and others, a respite from the grind of county matches and travel each summer, and the three or four months or more of touring some hot, dusty land most winters.

While Yorkshire crowds might have regarded Hutton as *their* new greatest batsman since his Test world-record 364 in 1938, in southern England Hammond was still supreme. While wartime matches were supposedly only for pleasure, any batsmen who happened to be the most senior of the 22 playing would feel the weight of having to put on a show for the spectators (who saw the players' names advertised beforehand). Hammond alone could *never* escape the pressure of being the one the crowd most wanted to see – to be exact, making runs, and not in any old way, but attractively.

Take for example a charity game at High Wycombe on Sunday, August 27, 1944. Hammond led a Services XII against a Buckinghamshire XII. Hammond went in at 4 pm, 'amidst a great ovation', according to the *Bucks Free Press* report the following Friday. Many were 'disappointed' that Hammond did not dominate the bowling. He was nearly caught first ball. Hammond showed 'glimpses of the master hand' in his 30, 'particularly in those forceful shots off the back foot which sent the ball speeding through the covers where lesser mortals would be content to play a defensive stroke'.

Hammond *was* mortal, however. He had returned from North and South Africa in January 1944 having put on weight, admitting he had lacked regular exercise. The air force had discharged him in the winter of 1944 after an attack of fibrositis. Between the first and second Victory

Tests he turned 42. That was old but not unusually so for an English cricketer, especially at war's end when many put off retiring, simply because clubs did not yet know who else to bring in. He was hardly the only sportsman to find it hard to know when to call it a day; Bradman, too, held off retiring. Hammond had reached the age when quite a few players were old enough to be his sons. His fame, like Bradman's, always carried the risk of distancing him from his fellow men. Hammond, besides, on the field was, in Hutton's words, 'an unusually quiet, almost taciturn man'. Hammond, you suspect, was partly so uncommunicative because he had done and seen everything and did not see the need to open his mouth about it.

That is not to say Hammond had had his fill of cricket, especially after five more or less blank seasons. He had come to a time when he had enough on his plate, keeping to the highest standards as a batsman, and saying no to the schoolboys forever asking for his autograph. To be a leader, giving some of himself to other men, was asking too much. Hammond's gifts did not necessarily qualify him to give time to all the newspaper reporters, photographers, mayors, club presidents and a thousand other worthies and know-all time-wasting nobodies that hung around as public a figure as the cricket captain of England. The likes of Sir Pelham Warner probably liked a 'modest' captain like Hammond who did not throw his weight around at selection meetings.

The Australian Victory Test men, by contrast, had the best of both worlds. Some were playing for their third summer in England, and had lost their awe of places and names, without – yet – losing their zest. As Douglas Jardine wrote in his 1933 book *In Quest of the Ashes*, after the notorious Bodyline tour of Australia, a team abroad might be easier to captain, for the men chosen for a home Test match often had not played together:

The Teams

Picture the feelings of a wicket-keeper 'taking' a spin bowler whom he has never seen in action before. Nor will an opening pair of batsmen, with no previous experience of each other's running and calling, have that reliance and confidence in each other which is half their battle.

International players playing for years only for their country and seldom turning out for lesser elevens are a recent development. As late as the 1990s, England players would play only at most about 30 days of cricket a summer together. They were more used to their county dressing room. In other words, the earlier international captain had quickly to understand and bring together his men. An oddity of the 1945 Victory series is that the men from overseas had had far more time in each other's company than the home team. Hammond as home captain was, as Jardine put it, having to improvise at a few days' notice.

That should not have mattered because England's eleven, for all the tragedies of war, looked far stronger than the Australian Services. Of the English, only Griffith, Robertson and Stephenson had yet to play in a Test; only Stephenson never would. By contrast the Australians had only one Test player, their captain Hassett. With such experience lay an English weakness: they were old. That was hardly the men's fault. Nor were the Australians all young; Whitington made his debut for South Australia, aged 20, against the MCC tourists in November 1932 (and was charmed by the interest Jardine took in him).

The English were bound to pick up where they left off: with pre-war players. To take that last Oval Test of 1938, and the last pre-war summer of 1939, of three Tests against the West Indies. At the Oval Ken Farnes took five wickets, Bill Bowes seven. In the summer of 1945, Bowes turned 37 and in any case felt unready for top-class cricket. He had been in captivity between June 20, 1942 at Tobruk and April 12, 1945 at Brunswick in Germany – the sort of exact dates any former prisoner would remember. England's other bowlers at the Oval had been Edrich; Hedley Verity, dead after an infantry attack in Sicily in 1943; and the occasional bowlers Maurice Leyland (still playing, though about to turn 45) and Hammond.

The England XI in the third and last Test against West Indies in August 1939 was, in batting order, Hutton, Walter Keeton, Norman Oldfield, Hammond, Denis Compton, Joe Hardstaff, Stan Nichols, Arthur Wood, Doug Wright, Tom Goddard and Reg Perks. Compton, the youngest – only 21 then – and Hardstaff were in the Far East by 1945. The second Test included the batsmen Arthur Fagg and Eddie Paynter, and Bill Bowes and another fast bowler, Bill Copson. Picked only for the first Test that year were the batsman Harold Gimblett; and Verity.

Of England's 17 players in 1939, eight were in their 20s, eight in their 30s, and Arthur Wood, the wicket-keeper, became 41 during the Tests. It sounded like a good mix of ages. By VE Day, however, only Hutton and Fagg were still in their (late) 20s and in England. Even if Farnes had lived, he would have been 33; had Verity survived his wounds he would have been 40 the day before the first Victory Test.

England was, as far as anyone knew, without Test fast bowlers in their best years. Lord Tennyson, the former Hampshire and England captain, told *News of the World* readers in August, 'the dearth of great bowlers is one of the problems of Test cricket as a whole … the Bradmans, the Hobbses at their best can only make things safe for their side'. *The Cricketer*, too, harked back to the 'fine England XI' of 1939, 'immensely powerful in batting'. The discovery of bowlers was the problem, the magazine agreed, but 'there must surely be some potential bowlers in our forces and mines'. Was anybody looking?

Most institutions in England require their followers to give the nod to some fraud or hypocrisy, typically a divide between Us and Them. In the case of English county cricket before and after 1945, you had to believe in amateurs and professionals; and that a flourishing alternative to the counties – the northern and Birmingham leagues – did not exist. The 'England' team, as all the newspapers called it, was in truth the MCC's. That meant a regional bias in that first Victory Test eleven, and others before and after. Apart from the openers Hutton and Washbrook, from Yorkshire and Lancashire, and the captain Hammond, of Gloucestershire, all the players came from London or southern counties. Historians have taken their cue from the *Wisden* annuals and London-based newspapers of the day and lavished attention on the first-class counties and Tests, when they could easily write a valid and full history of English cricket from the point of view of the Yorkshire and Lancashire leagues. The Second World War was the northern leagues' finest hour.

For the best players of Lancashire and Yorkshire, it was only natural to turn out for your local league club, the place you had come from. So it was that in July Washbrook (scoring 86 for Eccleshill) played at Pudsey in the Bradford League against Hutton (who made 81 for Pudsey St Lawrence). And the *Yorkshire Post* reported how, a fortnight after Victory in Europe, the returned prisoner of war Bill Bowes turned out for his village team, Menston, in the Airedale and Wharfedale League, against North Leeds. Menston made 140; Bowes batting at nine made three. Then Bowes opened the bowling, the reporter noting 'there was the old leisurely stroll to position, the same glint of sunshine on horn-rimmed spectacles as he took his run to the wicket'. Bowes took seven for 17, skittling North Leeds for 45. (Unusually, Bowes ended his first-class career, as on that day, with more wickets than runs.) As he regained his fitness, and weight, he declined invitations to play in the Victory Tests, playing instead for Yorkshire, and clubs.

County clubs cut professional cricketers adrift when the likely Nazi invasion of England in 1940 made travel difficult and cricket frivolous. War quite suited the counties: they did not have to pay their players, while some income still came from members. Players had no choice but to look north if they still wanted a living from cricket. The only other alternative in cricket was, as before the war, coaching at private schools. Leagues offered cricketers a decent life. The money was there; factories were offering work to everyone, and plenty of men were doing manual or skilled war work rather than serving in the armed forces, and were free to play or watch cricket on a Saturday afternoon. Instead of the county grind of perhaps hundreds of miles of travel around the country, week after week, weekend league games were single innings, hard fought but short. Most teams were a few miles apart. Alf Gover of Surrey and Leslie Todd of Kent, to name only two southerners, played in the leagues then travelled during the night to take part in charity games in the south of England; and did coaching in midweek.

The leagues had long attracted great names, such as the Staffordshire fast bowler Sydney Barnes and the West Indian all-rounder Learie Constantine; the war brought many more. To take the Bradford League alone, professionals included West Indian Ellis Achong; senior Englishmen such as James Langridge of the Sussex family, and Les Ames and Arthur Fagg of Kent. WH (Bill) Copson, the Derbyshire and England fast bowler, was playing for Saltaire; Tom Goddard of Gloucestershire and England for Keighley. The best Bradford League all-rounder according to the 1945 averages was Les Townsend of Derbyshire and England, now of Undercliffe; also in his team was Dennis Brookes of Northamptonshire, a batsman on the brink of playing for England, 12th man in the second Victory Test.

Besides established names, men making their names in the next few years were coming through, and noted. Playing for Saltaire that summer were JC (Jim) Laker; and Willie Watson, a Yorkshire colt and Huddersfield Town forward, and rated in the Yorkshire press as having a 'good chance of playing for Yorkshire some day'. Both played for England in the next decade. Richard Sparling of the *Sheffield Telegraph* pointed out (accurately) that JH Wardle, a 22-year-old ex-grammar school boy who played for nearby Denaby, was likely to take the place of Verity as a slow left-armer. Johnnie Wardle made the Yorkshire team later that summer. So if the London-based national selectors had truly wanted to, they could have mixed proven men like Hammond and Hutton with such known youths of promise. To pick the right northerners in 1945, though, selectors had to know the leagues, or ask people who did know, and there was no evidence they ever did.

The ruling class, whether in politics, business, or sporting pleasures, stuck to a yearly round of venues and associates within easy range of London. A Lord's selector would no more watch a northern league club than a lord would visit a fish and chip shop. In his memoir *Long Innings*, Sir Pelham Warner described attending the 1949 jubilee dinner of the North Staffordshire League in Stoke-on-Trent. While he said he enjoyed the occasion – he seemed to enjoy every occasion – he did leave the impression that Stoke was as exotic and as seldom-visited as Trinidad, New Zealand or Uruguay (all places he played in for MCC).

The three men who chose the England team for the second Victory Test – Lieutenant Colonel GO 'Gubby' Allen (the England captain before Hammond; here representing the Army), Wing Commander WHN Shakespeare (representing the RAF) and Sir Pelham Warner did make some gestures towards the north, perhaps because the venue was Sheffield. They picked George Pope of Derbyshire, and Lancashire bowlers Dick Pollard and WB (William) Roberts. Even so, you could claim that the selectors had to make some changes, because meanwhile Ames had fractured an elbow playing football; and Robins had a cracked rib. Miller had hit him there at Lord's.

The London-based cricket establishment did not ignore the northern leagues because they were not worth the look: the very opposite. The leagues, popular and commercially-minded, were a threat, not only as an alternative to the county set-up but to the leisurely, long-winded (three-day) sort of cricket the counties stood for. No wonder the counties voted against a cup competition; or rather, more in character, put off a decision for another year. A football-style knock-out would have been vulgar; and too much like a pale copy of the leagues. Worryingly for the county establishments, some professionals made noises that they might stick to the leagues. Alf Pope, the Derbyshire all-rounder, now with Baildon Green, told the *Bradford Telegraph & Argus* in July that he did not think he would play again for Derbyshire; and brother George might be leaving the county 'before long'. A month later, Bob Crisp, reporting on the Manchester Victory Test, told *Daily Express* readers how northerners reckoned that a team from the northern leagues could beat England. Few professionals, Crisp wrote, could turn down an offer from the leagues for a 'nebulous reputation' as a county or even an England cricketer.

The position of the Australians towards the leagues and what you could call the Lord's establishment was ambiguous. According to the northern press, in the summer of 1945 Bingley had hoped to field Hassett; Carmody was ready to play at Bingley, only to trip up on the rules; likewise Stanford, approached by several league clubs. Bob Cristofani for a long time was expected to turn out for Eccleshill when stationed near Lancashire and England wicket-keeper George Duckworth's home, but he never did. According to the *Manchester Evening News* during the fifth and final Victory Test, Lancashire League and Central Lancashire League clubs had men at Old Trafford on the Monday, unofficially sounding out Australian players. Pepper had already deputised at Nelson, and 'created a big impression with a forceful innings of 63'. Another spinning all-rounder, Jack Pettiford, also in demand, had played with Stockport in the Central League. He later played some years of league cricket, then six seasons for Kent. Once home in Australia, Miller did go so far as to sign a contract with Lancashire League club Rawtenstall, then bought himself out of it.

On the other hand, Stanford recalled: 'We considered Lord's to be our home ground because we played more matches at Lord's than any other ground when we were in England. That was one of the highlights of my cricket career, playing cricket at Lord's.'

London as a base had mundane advantages for the Australians. While the RAAF bomber men largely flew from east Yorkshire or Lincolnshire, or training units in the shires, London was a natural place to head for on leave, whether to catch up with mates, see the sights, or for shopping or cricket. The Australian players' delight at making Lord's, the home of cricket, their home, was genuine.

The hosts – Marylebone Cricket Club – were keen to have them, as the biggest attraction of the wartime and 1945 seasons. Even so conservative a club as MCC would not ignore the commercial possibilities, besides the honour of binding the Empire. Yet the different Australian and MCC outlooks could not help but clash. Whitington and Miller told the story of how in 1944 at Lord's a photographer was making the Australian team late to take the field. Carmody as skipper had to decide between abandoning the photo; keeping the umpires and 30,000 spectators waiting, including VIPs like Blamey and Curtin; or saving time another way. Instead of going through the Long Room, and out of the players' gate, Carmody led his men through a gap between pavilions and hurdled the rope-fence around the ground. At tea, 'Sir Pelham Warner cornered Carmody and told him he had committed a serious offence and that it was not to happen again'. The 21st-century visitor to Lord's, greeted by a gateman saying 'Hi!', can have no idea how fussy the place once was. It took courage – and violated the jacket, shirt and tie standards – for Carmody to tell Warner to 'break down the red tape and be practical'.

The Australian authorities no doubt gladly fell in with the British establishment. Meanwhile, the RAAF officers were as happy to rub shoulders with the mechanics who repaired their planes, as with MCC members in the Lord's pavilion. The most famous Australian of his generation, Keith Miller, came to be photographed often enough in a dinner jacket with royalty and lords; and they, as patrons of the aristocrats of sport and art, were happy to be in his company. Crucially, the Australians were usually only around for one summer in four; they never outstayed their welcome. If the Australians had been there to stay, they would have faced a difficult choice between northern leagues and southern establishment; between cocking their legs over the ropes, and toeing the line.

It's really a bomber team and it can truly be called a team for it must have those qualities which make a good football team, a good basketball team.
John Steinbeck, *Bombs Away:*
The Story of a Bomber Team (1942)

Meanwhile, for mundane, cricketing, reasons, these Australians could surpass England. One previously unknown batsman, Stanford, had excelled against England's best bowlers in the 1944 season. In old age, with assurance, he ran over the first Victory Test bowlers:

Alf Gover hadn't had much practice and was medium-fast, and Bill Edrich was medium-fast. Doug Wright; I never had much trouble with Doug Wright for some reason or other. He was very fast through the air and I could always pick his wrong 'un and for some reason he would bowl it off or middle stump and I leg-glanced him a lot of times, and I late-cut or square-cut a lot of his leg-breaks too.

As for bowling, Australia had lacked a fast bowler in the 1930s, and had relied on the spinners Grimmett and O'Reilly. So it was for the RAAF teams in the war. With the AIF reinforcements, the Australians picked three, even four from five slow bowlers: Ellis, Price, Cristofani, Pepper, Pettiford – the last four also useful batsmen. (Ellis in old age would claim he made a century in

England, and did make 23 against the RAF in May 1944, but was best described as a number eleven batsman.) As their crucially scene-setting first innings in the first Test showed, aggressive later batsmen such as Pepper could flog ageing, tiring bowlers.

A wicket-keeper is often unfairly taken for granted. Sismey was regularly praised, and could besides hold up an end with the bat. In his column before the first Test, Hammond spoke of only four Australians: Ellis, Cristofani, Miller, and Sismey, whom he called 'not a showy player. He does the job in an unassuming way and he does it well.' This was clearly something Hammond admired. Having taken over from Bert Oldfield as New South Wales wicket-keeper, Sismey – a western suburbs Sydney man – had flown Catalina flying boats in the war. The year before, the *Manchester Guardian* praised him as a 'strongly built' batsman who 'gets well on top of the ball' after he made 36 for the RAAF against the North before a nose-diving Learie Constantine caught him at short leg.

To surpass a stronger team, Australia would have to rise to the occasion. They could, because they had one other, invisible weapon: their team spirit, and inner character. Here as elsewhere on the private side of the Australians, Whitington is the source. As a journalist who put his name to several books with Keith Miller, and Miller's biographer in retirement, Whitington brought insight to his first-hand view of a team suddenly thrown together in May 1945. As Whitington, one of the Army newcomers, recalled, some of the airmen resented Hassett as captain. They wanted to keep their captain, Keith Carmody, who, however, was only just back in the country after almost a year away. Pulled from the sea and held prisoner by the Germans, liberated by the Russians, Carmody had what he called a 'grim month' with those supposed allies before he crossed the River Elbe to the American Army.

That the two possible rivals did not split the men into two halves – army and air force – was both a credit to them and the team's practical selflessness. The selection committee of five – Hassett, Whitington, Carmody, Mick Roper and Sismey – sensibly had a majority of airmen, matching the balance of personnel. The airmen saw that Hassett had not asked to come in for Carmody; and Hassett won them over with his integrity. Carmody for his part captained the RAAF once more, but did not seek the overall Services captaincy. All the players realised that they had to be united to hope to match England. As Miller said to Whitington long afterwards: 'And we were all servicemen happy just to be alive and fit and well.' By the Second Test, the *Sydney Morning Herald* noted that Hassett 'obviously' had his team's full confidence. Bowlers accepting the ball from him exchanged a mutual grin; fielders picked up the captain's slightest signal.

That does not mean that every Australian was great mates with every other Australian. By 1945 Miller had become someone with the charisma to pick up and drop people, however charmingly, as he went along. A couple of stories of Reg Ellis' in 2009 said a lot about Miller – and himself. He began by calling Hassett the best captain he ever played under:

> *And the reason that Miller was never a captain was that he was, ah, he was always so rash in the things that he did. I remember after one of the Tests, at Lord's, he said to me, 'What say you and I walk home,' and that meant to The Strand; and we were walking down the street and a chap came up the other way, he was absolutely inebriated, and he nearly knocked me over when we passed and Keith didn't say anything to me,*

*he just got hold of him and got a policeman and said,
'Do something about this, he had a go at my mate', and
that's the type of chap he was. And the policeman was
still with him [the drunk] when we left. We also went
to Epsom, to the races, and I didn't drink or anything,
and I don't know how we became friends, but we did;
and he lost £150 at Epsom and that night we were back
at Brighton, that was where we all were then; and he
won £250 at two-up. That's why he was never made
captain of Australia.*

As for two-up, as Reg said, its players put two shilling
pieces, or a penny, on a board: 'Whether it comes up heads
or tails, you bet on it. Australians will bet on anything.'

While Reg Ellis named Miller, Stanford and Hassett
as heavy drinkers in the group, Miller liked race course
gambling, and Hassett was a golfer. As among any set
of workers, some would be your friends; some, with
outside interests in common; some, you merely worked
with. It was the same on an airfield: some bomber crews
stuck together socially, some did not. Even comrades
eventually could tire of the sight of each other. All that
said, Miller recalled how he and fellow airmen Mick
Roper, Stan Sismey and Keith Carmody 'were chatting
over a round of drinks' when Carmody brought up the
idea of a ring of close fielders to catch snicks from the
new ball, at the risk of giving away fours. The 'umbrella
field', an arc of catchers, began in a pub in Shepherd's
Market, in London's Mayfair. While the stereotype of
the loud, heavy-drinking Australian man is, like all
stereotypes, based in fact, like all stereotypes it doesn't
apply to some. Ellis the non-drinker and non-smoker
roomed with the like-minded Eddie Williams: 'He
kept himself to himself like me,' Reg said revealingly
in 2009.

For all these subtle relations between men, Ellis stressed the togetherness of the English and Australian players: 'We played as a team, a real team, they were, oh, good guys, we used to knock together, like; in those days it was different altogether to what cricket is now. That's off the field; and on the field it was cricket.'

To see the Australian Victory Test team as two halves – airmen or AIF, boozers and puritans – is missing the point. For men who came from such an enormous country – a continent – they already knew of each other to a remarkable extent, having played weekend, grade cricket together. Take Sydney and the 1939–40 season as an example. Pepper and Roper played for Petersham. Cheetham opened the batting and bowling for Balmain. Carmody and Clive Calvert batted for Mosman – the next season, they were the openers. Those three suburbs are, as the crow flies, six miles apart. In Adelaide Reg Ellis played in the colts team with Hartley Craig, RAAF opener; and Bruce Stanford, Ross' brother.

Their paths had separated. Airmen were the ones already in England, that the AIF cricketers, after their weeks around Eastbourne, attached themselves to. And of the airmen, Bomber Command shaped most of them.

If some call Bomber Command 'controversial', it's because they feel vaguely that bombing was wrong, but they are too lazy to ask why. During the war and at its end, only a few (ignored) pacifists questioned the morality of bombing. Only later did anyone argue loudly, in effect, that young Australian (or English) men killing other young German, Italian and Japanese men in deserts and jungles – far away – were somehow more proper than young men killing with bombs the Germans' parents, wives and children in their homes. The tragedy for all was that despite the latest technology – in aircraft and bomb-aiming – Bomber Command was not very efficient. The glamour of aeroplanes hid the reality that bomber men were the 1939–45 equivalent of the infantrymen in the 1914–18 trenches. Weather permitting, most nights a bomber squadron went 'over the top', on a bombing mission, or expected to soon.

What does the bombing of Germany by night have to do with cricket? Arthur Doubleday was one of the first pilots to pass through RAF Lichfield. He survived, by a statistical miracle, the set 30 or so missions at RAAF 460 Squadron; and returned to Lichfield as station commander in 1943, returning later to a front-line squadron at RAF Waddington. When interviewed in old age by the Australian War Memorial, he had this to say about nerves before a mission:

> *There are people who are physically sick, every time before they went off. Had cramps in their stomachs ... I never felt any different, other than from waiting to go into bat at cricket. You know, a fast bowler looks a bit faster from the fence but when you get in there it's not so bad ...*

Fear of failure can similarly cramp a cricketer – or am I, the author, speaking only for myself? For I was a bad cricketer. It was only just before I stopped playing, in my mid-20s, that I understood why I was bad, and could start to become better – that is, to do enough so that I did not feel a fraud whenever I wore whites. What can get in the way of this insight, and what held me back for years, is the fact that a man may fail – knock a catch from an easy ball; be hit; or drop a catch in the field – not because of some mental anguish that you can remedy, but because you are not very good at the game, or you have bad fortune. Once a batsman is out, he has a long time to dwell on his failure before his next chance. If he drops a catch, it can stay with him until he next has a chance to take a catch – which he may dread. But at least the failing cricketer can expect to return home in one piece, unlike the wartime airmen.

Any flight was dangerous, let alone a bombing mission. This dawned on airmen before they reached a front-line squadron, even if the authorities never spelt it out. Keith Campbell, for instance, was at his operational training unit at Bassingbourn in Cambridgeshire in 1941 when the England fast bowler Ken Farnes died there, crashing on take-off.

A pilot had to master fear like a batsman – knowing that one chance could be your last, while at the same time accepting that there was only so much you could do. You gave yourself (and your crewmates) your best chance if you did what you could, without worrying about what you could not affect. A batsman could play a reasonable shot, even a great one, yet be out thanks to better bowling or some outstanding fielding, or a misunderstanding with the other batsman while running. So it was with flying a bomber. Despite your skill or concentration, you could not avoid flying through flak – anti-aircraft gunfire. Or, to take a combat report in 467 Squadron's records: on the night of October 20–21, 1943, on the way to Leipzig, another Lancaster below fired at Pilot Officer Stanford. He took a precautionary dive to port and the 'attacker' was shaken off. Stanford's gunners did not open fire 'believing the encounter to be one of mistaken identity'.

For a pilot or gunner as for a batsman, a mistake might go unnoticed, and unpunished. Or your wartime kit let you down. Your aircraft might have patched holes, and worn-out engines from past pilots handling the plane roughly in their efforts to survive. Or your bat was old and your pads flapped; you had to make do. You had to weigh up whether mechanical faults were so serious that you had to return without bombing – at the risk of being punished and called a coward – or you could press on regardless, at the risk of being shot down as a slower, lower, easier target.

Besides accepting that the odds were against you, the mechanics of piloting an aircraft required qualities that a cricketer could relate to, and use. Above all, pilots had to concentrate and attend to detail. In old age some pilots made light of their task, likening it to driving a bus. A bomber did have an automatic pilot, called 'George', but it was a brave or foolish man who relied on it for long. The first and last hour of say a six-hour (against Hamburg or the Ruhr) or nine- or ten-hour (to Berlin or Munich) mission might be over England and the North Sea, when you would not expect enemy night-fighters. Even so, only a fool took his eyes off the cockpit instruments or shut his ears to the two engines on each wing beyond the cockpit glass. Or your wireless operator would pass on a message about wind direction, or the navigator would give a change of course. Or, at any moment, the rear gunner would scream a warning over the radio of an approaching plane, and fire a couple of bursts of his guns. Then the wise pilot who wanted to live a moment longer would fling the aircraft into a 'corkscrew' to throw the enemy off, as Stanford did to evade a Junkers 88 on a mission to Mannheim on September 6, 1943.

The intelligent batsman, similarly, did more than play each ball carefully; he observed and encouraged his fellow batsman; he watched for changes in the fielders, and the weather, and tried to anticipate. If the star bowler was coming off and a young unknown coming on, was it time to have a go? What was the best way to a target

– was there safety in numbers in the 'bomber stream' or was it wiser, though against orders, to fly higher if you could?

The larger and more complicated the aircraft – and a four-engined bomber such as a Lancaster was as advanced as any in the world in its time – the more drills the pilot had to go through – as Doubleday recalled, three or four were essential on the most basic training aircraft, the Tiger Moth, ten or 12 in an Anson, and 22 or 23 in the front-line bombers he flew, a Wellington or a Lancaster.

What connected cricket with flying a bomber, or any 'plane come to that, was that you could train a man to follow drills, that were taught for a reason, so that the aircraft did not fall like a stone, or you were ready to evade an enemy fighter (or one of your planes that thought *you* were an enemy). Likewise a batsman learned the drills to hook, sweep, drive, play forward or back, and so on. For a batsman and a pilot alike, the skill came in picking which drill to do – whether to let a ball pass, or waft your bat at it. Sometimes there was no drill in the training manual. Based, it was true, on all you knew, you had to decide on the best, or the least worst, option. And you had to hurry, whether a ball was rising nastily towards your nose; or you saw the flames of a falling 'plane in the dark and wondered if you were next.

Crewing a bomber and surviving in a cricket team each required teamwork, which called for some unselfishness. True, in cricket you had to look after your own interests, and be sure to do well enough in your specialism. It did not pay to be too selfish. If a player dropped a catch off your bowling, it would not do to run him out, in revenge, the next time you batted together. In a crew, similarly, it paid to give each other a hand. On the other hand, while you wished every other crew well, minding your own business could be the difference between life and death, as Doubleday recognised on an early mission, while crossing the Continental coast:

> *After we'd passed Texel and my gunners were saying, 'Oh, you ought to see the stream of aircraft burning on the ground,' and I said, 'Look, keep your eyes in the sky. There is a quota tonight and your job is to keep us out of that quota' … and that's the attitude I always adopted. You could get back and sigh about it or go and get drunk or do what you like, but there was no point in trying to commiserate with people, and get your attention drawn away.*

Between missions, such were the responses of airmen to what one pilot called the fear 'in your system', the near misses and the loss of comrades. It had much in common with how batsmen came to terms with unavoidable failure and the nagging fear that, no matter how many runs you scored one day, the pressure would be there to score more runs the next. Grieving, thinking too deeply about it, not only was no help; it might harm your reflexes for next time.

Again, batting (and keeping wicket) and flying in combat had similarities. Say, for ease of arithmetic, you face a bowler of 60 miles an hour – slow to medium for the expert batsman, but fast enough for anyone else. The ball would travel, for the sake of argument, a mile in a minute, or 20 yards from release from the hand to the batsman – again, roughly, for ease of maths – in a second. It can take the brain longer than a second to take in the sensory data – where the ball is going and how fast; compute how to respond – move the legs and arms to meet the ball with the bat; and to do it, by sending the commands to the limbs. Sometimes, even the best batsmen are beaten for pace, as the saying goes. How can a batsman seemingly defy science, by putting the bat to the ball in time; and how did Hammond make batting look so easy?

Hutton reckoned that Hammond defied the principles of the game by making up his mind where to hit the ball before the bowler let go of it. Far from defying principles, Hammond was a supreme *reader* of bowlers. Sooner than lesser batsmen, Hammond picked up clues to how the ball would reach him, judging by the way the bowler held the ball in his hand, how fast or how wide of the stumps he ran. He worked from thousands of previous similar-looking balls. Putting it another way, Hammond was ruthless in rejecting all unnecessary data. So it was on a bomber mission.

'Pressure is a Messerschmitt up your arse,' said Keith Miller. It's much quoted; it sums up a truth. No peacetime worry could match the coarse urgency of avoiding sudden, violent death. And yet Miller, like any bomber veteran, knew pilots were not always, or even regularly, fighting off Messerschmitts. Most if not all survivors of Bomber Command, if they wish to talk about it, can relate near-misses, hits and injuries, and hair-raising hardships. Yet a bombing mission was seldom if ever one scrape after another, except, for sure, during the relatively few minutes over the target. Most telling of all, Miller was uncertain he ever came across an enemy – in his very short combat career, admittedly. As he put it to a 1981 National Library of Australia interviewer: 'I only saw up to bugger all, to use an expression, "aircraft, enemy" and if I did I was very happy if he got away from me rather than me trying to chase him.'

A combat mission, like a game of cricket, was above all a test of concentration. Bomber Command was, then, as good a finishing school for cricketers as anything. At the pilot's controls as on the cricket field, you had to keep a minimum alertness at all times, while being able at a moment's notice to flick to absolute concentration as some thunderbolt came at you. And the difference between being a hero or not at cricket, or returning safely in your 'kite', or not, could be the ability to respond efficiently for a few seconds after five or six hours or more of fatigue and cold and noise. As a sports fan and bomber wireless operator from Sydney, later a historian of Australians in Bomber Command, Ross Pearson, put it: 'There were no prizes for coming second.'

The cruel trick in combat and cricket was that you could be as gifted as a Hammond, a diligent and sober student. You stored your experience so that you could react sensibly if a similar emergency cropped up again. Sometimes, no matter how kind the weather, or undefended the target, or able your crew, you could crash and die because you were in the wrong place at the wrong time. Or, you could survive some mishap that others did not, until an umpire gave you out unfairly, whereas on another day you would be plumb out but another umpire would give you a 'life' – a significant word, recognising that the end of a batsman's innings was like a temporary death.

Batsmen and aircrew, like anyone trapped by fate that seemed beyond reason, retreated into fatalism and superstition. Men drank to forget; kept to rituals; or let off steam through high jinks, tolerated by the authorities if they understood the men's predicament. Aircrew released energy and their suppressed aggression through sport.

The month that Ross Stanford arrived at 467 Squadron, August 1943, it lost seven crews, roughly one in three, including the squadron commander. On the day of the news of the lost commander, described in the station log as the 'worst day in the squadron's history', there was an inter-flight aircrew cricket match; about 30 aircrew went swimming at Newark baths; and about 20 others went on an organised cycle tour. It was best not to mope.

Ross Pearson served on an RAF squadron at Pocklington in east Yorkshire in 1944 in a mixed Australian-British crew. He recalled an Australian chaplain in a game of rugby union:

> *I must say he was a wonderful padre for members of his flock, he saw them before they went on ops. But he played with the officers' team … and I have never played against a dirtier player. If they went on the ground, he would say, kick them off it! At half-time I said, 'I am sick of this. Forget the ball, kick the padre!'*

Even in sport, fatalism crept through. 'I can remember us playing cricket while stood down, or waiting to go away, Australians playing against an England team; we batted 14 and they didn't wake up to it. Or they didn't care,' Ross Pearson said. The nationalities on his squadron – Australians, Canadians, South Africans, Rhodesians, New Zealanders, a Jamaican – all got on. They were in the same boat. On the ground, men did not have so achingly, or at least not all the time, the gut-fear of the prospect of combat, like the fizzing of a hard, fast ball wanting them out. The mood on squadron was like any batsman's: 'How shall I put it?' asked Ross Pearson. 'Not even an air of apprehension; you were just conscious that you might not necessarily be there that much longer'.

Sport – as a quick release of muscular tension, and relaxation for the mind – suited nervy, impatient airmen while off duty in ways that longer-term, improving pursuits did not. Ross Pearson recalled: 'I was starting to study law by correspondence at the University of London. When I got on the squadron I gave it up. It sounds silly, but I felt I would never be able to use it. Just live for today and to hell with it.'

At least one crew forbade a comrade to carry on with such an academic course, when they found out about it, taking the view that it would take up his mind and endanger the crew. No airman would stop cricket; or a game of cards. Indeed, the air force encouraged sport. While Pocklington was a wartime airfield built in a hurry, lacking its own facilities, aircrew lucky enough to arrive at a pre-war, more solidly-built aerodrome could find squash courts, snooker tables and so on.

For a bomber man's life was not one mission after another; quite the opposite. Even a dedicated squadron commander like Leonard Cheshire, of 617 Squadron, allowed sports, because you could not fly and work all the time. While it might seem obvious to take young men's minds off their likely death by giving them sport, it's striking how many of the Australians were at home all-round sportsmen and men of the outdoors. Stan Sismey played tennis and rugby league; Mick Roper played for New South Wales at baseball and table tennis. Keith Miller, recalled fellow pilot and Invincibles tour all-rounder Colin McCool, was a 'red-hot' table tennis player.

Once on a bomber squadron, you had to do roughly 30 operations to earn yourself a respite as an instructor at a training squadron. Those 30 missions would total about 240 hours, the equivalent of ten days and nights. In fact the 'tour of operations' would take about six months. A crew had a week's leave about every six weeks; illnesses or faults in aircraft or bad weather might mean time off. A story about Ross Stanford that made the news in 1944 shows how a cricketing airman made the most of his time, while not forgetting that the air force came first; and if ignorant civilians spoiled things, there was no point in wasting your anger on them.

The Teams

In the *Yorkshire Observer* on Monday, August 7, 1944, sports reporter George Thompson described how Stanford – staying in Bradford with friends – was refused permission to play in the Bradford League on the Saturday, August 5, as a substitute for a player away. A second club had permission refused to take Stanford, although they had registered him as an amateur, six weeks before. According to the league, it would not allow a better player to replace the substituted man. Stanford was quoted saying, typically of a man risking his life, as Thompson put it, 'You can never tell which ball has your name on it.' Stanford might have been out for nought, and the other, supposedly lesser man might have scored more.

It was a telling comparison of the front-line airman's uncertain life with the unpredictability of cricket, ignored by the petty league officials. By the Thursday, Thompson reported that Stanford could play that weekend, for Great Horton, on the Saturday, as he had wanted to the Saturday before; only Stanford's leave ran out on the Friday. So the story closed on the Saturday, August 12, when George Thompson reflected that Stanford, 'probably still mystified', by now would be back at his 'drome. Stanford would not apply for an extra day's leave to play cricket, because, Thompson hinted, Stanford felt his job was with his 'air crew pals'.

Cricket and Bomber Command had one more thing in common: for all the books and broadcasts about them, veterans admit difficulty in putting into words what a combat mission, or the battle between batsman and bowler, is like. This is one reason for the quiet but deep and lasting comradeship between bomber veterans, like many men who have been through war. Not only did they share extreme experiences, but they found that civilians back home – like those Bradford cricket authorities – could not understand, or did not want to.

Museums try to bridge the existential gap. At the Australian War Memorial in Canberra you can view the 460 Squadron Lancaster 'G for George'. In 1999 the memorial offered a 'bomber experience': visitors stood inside a dark tube for a five-minute recorded drama. To be fair, much was accurate: the pilot's order over the radio (like Doubleday's) to shut up and keep watch; the worryingly mysterious rumbles; and the lightness of the aircraft once the bombs are dropped. But no matter how well-meaning the museum, you could not avoid the fact that everyone stepped out at the end, as they knew they would all along. The same with any cricket museum or commercial efforts to reproduce batting and bowling; even if you were to equip a batsman, fire a ball at him from a bowling machine, and broadcast the conversation of fielders and umpires; can it be the same as the real, dangerous, stomach-sickening thing? That your (sporting) life depends on?

Ross Stanford's two-year journey to the front line ended on August 26, 1943 when he arrived at 467 Squadron at RAF Bottesford near Nottingham. In November, the squadron flew their Lancasters a dozen miles north-east to RAF Waddington outside Lincoln.

Bomber Command for three years had flung itself at Germany, with (we know now) painfully little to show for it. Numbers and size of bombers had risen gradually and successes had come – the 1,000-bomber destruction of Cologne in 1942 and the firestorm raid that burned the centre of Hamburg in 1943. The cost was grim. In the year 1943, 467 squadron lost 40 crews; in other words, roughly all the crews it started with, and all the crews that replaced the lost ones.

The Teams

Stanford and his crew – mixed, as so many were; two gunners and the flight engineer were Royal Air Force, the other three were Australian – began with a raid against Mannheim, on September 5. Late that month they flew against Hanover; and Bochum – all 16 from the squadron back safely that night. On October 1 the mission was to Hagen – again, all returned; the next night, he flew to Munich, when two of 19 failed to return. After a fortnight's break, he had a burst of three missions in five nights: to Hanover, Leipzig and Kassel.

November saw Stanford fly to Dusseldorf, Modane and, four times in nine nights, Berlin. The head of Bomber Command, Arthur Harris, determined on sending hundreds of bombers at a time that winter against Hitler's capital, a distant but most prestigious target. Those nights were thankless, as the 467 log book recorded. And Stanford recalled:

> … *generally in ten-tenths cloud and you would be dropping your bombs on the sky markers because you couldn't see the ground. And the Pathfinders would drop their sky markers and bomb aimers had to aim their bombs on the sky markers and only once did I go over Berlin when it was clear and you could see the whole town, all the houses, and it was that lit up. They had 400 searchlights surrounding Berlin and it was just like daylight going across and I never thought I was going to get over the target.*

On one of those Berlin missions, Stanford had to turn back after an hour and jettison his bombs, because of ice on the engines: 'starboard inner out and starboard outer looked like cutting also due to icing', the station logged. December brought him three more raids on Berlin, two days of Christmas dinners, and a narrow escape before bombing practice on the Lincolnshire coast at Wainfleet, 'for just after taking off he ran into a flock of birds and one went right through the Perspex and hit him on the side of the head,' the station log book said. 'Being solid (hope he doesn't read this) no damage was done although it is learned that the bird did not survive.'

January saw more 'trips' to Berlin, and one even further east, to Stettin; two of the eleven sent there by 467 never came back. That month also brought snow: 'quite a spectacle; some of the Aussies had never seen it before', said the log. By February 1944, Stanford and his crew had flown 23 missions, which made them one of the most senior crews on the squadron. Put another way, most others were killed sooner.

Arguably the most famous squadron of all, 617, wanted volunteers. As Stanford recalled: 'There weren't many volunteers to 617 Squadron after the [1943] Dams raid, and the Dortmund-Ems canal, which was a worse result [that is, a higher ratio of bombers shot down] than the Dams raid.' The Waddington station commander flew with Stanford to the practice bombing range at Wainfleet. Stanford recalled: 'Funnily enough the bombing area was only 68 yards [wide] from 8,000 feet, which was the best result put in by the squadron for I don't know how long.' He and his crew had proved themselves – not least by staying alive for so long – to be one of the elite, fit to 'volunteer' for the Dambusters Squadron. 'And so about a week later my posting came up to go to 617 Squadron.'

As Bomber Command developed as it went along – as Britain's armed forces did in both world wars – long-lived crews went into special 'Pathfinder' units to drop markers on targets for the rest. Even more of an elite was 617: 'How shall I put it, perhaps a more friendly atmosphere among the blokes on 617 Squadron because more of a mixture; a few New Zealanders, about 40 Canadians, and there was one Rhodesian crew, about 20 Aussies, two Americans, and of course there was a lot of shy-acking between the blokes from the different countries.' The Canadians, Stanford recalled, used to play ice hockey, and dismiss his sport with: 'That game of cricket! You take three days to play a game!'

Leonard Cheshire had taken over the squadron from the original Dams raid commander Guy Gibson. Like others, Stanford regarded Cheshire highly as a leader: 'He was the greatest man I ever met in my life. He had a wonderful personality and of course he was an absolutely courageous man who went on nearly all the raids. The only reason he didn't go on a raid was if he had to go to headquarters. He was the same with the ground staff as with the aircrew. He knew a lot of the ground staff, got to know their names. We would have followed him anywhere.' Where 617 did go was on special missions, still at night, that called for exact bombing. Rather than anonymous mass bombing, a 617 raid of about 20 'planes knew whether they had 'knocked the target out or not', Stanford said:

> They picked out special operations, for training really; these targets were in France, mostly, and the Germans generally had French workers in these factories, you see? What Leonard Cheshire used to do was fly low over the factory to warn the French workers to get out, that we were going to bomb their factory. He made three or four runs, and the bomb-aimer would call up and tell him he reckoned that most of the French workers were out of the factory and so Leonard Cheshire would mark it then, and then call us up and tell us where his markers were exactly, and where to bomb, either in the centre of the factory or north-west or south-east of his markers, if he

didn't have them dead centre. We had very high [radio]
frequency and we could talk to one another.

Such targets might be undefended. After D-Day, the
Allied invasion of Normandy, 617 switched to other,
defended, French targets – the U-boat port of Brest;
flying-bomb sites; and the 'big guns' at Mimoyecques on
the coast that might have fired at England; 'We used to
get peppered there regularly'.

Stanford had a close escape on a daylight attack against
Mimoyecques: 'I went through the target the second
time. My first run wasn't any good, or my bomb-aimer
reckoned it wasn't, and he wouldn't drop the bomb.' On
his second try, Stanford's Lancaster was on its own 'and
I got hit in the coolant tank in the port outer [engine] on
the run over the target and I had to get it feathered, [get]
the engineer to feather that engine, and we also got hit in
the hydraulics. So that when I got out of the target area
I couldn't close the bomb doors.' A second engine seized
up: 'It had been hit in an oil pipe and so I came home on
two engines that day. And we had to pull the emergency
air bottle to push the wheels down. I landed at Bradwell
Bay just north of the Thames, which has a long runway,
because the starboard inner engine had cut once, but it
picked up as soon as we changed the petrol tanks ... on
other occasions I came home on three engines.'

Before and after D-Day was the busiest time for Bomber
Command, and Stanford, who flew six missions in April
alone. Meanwhile, Stanford was the most consistent
RAAF batsman of the 1944 season, topping their batting
averages for first-class matches with 275 runs at 55,
though Miller and Clive Calvert made more runs.

More than 50 years on, Stanford sighed at the memory:
'I had done 43 trips in 11 months, oh, I reckoned that was
enough.' Two of his crew stayed on; one was killed with

another crew. Stanford took an invitation to go on a tour of aircraft factories, to give speeches to the workers, for £10 a week, plus free rail warrants, far more money than he earned risking his life. Early in 1945, he became baggage and sports officer for returning Australian prisoners of war. 'I had to try and get sports equipment of all sorts, including golf clubs and golf balls and arrange games of cricket for PoWs as soon as they became well enough to become active again.'

Chapter Eight

Between the First and Second Tests

Nothing else in cricket quite approaches the importance of a Test match between England and Australia ... Nothing else will re-establish the game so thoroughly after the armistice as our best being pitted against their best.

Sir Home Gordon *The Cricketer*, May 6, 1944

An Ashes Test, even an unofficial one, was not supposed to be so exciting. If one side won, it was by the grim overcoming of the other; or by catching them on a 'sticky', a wet wicket impossible to bat on. While Hammond did not contrive the close finish to the first 'Test' – the Australians did have to throw the bat – Hammond did make it possible. His tactics mirrored the world, glad of the end of a war against tyranny, yet unsure of how to proceed. Strangely, at least while Hitler lived, the Allies had known what they had to do. Similarly, in a normal Ashes series, as Hammond wrote, both sides knew what was at risk, and played carefully. Would the world, and cricket, return to 'business as usual' – bearing in mind that the world after the 1914–18 war had, you could say, merely proved to be an inglorious 20-year respite before a still longer war? Cricket between the world wars had become a dead end of flat and over-prepared wickets – doped or dead, some said – to suit batsmen. The world could not undo the wartime changes – in politics, the advance of the Soviet armies into Germany, the Americans supreme on the Allied side. Likewise in cricket the war had meant that groundsmen lacked the labour and equipment to keep pitches so perfect for batting. Bowlers might have more hope, for the time being.

The Australians were the heroes of the moment – and were winners, people always worth knowing. They could expect even more courtesy and luxury, or at least what luxury a war-weary and patched-up country could offer. The Australians were not likely to have their heads turned. All along, they had enjoyed the natural hospitality of their English hosts, whose cousins or old friends had often migrated to Australia. The airmen in particular, as survivors, had reached quite high rank quickly on their squadrons. All airmen in any case were used to having everything done for them – their laundry, their parachutes packed (a skilled and long job best left to specialists), and being driven the half-mile from the aerodrome buildings to their waiting bombers. Being waited on at table was not new; only meals now came with speeches from cricket club presidents and mayors that always sounded the same.

Besides, the Australians did not have time to take on airs. On Wednesday, May 23, the day after the Lord's win, five of the Test Australians were in the AIF team against Dover Wanderers, as part of the town's Navy Week. The Australians batted first for 151, two of the Test men top-scoring – Price 66 and Hassett 51 – and Dover, bolstered by several county men, won by two wickets, batting on to 166 all out. The following weekend, the AIF played two one-day games in High Wycombe. First, against High Wycombe, the AIF helped themselves to 165 for two, Whitington with 84 and Price with 58 being the only men out. Pepper with four for 14 bowled High Wycombe for 82. Hassett and Cheetham were the other Test men of the eleven. On the Sunday, Buckinghamshire, batting first, lunched at 73 for five, but were able to declare at 162 for nine. Cheetham took four for 41 and the occasional bowler Whitington three for 37, which suggested not for the last time that summer that Hassett gave struggling lesser teams some friendlier bowling; or the friendly bowling was all he had. It gave the crowd something to watch later. According to the local *Bucks Free Press*, Pepper 'knocked up a brilliant century in a very short time', and was 'especially severe on the slow bowling'. The trees stopped sixes landing on the nearby London Road. The only other men in double figures were Whitington with 39 and Cheetham with 48.

The AIF and the RAAF cricketers' paths seldom crossed in the next few weeks before the second Test, due to start on June 23 at Bramall Lane, Sheffield. The AIF largely played teams below county standard, in Sussex. Typical was a Saturday, June 9 game at the Saffrons when, in the *Eastbourne Gazette*'s verdict, 'the Australian Imperial Forces team were much too good for a side representing the Sussex Cricket Association'. The five Test men, Whitington, Price, Cheetham, Hassett and Pepper, all made runs and two bowlers, Holmes, 'an enterprising left-hander' who 'hit a couple of sixes to long on' and Kennedy added 43 before Hassett declared at 224 for ten – each team batting 12 a side. The dozen Sussex club players took an hour and a half to fold for 67. One of their opening batsmen was a 16-year-old, Ken Suttle, of Broadwater, later of Sussex until 1971. All went well, according to the *Eastbourne Herald*, against the opening bowlers Holmes and Cheetham, 'until the gloss went off the ball and Pepper and Price were let loose. Pepper's fast leg break which some critics have been rude enough to describe as a shooter soon had Suttle lbw.'

Pepper took six wickets for 23, Price five for 18. The spinners were Hassett's main bowlers and they had a long summer ahead of them. Holmes, incidentally, recently freed from four years in a German prison camp, was ambidextrous at bowling. He was right arm fast and was a slow left arm spinner and left-handed batsman. His father had converted him, saying Australia needed fast bowlers more than slow.

The weekend before the Sheffield Test, the AIF were hosting RAAF Brighton at the Saffrons, in a two-day, two-innings game. Hassett took five wickets for 35 in RAAF Brighton's first innings of 107. While Hassett as an experienced tourist understood that he had to save his concentration for the most important games, you suspect that among his countrymen he relaxed.

That Brighton side did not include any RAAF first-teamers, though TD (David) Beyer, the 39-year-old air force chaplain, had been playing cricket in England for a good couple of years. John Papayanni and Colin Bremner shared the wicket-keeping; indeed each took a stumping in the AIF's first innings of 215. The Australian air force was spoiled for wicket-keepers – both stood in for Sismey over the summer. Once again, the Test players made most of the AIF runs: Whitington 60, Price 30, and Hassett 81 not out. RAAF Brighton closed the first day on 23 for one. Resuming 'in glorious weather', so the *Eastbourne Gazette* reported, the airmen batted until mid-afternoon, making 211, Speakman top scoring with 55. That left the AIF to make 104, which they did by 5.15pm. 'Presumably to please the spectators, the teams continued playing for a little over an hour longer, during which six fresh bowlers were tried.' Again, the suspicion is that Hassett enjoyed himself, playing 'free but perfectly correct cricket' the

Gazette wrote approvingly, making 112 not out of 244 for five.

The RAAF, meanwhile, met tougher teams. During the first Test, the RAAF faced Glamorgan at Cardiff Arms Park. For the Welsh county, the 47-year-old JE Clay took four for 29 in a two-hour spell on the first day, and 10 for 79 in the match. The RAAF's first innings of 128 was the highest of the match, and Papayanni's 26 the Australians' joint highest score. The RAAF won by 56 runs.

Next, on Saturday, June 2, the RAAF faced the Royal Air Force in a one-day match at Gloucester, the first visit to the city by an Australian team. Traditionally the Ashes tourists began their summer down the road, at Worcester; as it happened a New Zealand Services side was playing there, captained by a 41-year-old former Test player now a flying officer, Ken James, and starring the Test batsman, now an army major, Martin Donnelly. Cricket-watchers with cars could choose between the two, because as *The Citizen* reported beforehand: 'It is expected that the basic petrol ration will bring an extra large number to see the game.'

Life was beginning to return to normal in some ways; a petrol ration began again – previously, private car use for pleasure was not allowed – on June 1. As the local paper was hinting, such a high class of cricket came to Gloucester only because it paid. Three previous wartime first class matches in Gloucester resulted in £733 for the RAF Benevolent Fund, tens of thousands of pounds in 21st-century money; and Gloucester came close to the top in profits made from such wartime games.

For their money the city saw county players – Dennis Brookes of Northamptonshire came in for Ames of Kent, owing to what the newspaper termed 'services calls'. Bill Edrich won the toss for the RAF, and 'decided to bat on a soft wicket' as *The Citizen* reported later that day. The

Australian spinners kept the score down but 'Miller the fast bowler' took the first wicket, Brookes, yorked middle stump for 41, just before lunch.

Two heavy showers came but, as the paper reported on the Monday, 'the players possessed hardier spirits than the usual peacetime County teams and played through ...' The first rain while the RAF batted did mean a drying pitch and Ellis 'proved too dangerous'. Edrich was 'in fact the only batsman who could do anything with him. He hit one ball on to the club building for a beautiful six and took quite a number of fours.'

The RAF made 175, Washbrook top scoring with 50 and Edrich making 36. It left the Australians with two and a half hours. 'The Australians made a gallant effort to win but Warburton and Edrich bowling fast in the rain beat them with ten minutes to spare ... There were several thousand spectators present during the afternoon and they had full cricket value for their money. It was a bright and interesting game and thanks to the Australians there was a fine fighting finish,' *The Citizen* reported appreciatively.

Miller was out first ball to a brilliant catch in the slips off Edrich: 'Miller meant to drive the ball but it struck the corner of his bat and flew like a bullet to Warburton who held it.' Warburton took a similar catch to dismiss Workman, who nearly carried his bat. Workman (68) and Pettiford (40) put on 87 for the third wicket. Later Cristofani made a run-a-minute 28 until Brookes caught him at extra cover, high up with one hand. The Australian airmen needed 20 in the last 20 minutes, with two wickets left, but could only manage three and were all out for 159. Edrich took five for 26, Leslie Warburton of Lancashire four for 52.

One innovation later taken for granted had a trial at Gloucester. Flying Officer HS (Stan) Squires scored 16 for the RAF, wearing as an experiment 'contact lenses (invisible glasses) that adhere directly to the eyeballs and which have been worn by airmen with great success', *The Citizen* said. It and many other newspapers explained that the Surrey batsman, who had returned to the mainland a fortnight before after two years' service in the Hebrides, found the lenses a big advantage over ordinary spectacles. Squires said: 'Besides cricket I have boxed and played squash rackets, rugby and association football wearing contact lenses. Troubles experienced by a batsman wearing glasses during wet weather appear for myself at least to have been overcome.'

Squires as an air force sports officer had laid a concrete wicket with matting at an RAF station in the Hebrides. It had a local rule; because of a sand dune the size of a house at cover point, a fielder could hide out of sight and take his pick of running out the batsmen taking a second run.

By the Tuesday, June 5, Workman and Pettiford were walking to the wicket at Old Trafford, Manchester to open the RAAF innings against Lancashire. In keeping with the city's reputation – the entire 1938 Test was rained off – heavy rain sent players running for shelter for the day. The teams agreed to an extra day's play so that in fact the original two-day game went ahead.

Play was as grim as against Glamorgan. The Lancashire spinners, William Roberts and Jack Ikin, took seven wickets between them as the RAAF reached 109 in 55.1 overs. The only run-makers were Miller with 52 and Keith Carmody with 21 – returning to cricket after his year as a German prisoner of war. Two England batsmen, Washbrook and Eddie Paynter, opened with 71 before the spinners Ellis and Cristofani took eight wickets. Late in the innings Barry Howard – the 21-year-old Manchester University student son of the county secretary – tried to swing to leg, accidentally hitting Sismey on the forehead. Workman took over as wicket-keeper and Hartley Craig was allowed to field and bat in Sismey's place. Lancashire declared at 137 for nine. The RAAF found the going even harder on the second afternoon, falling to 27 for five, still one run behind Lancashire. Stanford batting at five and Craig, batting last out of courtesy, added 20 'difficult' runs, according to the *Manchester Guardian*. The RAAF eked their 90 all out from 56.1 overs; Stanford was 32 not out. That left Lancashire 63 to win in two hours, 10 minutes. By the standards of the match, Lancashire were racing at 38 for two in 13.1 overs when a downpour ended the day at 5pm.

The Lancashire men had careers to re-establish, and were not the sort to give anything away anyway. By contrast, the RAAF's following weekend game against LN Constantine's eleven at Edgbaston was altogether friendlier, because both sides knew they were there to entertain the crowd; and Learie Constantine's team was not as strong as a county's. On the Saturday, RAAF made 275, and the West Indians 23 for three. After 70 more minutes on the Sunday, the West Indians were all out for 55, and out again for 75 in less than two hours. Yet again, the spinners – Cristofani, Papayanni's teammate at St George in south Sydney; Ellis; and Pettiford – took all 20 wickets.

An exhibition game for the 3,500 spectators followed on the Sunday afternoon. The West Indians were stronger in bowling – besides Constantine, the spinner Bertie Clarke and the opening bowler Edwin St Hill had played Tests for West Indies before the war. Constantine was, even aged 43, their most dangerous bowler. In the words of the *Birmingham Post*, Constantine was 'no longer a fast bowler, he relied on variety and deception of delivery and never allowed opponents to be comfortable'.

The RAAF gave more proof of their strength in depth. Their three highest scorers were the incomers: Craig with 64, Papayanni with 40 and Eddie Williams – no relation to Graham Williams who had earned the ovation at Lord's – 35. Eddie Williams, incidentally, had made his debut for Victoria against Tasmania in Melbourne, the week before Tasmania travelled on to Adelaide where Stanford made his unfortunate debut. Both men had not played for their state since – indeed Eddie Williams never would; but at least he had scored 78 in February 1936.

While the AIF and RAAF Brighton met at Eastbourne, the RAAF had the better of the Royal Air Force at Lord's. As usual in a one-day, one-innings match, the RAAF, batting first, took up most overs, declaring on 243 for seven after 83.2 overs. All the batsmen made runs except Stanford, out for a duck, the same as against the West Indies. Carmody, though described by the *Daily Telegraph* 'as only natural … somewhat out of practice', was captain of the RAAF again and looked like returning to the Test team in Stanford's place. Cristofani again made runs and took wickets. The RAF closed on 162 for seven in 55 overs, saved by the 44-year-old former England captain Bob Wyatt, who opened with 94.

Whether playing as AIF or RAAF, or combined, the summer lifestyle of the Australian (or indeed the Royal Air Force) cricketers was in place. It had much in common with their wartime routine. Sometimes they were awake and away while citizens with any sense were still in bed. Often they had to sit on a train for hours, or wait with their feet up, passing the time with conversation, a pack of cards, letters or a passed-around newspaper; or padded up, thinking about what was ahead. For the bomber men, only the kit and the daylight were different.

Chapter Nine

Second Test, Bramall Lane, June 23, 25 and 26 1945

Outside the walls of the ground, tramcars clattered along cobbled streets and hissed like ganders as they stopped to pick up passengers. The ugly fingers of soot-blackened chimneys forever pointing at the sky belched great fugs of yellowy-brown smoke into the atmosphere.

Fred Trueman, *As It Was* (2004)

Wally Hammond wondered aloud in his newspaper column between the first and second Tests: 'Whom have we to take the place of Farnes as a fast bowler, Verity as slow left arm bowler and who can replace Leyland as the left handed batsmen in the side? ... I have not seen a real fast bowler among the present generation. Friends tell me that Alec Bedser one of the Surrey twins has possibilities but I have not seen him play. He is now in Italy.'

Hammond put younger batsmen in order on merit: Hutton, Hardstaff, Compton, Robertson, Washbrook, Edrich and his Gloucestershire colleague Charlie Barnett; and of the 'newcomers', Dewes, Carr, Simpson, Brookes and White. He summed up: 'The outlook does not look bright but we have been in this position before.'

George Pope, William Roberts and Maurice Leyland replaced Gover, Robins and Ames. Stephenson remained but Dick Pollard later took his place. George Pope, a six-foot 'medium fast bowler', 'of tireless energy', had shown fine form for Colne in the Lancashire League, according to the Press Association. He was besides 'a Wellard-like hitter of sixes', harking back to the Somerset and England all-rounder of the 1930s. He and two brothers had played for Derbyshire in the same match in 1939; George by that season had risen in the county batting order to five. The nearest he had come to Tests was at Nottingham in 1938, when he made the final 13. Apart from Hassett, the Australians were meeting him for the first time; a sign that the official fixture-setters had kept the Australians and the northern leagues apart.

Roberts, a left-arm slow bowler, had had 'good performances against West Indies at Lord's and for Lancashire against RAAF at Old Trafford', PA said. As did happen at some of the strongest counties, Roberts had had a long apprenticeship. Before he first appeared for his county in 1939, he had six years on Lancashire ground staff. Also of Lancashire was Pollard, who 'bowls straight of good length and can move the ball each way', the news agency reported. While none of the three were youthful, the two seamers could expect to take advantage of a seaming pitch, while Roberts would be a spinning alternative to Wright, filling the gap left by the dead Verity.

Now that English towns and cities look ever more alike, it takes some imagination to arrive like the Australian eleven, and the many visitors that followed them, in Sheffield, on Friday, June 22, the day before the second Test.

The Australians left London St Pancras by train at noon. The AIF members of the team had an even earlier start, leaving Eastbourne before 8am. The party arrived at 5pm, left their belongings at the Grand Hotel, had a cup of tea, and by 6.15pm were at Bramall Lane, for a knock in the nets. The ground staff had prepared matting wickets for practice, by the football stand. Bramall Lane, the home of Sheffield United cricket and football clubs, had hosted its last Test match in 1902. The city's press, plainly jealous that the Headingley ground in Leeds had taken Tests since, reported how the Bramall Lane seats, fortunately, had been stored, whereas Headingley's permanent wooden fixtures had perished. German prisoners of war washed the Bramall Lane benches and put them back in place; and washed the paintwork and white-washed. There was justice in such work. German bombs in the winter of 1940–1 had half destroyed the football stand. Years on, a pile of rubble lay in one corner and sand filled a bomb crater on the terraces. Australian and English players had to share one dressing room, because government ministries were working in the pavilion.

On that Friday the *Sheffield Telegraph* gossiped that 'Tonight an army of cricket journalists and photographers will invade the city'. A flash message about the Test would reach Australia in four minutes. The newspaper told readers: 'Special lines of communication will link up the ground with Australia and the game is to be broadcast ... what a priceless advertisement for Sheffield!'

Either the newspaper did not want to remind its readers, or the people of south Yorkshire took their surrounds for granted, but the truth was that those visitors, hard-to-impress Fleet Street reporters, might not see Sheffield in the best light. One of those visiting journalists – Bob Crisp of the *Express*, the sort who boasted he kept a taxi waiting on the last day of a match so he left as soon as he could – repeated an old tale about the 'belching' chimneys. 'For as every county cricketer knows, when the visiting side is batting in Yorkshire, the word goes round the factories and fresh shovels of coal go on the foundries to fog the atmosphere and reduce the visibility.'

Crisp had a point. When a couple of years later the teenage Fred Trueman entered the nets at Bramall Lane – the first time he set foot inside a county cricket ground – he gloried in the place's history while noticing 'the yeasty odour of a nearby brewery'. During the Victory Test, those brewery workers could watch the cricket during their lunch hour, from – inevitably – a chimney.

The press had the usual two questions to chew over beforehand: how would the pitch play, and how good were the visitors? Fred Kean, the groundsman, told the *Sheffield Telegraph*, defensively: 'It's a natural wicket, no dope of any kind has been used. We have never used dope at Bramall Lane in my time.'

As for the Australians, KE Hooper, an Australian sporting journalist, talked up Ellis the googly bowler, one of four bowlers who had each taken four wickets during the first Victory Test. Ellis was a 'protégé of the great Clarrie Grimmett', 'as full of guile as the immortal Grimmett' who, Hooper added darkly, 'understands to the full the timidity of British batsmen against left arm googly bowling'. Hooper seemed to veer like many sports reporters between professional accuracy, and patriotically trying to frighten the other side. Dick Whitington, for example, had been 'long enough in England to show the form which lifted him from district cricket to opening bat for South Australia'.

Some of the players the readers would have known from the papers. Pepper was the 'blitz bat of the team', the 'husky hurricane from Sydney'. Carmody, shot down over the North Sea the year before, was reportedly saying that captivity did not impair his cricket form, as he managed to keep fairly fit although, he added, 'war prison diet does not permit much of that sort of thing'.

Their captain, 'dapper little Hassett, and the only member of the team who has played at Bramall Lane', on the last Australian tour, had his back massaged before taking a turn with the bat in the early evening nets. 'He showed all the attractive and forceful shots which featured his batting during 1938.'

Visiting players, as was only right for young men providing the city's sporting occasion of the year, were invited to the best Sheffield could offer that weekend: a dance at the Abbeydale Park pavilion; and a day's golf at Bamford in the nearby Peak District. Several England players meanwhile were watching the Friday evening game at Parkhead cricket club, the last in a lucrative festival week on the outskirts of the city. George Pope was run out for 157, out of Norton Woodseats' 237 for five in 20 overs. Parkhead replied with 210 for four. Two more of the festival's professionals starred, George Gunn of Nottinghamshire with 82 and Bill Bowes, still not feeling ready to play for England, with 45. While plainly the event was all about big name cricketers showing off with the bat, would a man due to make his debut for England this century be allowed to play the equivalent of a Twenty20 game, the night before?!

When Hassett won the toss on the Saturday morning, June 23, he grinned and asked England to bat. Australia made one change, bringing back Carmody for Stanford. Hassett was perhaps glad his batsmen did not have to face the wet pitch – maybe what the groundsman meant by 'natural'. Hammond had spoken of the need for a left-handed batsman; the Yorkshireman Maurice Leyland, however, had strained a tendon in his right leg, and ERT (Errol) Holmes, the Surrey amateur right-hander, took his place.

Washbrook on two was dropped by Cheetham at cover. Sismey – he was in the wars in the summer of 1945 – had to leave the field in the sixth over when the ball came off Hutton's pads and split the wicket-keeper's chin. Stanford came on to field as 12th man and Carmody took Sismey's gloves – ironically, because Carmody was due to be best man at Sismey's marriage in August.

Just when the openers seemed to have settled, Hutton tried to force the ball past cover and was out to a smart catch by Cheetham at backward point. The crowd of 15,000 groaned at Hutton's cheap dismissal for 11, on his 29th birthday. Graham Williams had taken his wicket for the second time. While Williams was Australia's most expensive bowler in all five Tests – his ten wickets cost 40 runs each – he did get Hutton out four times in all. Miller's memory was at fault in his 1956 memoir when he wrote that Williams and Cheetham 'went home after one or two Victory Tests and left us without a pace attack. That was the reason I took up bowling seriously.' Miller, however, did have a point when he went on to recall: 'Graham Williams told me of a chink in the Hutton armour ... Williams said to me before he left England, "Where you want to get him out is just behind square leg". He was right ...' That contest between Miller the bowler and Hutton the bat would define much of the Ashes cricket of the next ten years.

Ellis came into the attack at 41, and Miller at 46. At this, according to George Harrison in the *News of the World*, Robertson had his tongue sticking out of the side of his mouth, 'like a schoolboy painfully writing his exercises'. On 20 Robertson stood his ground when Hassett thought he had caught him at square leg off Miller; the umpires doubted whether the ball was on the floor or not. It mattered little because at 81 Robertson rather carelessly touched a wide ball and was caught off Ellis, for 26. 'Robertson gives every indication of being an England batsman of the future but it is noticeable how frequently he is dismissed between 20 and 40 ...' said *The Cricketer* in its next issue. Hammond joined Washbrook and, when on seven, edged Ellis close to Pepper the lone slip. Pepper rolled over in his effort to catch it and kicked his legs in the air in vexation. Without more alarms England went to lunch at 113 for two. Hammond, according to the *Daily Telegraph* reporter Sir Guy Campbell, was 'none too comfortable at first but once he had sized up the pitch and bowlers it was the pre-war Hammond and what fun!'

Hammond did have to save England, as Washbrook fell for 63, and Errol Holmes and Edrich cheaply, to the spinners Ellis and Pepper during their long spells. Washbrook just touched one from Pepper which Carmody as wicket-keeper held with delight. Holmes played Ellis with a cross bat and turned around in time to see his stumps go down. When Pope on debut came in at 3pm, with the score 141 for five, Norman Preston in *The Observer* the next day felt that Australia were 'shaping for a quick kill'. Australians in the crowd could be heard offering to bet that England would be out for 200 or less. As the last specialist batsman, Hammond sneaked singles off the fifth and sixth ball of overs to keep the bowling from Pope, who took time to settle. Hassett set an offside field, but Hammond beat it with his placing. Norman Preston reported: 'Alert in defence, Hammond saved his wicket time and again by the very lateness of his swift wristy chop on the ball and when the right ball came to drive we saw the bat flow majestically.'

Hammond changed his bat at 88, then Pope was caught, having made 35 out of a sixth-wicket stand of 107. England were well placed now on 248 for six. 'Nothing was more certain than Hammond's century,' wrote the veteran Bertie Lawton in the *Sheffield Telegraph*. To reach it, Hammond stepped out to Williams and hit an on-drive for three at 5.05pm, out of 259 for six. 'The hurricane of cheering which greeted Hammond's 100 was something to warm the heart,' wrote George Harrison in the *News of the World*. 'It shook the roofless stands of this bomb-blasted ground until they rattled.'

Almost at once Hammond was caught off a skier by the running Hassett. He was going for a big hit off the returning Cheetham, 'probably to see if his bowlers could take a wicket before the close', Lawton suggested.

Out for exactly 100, Hammond batted just under three hours, and hit two sixes and eight fours. The crowd rose, and the reporters competed to give praise. Crisp wrote: 'I have never seen a ball played so late as Hammond played it on Saturday afternoon.' And George Thompson, reporting for the *Yorkshire Observer*, called Hammond's 100 'as grand as any among the 156 centuries he has scored in first class cricket', 'delightful in his late shots of varied character'. In his 1958 book *Cricket My World*, Hammond too looked back on the century as 'one of the most satisfactory innings in my career'.

Then came anti-climax. England were soon all out, for 286.

The press box seemed agreed also in their downgrading of Australia's opening bowlers, and praise for the rest. Crisp called Pepper 'keen as mustard and as vociferous as Duckworth on a slightly lower key'. George Duckworth, the Lancashire and England wicket-keeper between the wars, was infamous for his loud appeals. Lawton dismissed Cheetham and Williams as 'nothing out of the ordinary ... who seemed to do little beyond cut up the surface of the pitch ready for Pope and Pollard.' Lawton found Miller 'impressive in that he put his whole soul into every delivery. A short run up and beautiful follow through and he fairly hurls the ball at the batsman.' The openers Whitington and Workman survived half an hour of accurate bowling by Pope and Pollard to reach 23. *The Times* called it 'one of the best days' play seen in this country for many years'.

On the Sunday, Hammond captained an eleven at Roundhay Park in Leeds in a charity game in front of tens of thousands. Hammond included Stanford, and the English county veterans Tom Goddard and George Gunn.

In Sheffield meanwhile, the match took a sharp turn against Australia, without them doing a thing, because only the ends of the Bramall Lane pitch were covered; the ground lacked full-length covers.

In Pope and Dick Pollard, Hammond had a pair of northern opening bowlers who knew how to bowl in the north. Pope, from the pavilion, was bowling to a cordon of three men just over the batsman's shoulder.

'Quite a humorist this George,' noted Frank Stainton in the *Sheffield Star*, 'for when a wag in the Bramall Lane stand called out "Keep it up, curly", Pope went through the motions of sweeping back his hair from his brow much as though he were a concert pianist at a recital. The joke of course is that those who know George realise he is almost naked on top.' Pope may have been bald – he was 34 – but he soon had the openers in his traps after his first over went for six runs. Workman was first out, for six, pushing the ball into Pollard's hands at silly mid-on. Next, Whitington turned a late in-swinging ball round the corner to Wright, taking the ball on his toes, at short fine leg. Whitington, out for 17, had earlier lobbed a ball from Pollard gently towards the bowler, who just failed to get his hands to the catch.

Pollard bowled Hassett for five, to leave Australia 44 for three, and some way from the follow-on total of 136. Miller and Carmody added 36 – the second highest stand of the innings – until, watchers agreed, Miller ran himself out, for 17. Miller, facing Pope, raced for a single when the ball went straight to Robertson at forward short leg. Robertson stopped the ball, Carmody properly stood his ground, and Miller did not try to save himself.

After Carmody and Pepper came together at 80 for four, Hammond made his first change of bowling – Wright at the brewery end for Pollard and Edrich at the pavilion end for Pope. Carmody and Pepper made what was to prove the highest partnership of the innings, not without alarms. Pepper began restrained, then hooked Pope for four and a two, to bring up 100. Clouds rolled over.

At 122 Carmody was out for 42, caught by Hammond at short slip, low down, off Wright. Carmody might have been out at 38, only Griffith did not gather. Hammond caught Pepper off Wright; Sismey, facing Pope, like Workman pushed the ball straight to Pollard at silly mid-off, and Price in the same over fell in the same leg trap. With only two wickets to fall, Australia were still five runs short of making England bat again. Pope bowled a no-ball to Cheetham; then Cheetham popped up the ball towards Robertson in the leg trap, only it fell short. The crowd oohed. Cheetham drove Pope and got a snick through the slips for four, saving the follow-on. Australia were 147 all out shortly after lunch, when a return by Edrich ran out last man Reg Ellis.

England had only to bat the rest of the day and Australia would have to bat all the third, last day simply to draw. Whether the Yorkshire crowd was satisfied that England were doing so well, or out of annoyance that Yorkshire players had little to do with it, some in the crowd picked on two lapses behind the wicket that, according to George Thompson of the *Yorkshire Observer*, 'gave the Sheffield crowd the opportunity they like with one reference being to Woody coming back', Woody being the Yorkshire and England wicket-keeper Arthur Wood. 'But it was when Miller bowled for Australia that they had their best time,' Thompson added, meaning that the crowd had something to shout about. 'England's opening pair Hutton and Washbrook were making good though steady progress when he went on to bowl and in one over from him Hutton was hit on the arm (the one that has caused him so much trouble) and Washbrook was hit on the foot and the head.'

That Miller – who had soon taken over from the wicketless Williams and Cheetham – dared to hit the Yorkshireman Hutton provoked uproar in the crowd. The way the *Sydney Morning Herald* told it, the ball that hit Hutton flew to fine leg and Hutton, obviously in pain, took a slow single. Miller took Carmody's smart return but did not try to run out Hutton, and instead rubbed Hutton's injury. The crowd yelled, 'Come on Larwood!', evoking the name of the last English fast bowler to trouble batsmen. Miller then kept a better length; he had made his point.

What the spectators had not heard was a jokey yet telling remark inside the shared dressing room, as Hutton combed his hair before going out to open England's second innings. Miller grinned and said: 'That's right Len, if you can't be a batsman at least try and look like one.'

Such banter had many meanings. Miller sought to cast doubt on Hutton's ability to bat, after he had made only 33 in his first three Victory Test innings. In effect Miller was asserting his right to speak informally as an equal to Hutton, though Miller had not played any Tests, yet. And, on behalf of his team, Miller, as his team's fastest bowler, was having a dig at the opposition's best batsman. For all the goodwill off the field, on the field it was you or him. Either the batsman or the bowler succeeded, seldom both. Or was it simply that Hutton's act of vanity provoked Miller, a hair-comber himself, to say something? Hutton replied in character – or rather, according to our witness, Whitington, Hutton did not reply: he smiled, inscrutably.

On the field, Miller got results: Washbrook was out for 24 and Robertson for one within two overs and Miller 'gave Hammond an uncomfortable spell', Crisp reported. Whether because he was a neutral South African or a biased former fast bowler, Crisp argued for the occasional fast bumper, for 'psychological upset', 'especially as I did it myself'.

At tea, England were 76 for two, 215 ahead. They did not have to bat much longer to set Australia a daunting target. Then Hutton, Holmes, Hammond, Pope and Edrich were quickly out, leaving England 122 for seven, or 259 ahead. Griffith and Pollard went for the bowling to deny Australia their faint chance. Hassett brought on Price, the least-used of Australia's spinners. Price did the trick in no time; he had Griffith stumped by his opposite number – Sismey was back on the field – and a running catch by Carmody at long on – 'a thing to remember', Sir Guy Campbell called it – saw the back of Roberts. Day two had seen 314 runs scored for 20 wickets.

Australia began their innings on the third day, needing 330 or, not much more hopefully, to last all day. Bruce Harris, up north for the London *Evening Standard*, called it a 'forlorn hope'. Whitington, despite hay fever, and Workman this time saw off Pope and Pollard, under cloud that made the scene 'as drab as December'. Hammond brought on the change bowlers Wright and Edrich. Whitington gained four through the slips off Edrich, the ball thumping into the sightscreen. Hardly a run came in front of the wicket; an Edrich bumper over Workman's head went for four byes.

Edrich had bowled only four overs when he stopped during his long, energetic run up and felt the back of his thigh. He left with a torn muscle. Hammond brought

Roberts into the attack for the first time in the match at 50 for no wicket, after an hour on day three. The first ball by Roberts on his debut was what Frank Stainton termed 'a very rank long hop which Whitington gratefully pulled to the boundary'.

Roberts, lean and wiry with a gentle run-up, did settle, bringing the ball characteristically over from the small of his back. Runs were coming steadily as the openers hit the loose balls. Wright was giving no trouble, so Hammond replaced him with a more occasional spinner, Hutton, at the football end. Whitington hit the first ball to third man, for four, and the second, very short one was 'contemptuously despatched to long leg'. That first over of Hutton's leg breaks gave away ten runs. One presumably Australian spectator shouted, 'Keep him on Wally, we like it!' After an hour and three-quarters Whitington was first out, for 61, the lion's share of the opening stand of 108, leg before trying to pull a short ball from Wright. Hassett sent in Miller instead of himself; was it a sign that the captain saw a chance of victory and wanted to hurry?

Soon after lunch, Pollard twice hit Miller on the same thigh and obviously left Miller in pain – revenge, perhaps, for hitting English batsmen. In his next over Pollard swung one in a foot and Miller, late with his stroke, was bowled for eight.

Workman had so far made 42 out of 121. Hassett now came in and, though beaten by Pollard, hooked two of his no-balls to the boundary. A two and two fours and four leg byes – 14 in all – came from one Pope over and the total passed half what was needed to win for only two men out.

Hassett had hit five fours to all parts of the ground and made 32 of a stand of 50 with Workman when Pope took his first wicket at 171. The former England captain CB Fry, wearing his naval uniform, was watching from the top tier of the stand behind the bowler's arm, by telescope. 'Upon Hassett's return to the dressing room Fry poked his naval cap and monocle around the door and said, "Thought you might like to know what that one did, Lindsay. It swung from the leg". He was gone before the dejected Hassett could smile,' Whitington wrote later.

Carmody made 14 of the next 18 until he was run out by a return from Hutton at cover point: 189 for four. Workman was still going, while others went for the runs. George Thompson reported: 'The outlook for England was beginning to look a little doubtful.' The switch in fortunes came at last with a rising ball from Pollard. The wicket-keeper Griffith could not hold the catch but Hammond at short slip did. Workman was out, for 63 out of 221 for five. Pepper drove the next ball from Pope for four. Cheetham, the new batsman, turned Pollard to leg for three. A single left Australia needing 100 with five wickets in hand. In the last over before tea, a ball from Pope popped and Pepper gave Pollard a simple catch at silly mid-on. The incoming Sismey played out the rest of the over: 231 for six.

Hammond trusted to his opening bowlers to chip away at the later batsmen. Australia defied England for five and a half hours, but not for quite long enough. Pope bowled Price to win the game by 41 runs and draw the series, but Hammond gave the honour of walking off the field to Pollard, who bowled almost a third of the overs and took five wickets for 76. The newcomers Pope and Pollard had taken 14 wickets between them and had been the difference between the two sides.

Not that all was well with England yet. Australia had made England work. Bob Crisp, who was admittedly easily bored, claimed that the most exciting moment of the day came when a Mustang fighter 'plane 'scraped the top of the pavilion'. Crisp reckoned the pilot had come down to see the scoreboard. He was on surer ground when he canvassed opinions. The great all-rounder Wilfred Rhodes told Crisp that he was impressed only by the fast bowling of Keith Miller. Herbert Sutcliffe, newly elected as the first professional cricketer to the Yorkshire committee, had just returned from Australia on business and reckoned there were many better young Australian players in Australia.

George Thompson knew well that his Yorkshire readers would want to know where their entrance money went. The first day's receipts alone were £3,562 from 22,561 paying customers. Sheffield's Test expenses came to £400, and total receipts more than £7,000, meaning an enormous profit for army, navy and air force and Australian welfare funds. Players only had expenses; in other words they gave their services free. One man's rebellion against that would not last long but would change the course of the Victory summer.

Second Test, Bramall Lane, Sheffield, June 23, 25 and 26

Australian Services won the toss

England first innings

L Hutton	ct Cheetham	b Williams	11
C Washbrook	ct Carmody	b Pepper	63
JDB Robertson	ct Whitington	b Ellis	26
WR Hammond	ct Hassett	b Cheetham	100
ERT Holmes		b Ellis	6
WJ Edrich	lbw	b Pepper	1
GH Pope	ct Ellis	b Cheetham	35
†SC Griffith	ct Hassett	b Cheetham	2
R Pollard		b Pepper	11
WB Roberts		b Williams	4
DVP Wright	not out		7
Extras (3 b, 10 lb, 5 nb, 2 w)			20
Total (all out, 110.5 overs)			286

Fall of wickets: 1-28, 2-81, 3-129, 4-136, 5-141, 6-248, 7-262, 8-264, 9-272, 10-286.

The Victory Tests

Bowling

Cheetham	15	3	47	3
Williams	16	4	31	2
Ellis	33	9	66	2
Miller	13	3	19	0
Pepper	30.5	6	86	3
Price	3	0	17	0

Australian Services first innings

RS Whitington	ct Wright	b Pope 17	
JA Workman	ct Pollard	b Pope	6
*AL Hassett		b Pollard	5
KR Miller	run out		17
DK Carmody	ct Hammond	b Wright	42
CG Pepper	ct Hammond	b Wright	21
AG Cheetham		b Pope	10
†SG Sismey	ct Pollard	b Pope	0
CFT Price	ct Pollard	b Pope	0
RG Williams	not out		5
RS Ellis	run out		1
Extras (5 b, 12 lb, 6 nb)			23
Total (all out, 52.5 overs)			147

Fall of wickets: 1-33, 2-36, 3-44, 4-80, 5-122, 6-131, 7-132, 8-132, 9-145, 10-147

Bowling

Pope	21.5	4	58	5
Pollard	17	5	42	1
Wright	9	3	14	2
Edrich	5	0	10	0

England second innings

L Hutton		b Ellis	46
C Washbrook	ct Sismey	b Miller	24
JDB Robertson	lbw	b Miller	1
WR Hammond		b Ellis	38
ERT Holmes	ct Sismey	b Pepper	2
WJ Edrich	ct Hassett	b Pepper	1
GH Pope	ct Pepper	b Ellis	2
†SC Griffith	st Sismey	b Price	35
R Pollard	ct Whitington	b Price	25
WB Roberts	ct Carmody	b Price	6

Second Test, Bramall Lane

DVP Wright   not out   1
Extras (1 b, 4 lb, 4 nb)   9
Total (all out, 73.4 overs)   190
Fall of wickets: 1-56, 2-62, 3-97, 4-104, 5-120, 6-122, 7-122,
8-177, 9-184, 10-190

Bowling

Cheetham	7	1	19	0
Williams	9	2	23	0
Ellis	25	5	47	3
Miller	13	2	28	2
Pepper	15	3	46	2
Price	4.4	0	18	3

Australian Services second innings

RS Whitington	lbw	b Wright	61
JA Workman	ct Hammond	b Pollard	63
KR Miller		b Pollard	8
*AL Hassett		b Pope	32
DK Carmody	run out		14
CG Pepper	ct Pollard	b Pope	27
AG Cheetham	ct Hammond	b Pollard	18
†SG Sismey		b Pollard	17
RG Williams	lbw	b Pollard	2
CFT Price		b Pope	11
RS Ellis	not out		9

Extras (17 b, 6 lb, 3 nb)   26
Total (all out, 102.4 overs)   288
Fall of wickets: 1-108, 2-121, 3-171, 4-189, 5-221, 6-231, 7-244,
8-260, 9-280, 10-288

Bowling

Pope	28.4	9	69	3
Pollard	33	6	76	5
Wright	22	6	50	1
Edrich	4	1	13	0
Roberts	13	4	40	0
Hutton	2	0	14	0

England won by 41 runs. Close day one: Australian Services
23-0 (Whitington 13 not out, Workman 3 not out). Close, day two:
England 190 all out.

Chapter Ten

Amateurs and Professionals

Our only criterion of judgement should not be whether or not a man's actions are justified in the light of subsequent evolution. After all, we are not at the end of social evolution ourselves.

EP Thompson, *The Making of the English Working Class* (1963)

As John Dewes went into teaching, it was appropriate that I learned a lesson from him. I had assumed that Dewes was not expecting to be picked for England in 1945, when in fact he recalled: 'Well, I was up at Cambridge and the professionals hadn't got back into their stride; I was playing for the Combined Services – although I was at Cambridge I was in the Navy. I thought I had a chance; but I wasn't sure.'

This was a reminder, not for the last time, how easy it is to forget that the past might have been unlike the present.

These days Oxbridge cricket is irrelevant to the English professional and international game, yet for generations before 1945, and for a good while after, the obvious steps for an excelling cricketer were from private school to Oxford or Cambridge and to a county or MCC; and from there, maybe, England.

To a 21st century determined to stand against racism, sexism or any other -ism, the old class-based division in English county and international cricket between amateurs and professionals may seem grotesque, even unlawful: separate dressing rooms, hotels and gates to and from the field of play; your initials before (amateur) or after your name (professional) on a scorecard and in *Wisden*.

Hence it's as well to define the two words. Professional has come to mean someone belonging to a profession, or someone with the qualities or qualifications to so belong; contrasted with an amateur, who does not. The unspoken judgement may be that amateurs do not try hard enough; or could not make the grade if they tried; or they simply lack the time to. The English had long noted the Australians' dedicated approach to sport. A news agency before the second Test reported from Sheffield: 'Like WG Grace, the Australians practise every morning before play begins. Another illustration of the serious manner in which they treat the game is shown in the fact they brought their own masseur [Sergeant LW Maddison, an Australian Army veteran of El Alamein] all the way from Eastbourne.'

WG Grace was, officially, an amateur. In county and international cricket from its mid-Victorian beginnings to 1945, and for a few years after, professional and amateur meant, narrowly, someone who played for pay; and someone who did not.

Cricket mirrored much in English life, and so did the divide, practical and moral, between professional and amateur – or pro' and amateur; significantly, no-one in cricket shortened (and became over-familiar with?) the word amateur.

In a century when a professional footballer can earn more in a week than a working man can earn in a decade, and amateur can be another word for a fool, you can overlook how powerful and valid amateurism once was in England, and not only in sport. The Home Guard in 1940 came together as an unpaid army against a likely German invasion. The belief was that free people could do something better because they wanted to do it. That also suited the authorities because it was home defence on the cheap. A similar mix of the sublime and the mundane explained amateurism in team sports, including cricket.

Amateurism drew on an ideal classical civilisation, much taught in private schools and universities. The ancient Greeks as free men competed at athletics not for money but for the glory of being the best. The translation from ancient to modern was not so neat – Athens never played Sparta at cricket.

The appeal, however, was to all, those good at sports and not, because you could be pure in spirit (or putting it another way, not brainy) and be healthy in body. Hence the revival of the amateur Olympics, hosted in London in 1908 and 1948; and the frieze outside Lord's on the corner of St John's Wood Road. Carved are some men, and a woman, standing alongside another man carrying a tennis racquet. Others are carrying golf clubs. In the middle are cricketers, and most central of all is a batsman wearing pads and holding the Ashes urn. Other figures wear classical robes. Dating from 1934, it suggests powerfully that cricket harked back to a (fake) antique past – so did the burnt bails of the Ashes, even – and Ashes matches against Australia were central to cricket's exalted image of itself.

Amateurs and Professionals

In most sports, though, amateurism had collided unhappily with commercial reality. Rugby had split between professional league and amateur union. The Victorian days of amateur Corinthian football teams – another name harking back to the classical past – winning the FA Cup were long gone. Unlike rugby, cricket kept to one code of play; unlike football, amateurs could attain high rank, although professionals like Jack Hobbs and Wilfred Rhodes tended to reach the highest. And to return to WG Grace, once, or arguably still, the greatest; was he an amateur, or a professional? He called himself an amateur; to sceptics he looked like a professional. Most English institutions, to repeat, give the nod to some fraud or hypocrisy. Amateurism in cricket had lost its way before the war because the authorities tried to shoehorn the ideal into badly-fitting economic reality.

Amateurism had a point. The authorities reckoned that the game needed some amateurs, above all an amateur captain, as a leaven for the professionals. An amateur who did not have to worry about making a living from the game might be better able to shrug off any individual failure and do a captain's unselfish job of bringing out the best in others. Of the professionals playing for pay, you could rely on pro' bowlers to do the right things – they always wanted to take wickets – but the pro' batsmen would play for safety, their own safety, whereas sometimes for the sake of the team batsmen ought to take risks, to score runs quickly.

The professionals could answer that it was unfair to judge them by the amateur ideal; a pro' was batting to put bread on the table for his family, while amateur school teachers, students, vicars and businessmen were batting during their summer holiday, expenses paid. In any case, like any ideal, amateurism did not necessarily look so glorious when you looked at the people.

Professionals took no chances because too much failure would mean the sack, as in any job; yet plenty of amateurs achieved less than a professional and were tolerated because of who they were. Double standards riddled amateurism. There was long an unreality about amateurism because the believers in it, significantly, were often the older county club and MCC members, and the committees and team selectors they elected, who wished things would stay as they were two or three generations before, and not only in cricket.

The political equivalent was the belief that only the Conservative Party could rule the country, because the Labour Party or labour movement would either bring ruin or Communist tyranny. Similarly, only an amateur could be trusted with captaincy of a county, or England. Why? Believers tended to be vague. It was to do with character; only a disinterested amateur could inject flair and fun; a professional as captain would not be able to keep discipline at the proper distance from his former fellows as an amateur could.

It was unproven and it had become humbug. The pro' Hutton blocked for hour after hour for 364 at that 1938 timeless Test on the orders of the amateur Hammond, a former pro'. It was 'Them and Us' prejudice. The retired colonels and solicitors who ran county cricket clubs did not want a former railwayman or factory worker in charge. Bolsheviks did that. In truth a good captain, who understood the game and his fellow men, could be an amateur or professional. County pros carried their hopeless amateur captains, and because many counties did the same, no-one was too embarrassed.

Oddly, while war was a time of rapid social change and personal upheaval, the hibernation of county cricket in the 1939–45 war postponed a reckoning for amateurism, just as horse-drawn carts ran a few more years on English streets because the Army wanted motor lorries. If most young men were in uniform, whether they could play cricket or not was merely a matter of their units giving them leave. Leading cricketers such as Hammond could serve in the Royal Air Force while more or less taking the summer off to play cricket. Hammond was a sign of the humbug – not that he or any amateur or professional was at all to blame.

Young men of ambition did not want to change the world; they wanted to rise as far as they could in the game, whether amateur or professional. Whichever path they chose, they were inside a system. Some might resent it, some enjoy it, the same as any workplace; who knows how many merely accepted it? Pros might be a mix of rough or respectable working-class men; even cricket's famous, mystical ability to draw men of all sorts together was unproven.

Did cricket have a knack of keeping everyone together on the same field because men of otherwise utterly unfamiliar backgrounds, when close, learned to like each other; or did the outdoor spaces of cricket allow people to stay apart enough to tolerate each other? The intimacies of a changing room were least spoken of – but perhaps for that very reason most important. Men had to be comfortable with taking off their clothes and showing their bodies in front of their fellows; the other men had to not laugh or pretend not to notice if anything was too small or too flabby. This could not be a problem for the Australian Victory cricketers or anyone who had been in the services for years, and who seldom were allowed any privacy.

County cricket and MCC selection of England teams had bumbled along until the war. If any cricketer tired of it, just as if anyone tired of class-ridden England, rather than agitate they could emigrate: cricketers to the northern leagues, Englishmen to Canada or Australia. What undermined amateurism was not any internal hypocrisy – Englishmen could always come to terms with that – but the fact that foreigners showed it up; the Australians kept winning.

Like any hierarchical system, cricket's had to work from top to bottom: as Hammond put it in his 1952 book *Cricket's Secret History*, if the captain of England had to be an amateur, he had to learn as a county captain. As only one county could finish bottom of the championship each summer, most county elevens could carry an amateur or two who were not worth their place on merit; England, against Australia, could not.

The case of Hammond showed the handicap of any economic system that judged men as one thing or another. As Hammond wrote in his *Secret History*, he was the same man when he captained England as an amateur as he was in most of his cricket lifetime as a professional. 'But because I had changed my label all was well. I submit that this is illogical.' Ironically, changes in Hammond's personality, regardless of his status as amateur or pro', were fast making him a bad captain of England.

Donald Carr said in 2008:

The first thing I remember of it is the surprise at being asked to play. I was a substitute, really, for George Pope, the old Derbyshire player who had apparently turned down the invitation. Of course he used to be earning more money in the Bradford League than playing for England! A rather peculiar substitute, I was, for him. He was six foot three, fastish bowler and big hitter, and there was I, little 19-year-old, coming in, in place of him!

Main picture: Reg Ellis in 2009. Inset: Ellis in 1945.

Reg Ellis, Cec Pepper and Gordon Schwartz, gunner, sportswriter and a South Australia and Australia tennis player.

Rex Kenyon, Bert Hollings, Reg Ellis and Ron Gibson, wearing pilot helmets during training at Deniliquin, New South Wales.

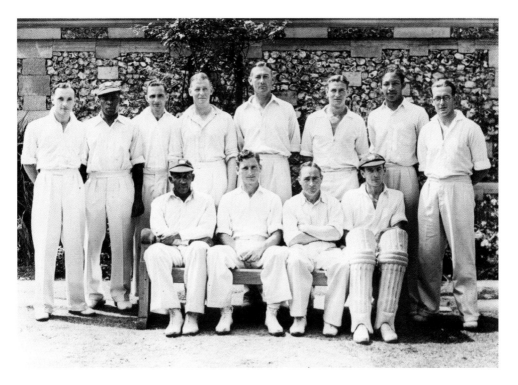

1943: the Dominions team to face England at Lord's. Left to right, back: Flight Lieutenant Keith Campbell DFC; EA Martindale, West Indies; Sergeant Jim Workman of Largs Bay, SA; Flying Officer (FO) AW Roper of Punchbowl, NSW; Cadet Officer Denijs Morkel, South Africa; Sergeant Keith Miller; CB Clarke, West Indies; Pilot Officer (PO) AD MacDonald of Ballarat. Front: Learie Constantine, West Indies; PO DK Carmody of Sydney, team captain; GS Dempster, New Zealand; FO SG Sismey of Concord, NSW.

The captains, at Lord's: Keith Carmody and Walter Robins, England. The Dominions were all out for 351 in their second innings, losing by eight runs.

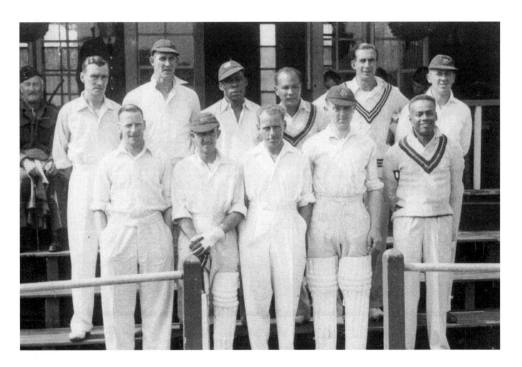

Charles Leatherbarrow's XI at Burton upon Trent in 1943 – Hallows, Pope, Martindale, Achong, Andrews, Cox. Farrimond, Paynter, Leatherbarrow, Place, St Hill. Paynter and Place are padded up, evidently about to go out to open the batting.

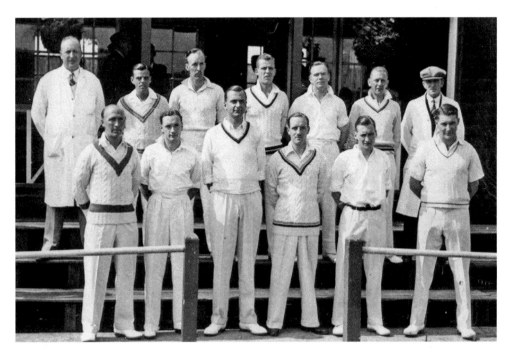

The Services XI that day – Milnes (umpire), Bulcock (Bradford League), Rymill (Northants), Page, Reg Ellis, Illingworth (Somerset), Raymond (umpire). Copley (Notts), Keith Campbell, Ward (Hampshire, captain), Tedder (Essex), Pollard (Yorkshire), Padden (NSW).

Maidstone, May 1945: Group portrait during a match between Kent and RAAF. Left to right: Sq Leader Stan Sismey; Sq Leader Bill Edrich, Mr Larkin, the Mayor of Maidstone, Hopper Levett, captain of Kent, and Flight Lieutenant PN Cochrane of Perth, an RAAF welfare officer.

Bacxk row (l to r) M Roper, J Pettiford, K Miller, C Pepper, E Williams
Front row R Cristofani, R Ellis, C Bremner, L Hassett, R Whitington, C Price.

Old Trafford, Manchester, August 20, 1945. Keith Miller and Ces Pepper go out to bat for Australia, during the first day's play of the fifth and last Test.

Reg Ellis, Dick Pollard and Bob Cristofani about to make a small boy very happy.

Flying Officer Jack Pettiford, a member of the RAAF team who in August was picked for the last two Victory Tests.

Australian captain Lindsay Hassett on the boat home – but only part of the way home: from England to India.

'S for Sugar', a 467 Squadron Lancaster piloted by Australians, on display at the RAF Museum, Hendon, north London, famous for surviving more than 100 missions, each one marked by a painted bomb below the cockpit. Also painted, the wartime claim by Luftwaffe leader Herman Goering: 'No enemy plane will fly over the Reich territory.'

That was the first thing, the surprise.

Another recollection I have is when I arrived at Lord's on the first day of the game. I was carrying my big rather old-fashioned and old cricket bag and I was in uniform, I was an officer cadet at the time, and I walked in into the dressing room; and I remember I opened the door; the first figure I saw and recognised was WR Hammond, our captain. He was chatting to one of his friends, not a player, some friend who had got in there; he turned around and saw me and looked away again; he obviously didn't think I was one of his players; thought I was carrying somebody else's bag, I think.

I looked around rather nervously – I knew Luke White, and John Dewes, the other two youngsters who were playing.

Bill Edrich had been – about three or four years before this match, he was at an aerodrome just outside Derby [Burnaston] where he was training to become a flier; and our family lived at Repton. We got a schoolboy team up to play against the local RAF blokes; we were horrified or excited to hear that the great cricketer Edrich was training there and he played against us; I was only 13, I think. And my elder brother was about 16 and running this boys' team. I know my brother bowled Edrich out for about ten or something.

When four years later I walked into that dressing room at Lord's Bill said, 'Hello, we've met before, haven't we?' I was absolutely amazed that he recognised me from the age of 13 or something and he said, 'Come and stretch next to me down here.' And put me at my ease and couldn't have been nicer. I was always grateful to him for the rest of my cricketing career; [laughs] he was a very nice chap.

To introduce Donald Carr: he was walking into the Lord's dressing room on the morning of Saturday, July 14, because he was the third of the three teenage amateur batsmen called up for the third Victory Test. As he recalled correctly, he was a late addition to the eleven, for Pope. Carr's memory may be, after more than 60 years, partly at fault, because he had played in the same team as Edrich five weeks before, for a Lord's eleven, against New Zealand Services. Carr took four wickets, including the openers with Test experience, CS (Stewie) Dempster and Roger Blunt. Like Dewes and White, Carr had excelled at the biggest occasions cricket could put on in wartime, alongside the most influential players. All three had played for Public Schools against a Lord's eleven starring Walter Robins in August 1944: White had scored 102. Carr took seven wickets for Surrey Colts at Lord's in September 1944, playing in the same team as Gubby Allen and the 54-year-old Lord Tennyson.

At Lord's on June 2, 1945, White scored 58 not out and Carr 21 not out as an England eleven captained by Hammond easily beat a West Indies eleven. That was, as Hammond admitted in his weekly column beforehand, the first time he saw Carr, and the spinner William Roberts, play. Hammond said of Carr: 'I liked this boy very much indeed, particularly as a batsman. He always seemed to have plenty of time to play his strokes, which is a very good sign.' And a quality that Hammond had, we might add. 'He uses plenty of air in his bowling and I think that with the right experience he will become a very good all-rounder.'

So when in early July for the third Test the selectors dropped ERT Holmes in favour of Dewes and White, the selectors had their reasons, as the press reported when chewing traditionally over the team in the days before the game. Dewes began the 1945 season in outstanding form at university. The *Express* praised his 'rock-like defence and unlimited patience'. During the first Victory Test he was averaging 257.5 after a 128 not out against the RAF, having scored 515 runs for twice out. By early July he had scored 1,002 runs for Cambridge, at an average of more than 100. You could quibble that he had made some runs against lesser-ranking teams than counties. For instance, at the end of May Dewes made his fourth century in five innings, against the Metropolitan Police, at Cambridge. 'It was a beautiful wicket,' he recalled in 2009; well kept, that is, for batting. In fairness, Dewes could only score runs against the teams he faced, the same as anyone else; and, newly-selected for England, he made 54 for Hammond's Young England eleven, which beat a New Zealand eleven at Edgbaston on July 8. Just before selection White, too, showed form, making 132 not out for Sir Pelham Warner's eleven against Second Army.

On the eve of the third Test, the Press Association described Carr, Dewes and White as the 'three best schoolboy cricketers of 1944'. The selectors were 'giving youth its chance'. The PA did voice some criticism of dropping Robertson, who 'needed every opportunity of big match play' before real Tests started again. Regional newspapers took their cue from the agencies; the *Bradford Telegraph & Argus* for instance claimed that England could afford to try out new players. All three 18-year-olds had topped their school averages the previous season: Dewes at Aldenham played 10 innings, averaged 74; White at Eton played 13 innings, averaged 50.3; and Carr at Repton, 14 innings, averaged 37.75 and was runner-up in bowling averages, with 35 wickets at 11.17. 'Carr's usefulness with the ball – he bowls slow left-arm – would probably be more tried than his ability with the bat if he gets in the final Test eleven. England will have a lop-sided attack with only one recognised pace bowler in Pollard,' the newspaper told readers.

How had two youths, enough of an experiment, become three? And where had Pope gone, after his all-round success at Sheffield? To repeat, Pope was in the original twelve. An alternative, Bill Bowes, was not bowling at top speed, on medical advice, and declined the invitation to play in the third Test, Yorkshire newspapers loyally reported. Most newspapers a few days later merely reported that Pope had similarly declined or 'vacated' his place. The *Daily Express* gave the full tale: Pope was under contract with Colne, his Lancashire League club, and when he could not play he had to pay for a professional to take his place. Fees from a Test match did not cover this. 'Pope made a stand on behalf of his fellow professionals,' the *Express* reported.

It did seem to make no sense that the selectors had replaced a protesting fast bowler with a teenage batsman who had bowled slow left-arm with some success for his school, but not for long spells in big-name cricket so far. It only made sense in MCC terms; that it was better to bring on untried but talented amateurs than proven county professionals.

Selecting a sporting team is like eating in the dark: you always wonder what you're getting. Another man, or men, not chosen may have done better than those you picked; you can never know. Anyone can be wise afterwards; hence so many people are, as they were after the third Test.

Another truth for a captain is that once you have your team, that's yours and no other. Ideally, you lead by example; but there's more to captaincy, as even teenagers starting in the game who have experience of captaincy, like Carr, soon grasp. For an absolute start, you ought to know your players, although Hammond may simply not have recognised Carr.

A lifetime on, Carr could no more than anyone else articulate the strongest emotion that anyone can ever go through, in sport or anywhere else: the nervousness of crossing the threshold and taking your place somewhere for the first time. It's no good telling yourself that you are there on merit, because someone has decided that you ought to be there; or, that others are in the same boat as you, and everyone was in the same boat once. Whether it's a workplace, or the first day at school, until you belong, you feel deeply unsure.

Carr, in recollection, did not hold anything against Hammond: 'I became good friends with him later on, but that was the first time I had come across him. He was very pleasant, but fairly surprised to see me, I think.'

It was not mere good manners to welcome a new boy; it made sporting sense. The sooner a newcomer felt at home, the more he could concentrate on doing well. That was not how a cricket dressing room or many other English workplaces ran in 1945, as another recollection of Carr's suggested.

> On the Saturday night, after the first day's play, we all
> were invited to the White City to watch the dog racing.
> And I had never been to dog racing before in my life,
> nor had the other two youngsters. There was a big table
> laid at the White City for the two teams especially and
> one or two directors or something of the White City
> were there as well and chatting to Walter Hammond.
> And I remember we had – melon I think was on the
> menu, which ... rather posh meal set-up, and one of
> the things to eat I had never seen before; I had only

been at school during the war and the food was very basic. Anyway we were enjoying our special occasion and all rather important and the racing started. And Wally was talking to one or two of these directors of the place, who were giving him tips. The first race came along and he shouted, 'White!' And Luke White: 'Yes, captain, yes sir?' 'Will you put five shillings on dog number three?' And Luke didn't know where it was or anything; he went and got the money on for the captain. And went back and gave him the slip. And anyway the dog didn't win.

Then the next race came along. 'Dewes! Get me £7 on dog number' – whatever it was. And John Dewes toddled off and found the right place to put it on and took it back to Wally and anyway that one lost as well. Next race: 'Carr! Will you' ...I am not sure how much money it was, really, about a fiver, I think, on dog number whatever, and this animal came in. so he shouted at me again, go and collect my winnings! Ten shillings or something; and I took them to him and he gave me sixpence; I kept that sixpence for a long time! My winnings from the great WR Hammond. That was a good memory.

As a starter, to explain the melon: Carr was completely accurate in his memory of how remarkable a sight it was on an English dining table in 1945. Throughout the war, imports had to cross the oceans by ship and miss the U-boats. Guns came before tropical fruit. The German submarines had surrendered, but, if anything, rationing became even more severe in the first years after the war.

Carr's story also brings out how the England cricketers were a star attraction in 1945. Any leading venue such as the White City race track in west London would welcome Walter Hammond, for the sake of publicity or for the sheer thrill of treating one of the most famous men in the country.

Besides Hammond's abrupt manner, it is hard not to dwell on the reason he made the three junior members of his team run his errands. If Hammond had wanted to stay at the table, surely a stadium employee could have placed the bets? It does look as if Hammond wanted to put the youths in their place, and let them, and everyone else around the table, know it. It was Hammond asserting himself – it may have been his rebellion, of sorts, against the formalities that he above all as England captain had to observe.

John Dewes recalled differences between the amateurs and professionals: 'I could go up to Hammond, even, and call him Hammond; but he had to be careful what he said to me.' Hammond would have to call Dewes, as an amateur, mister; at least at first. Again, as with so much of this story, it's misleading and unfair to judge the men of 1945 by later standards. The standards of those days were there for reasons. Cricket was hardly the only world with its own formalities. A German ought to address a fellow German properly as *Sie* until both agree (formally, naturally!) on the less formal *Du* – admittedly not the best example to use in a story of 1945.

Hammond had to abide by the conventions that marked any amateur apart from any professional – otherwise he would never have gained the premier job in English cricket. As Carr's story from White City and another story of Dewes' suggested, other currents ran in cricket, depending on your wealth; schooling; and influence. As so often, it was not what you knew but who you knew.

Important background for this following story of John Dewes is that – unlike later county cricket – you were supposed to play for 'your' county by birth or residence – in Dewes' case, Lancashire. He recalled: 'I played at my school, Aldenham. Walter Robins came and said, "John, would you like to play for Middlesex?" and I said, "Yes, I would," and he got me in; I played once for Lancashire [in 1945], but not again.'

Walter Robins, to repeat, was one of English cricket's most senior amateurs; a former captain of Middlesex and England. John Dewes indeed went on to play for Middlesex for the rest of his career, into the 1950s.

On a second reading, what's intriguing is how Robins could call Dewes by his first name. On further thought, we might be reading too much into all this, if Dewes was a schoolboy when Robins spoke to him. On his England debut Dewes was no floppy-wristed student; he was starting two years in the Navy, which included a winter mine-sweeping off the Faroes. The least we can say is that cricket's class system made you sensitive to nuances.

So while it seems that some amateurs could assume a familiarity with another in a way that Hammond, a former professional, could not, Hammond had the right, unquestioned, to tell other people what to do because he was the man in charge. Not for nothing was captain a military term. 'But although there was that distinction they were all members of the team. The captain was the boss of the amateurs as well as the pros,' John Dewes recalled.

The three newcomers' place was at the bottom of the proverbial ladder. Their captain did not take the trouble to tell them apart. They were different: although Carr and Dewes came from families well-off enough to put them through university, only White was the son of a lord, and would in time become Lord Annaly himself. We can speculate that Hammond enjoyed having the Honorable Luke White placing a bet for him at a dog track – presumably a new experience for White. Or, less to Hammond's credit in a way, perhaps he only thought of the lad as someone to do as he was told. Hammond would not have ordered his more senior players about so publicly. This was something primitive, like a lion asserting himself over the younger members of the pride. This was what British workplaces were like.

You started at the bottom, as Hammond once did, and worked your way up. If you lasted, and older players left – as everyone did eventually – you became gradually more senior. Bill Edrich had been sympathetic enough to show the new boy Donald Carr to his place – literally and symbolically – yet there were further markings of territory in the dressing room. John Dewes recalled: 'In the home team dressing room at Lord's there was a nice sofa [like the one I as his guest in 2009 was sitting on in his living room], only in leather; that was restricted for the Hammonds and Allens, and people who were the ordinaries had to go on the other side.'

John Dewes agreed with an analogy his wife Shirley offered: of the prefects' room. Even when you became one of the prefects, it took time to belong fully. No wonder then that conversation in the dressing room was limited, as Dewes recalled: 'We talked cricket, but we didn't talk.' Like in any workplace, it was one thing to talk shop, another to share your life.

It made sense. The juniors were seen and not heard. They listened, and learned on the job – that traditional way that the British did everything, including fighting world wars. And the youth making his way in the game, as an amateur or pro', knew he could not get a better cricketing education than from the men who had achieved everything a man could in the game.

'Having played for the Combined Services; that was my finishing school,' John Dewes recalled. 'I shared a room with Bill Voce and I thought, "My goodness me", and it was a very good way of learning.'

Voce, someone else nearly old enough to be Dewes' father, went on the Bodyline tour, with the Lancashire left-handed batsman Eddie Paynter, and, as Dewes, a fellow left-handed batsman, recalled: 'Eddie Paynter was the one I looked up to.' For all the hierarchy, English cricket provided – had to, for one generation to pass into another – a channel whereby the young hopefuls became, so gradually that they did not notice, like the old hands they admired as boys.

To be fair to Hammond, there is doubt, though no evidence at this distance, whether he wanted the three teenagers. In his weekly column printed a couple of days after the third Test, Hammond said that although he was 'a firm believer in giving opportunities to young players', the 'three teenagers weakened the side'. That was not any fault of the boys, he added … which did imply it was someone else's fault (the selectors', for picking them?). 'We must remember it was a very big occasion for them and a tremendous ordeal. They no doubt felt over-anxious to do well and make a good impression and we could not expect them to do more than they did.' As Carr's recollection has shown, Hammond hardly went out of his way to make the match less of an ordeal!

Hammond was not necessarily particularly, or deliberately, harsh; it was the way of cricket: you were either an amateur who could afford to play for the love of it, or you were one of the workers. The exception was a grammar school boy, who belonged to neither of those two classes, like Washbrook. You could not quite place Cyril Washbrook. He was born in Lancashire, and played for that northern county; yet his family had moved to Shropshire and he had gone to Bridgnorth Grammar School. You never saw him smile – hence the crowds called him Smiler – yet he wore his cap at an angle. He was able; he had the stern face and cautious approach of a pro', yet he had more schooling than most professionals. Significantly, he served six years in the air force as a physical training (PT) instructor, the sort of middle-ranking job that put distance between you and everyone else.

For all the romance of amateurism – of playing for the love of the game, not the money – once inside the dressing room a grimmer reality applied, and here was the final grading of everyone in the dressing room, no matter how famous: between those excelling, and those falling short. Even if the young men of ambition proved they were worthy of a place, the reward was a grinding routine of forever having to prove yourself, until you chose to give up or, more likely, had the choice made for you by selectors. Such was the deal for a sportsman, with its parallel in military combat – and Hammond's father, a soldier, had died in the 1914–18 war. You could have training, and good wishes from your teammates; but they could not go out there for you. Sooner or later you had to jump in, and sink or swim – as Ross Stanford could have told them.

Chapter Eleven

Third Test, Lord's, July 14, 16 and 17, 1945

Things are not revolutionised by making revolutions. The real revolution lies in the solution of existing problems.

Le Corbusier, *The City of Tomorrow*

Though the clouds were dense and low in London on the morning of Saturday, July 14, Lord's was full for the first day of the third Test. The two captains had the covers removed to see what the wicket looked like, before the toss, won by Hammond. The groundsmen put the covers back in case of more rain; more rain came.

The sun came out, and the crowd in their shirt sleeves saw groundstaff take off the covers, piece by piece. Play began after midday. The air was still and humid; it turned so hot that even Hassett took off his sweater. Of the twelve, England left out Robertson, more, so it was claimed, to give the youths a chance than to drop him. Williams began among the sawdust, the ball slippery, with a maiden to Hutton.

Cheetham, the other opening bowler, beat Washbrook. He hooked a no-ball to the boundary; another ball he stopped dead. 'Pick it up!' urged a voice in the crowd – unfriendly, because of an unusual event a fortnight earlier at Lord's. Gubby Allen, captaining South of England against the RAAF, had been batting against Roper. Allen hit the ball onto his pads and it was trickling on to his wicket when he stopped it with his bat. He picked it up and threw it back to the bowler. Roper, thinking the wicket was broken, being hidden by Allen's body, called how's that and the umpire had to give Allen out, handled the ball. Fleet Street was there because it was the main game of the weekend. Reporters having checked afterwards agreed it was a genuine misunderstanding by Roper. That had not stopped the crowd booing at the time. Mick Roper and Hartley Craig were, in the newspapers at least, two possible newcomers for the Australians, but the only change was one spinner and capable lower-order batsman for another – Bob Cristofani in place of the injured Price. Newspaper suggestions of Norman Oldfield or the Surrey all-rounder John Parker, men on the brink of playing for England when war broke out, came to nothing.

Washbrook hooked another four; the openers seemed settled. Then Washbrook tried to cut a rising short ball from Williams; Sismey took the catch.

Dewes, the first of England's three new teenagers, walked to the wicket in a Cambridge Crusaders cap. The crowd clapped in welcome; Hutton, chewing gum in mouth, gave him a wide grin and a word of encouragement. Dewes took two to fine leg off Williams and a hefty off-drive for four, off Cheetham. At 25 for one, Dewes had nine to Hutton's eight.

The BBC radio broadcaster Chester Wilmot went to some trouble to tell Australian listeners about the newcomer:

Dewes is not a pretty batsman but he goes about his job in a workmanlike fashion. He has rather a stiff stance ... he crouches over his bat with his cap pulled hard down ... right elbow jutting awkwardly forward and then just as the bowler delivers the ball he shifts his forward foot across a little as though he was about to hook the ball. Dewes is stocky, well-built and has really powerful wrists. He watches the ball closely, gets right behind it and plays his shots very late using his wrists to get power in his shots. He barely seems to hit the ball and yet it goes from his bat swiftly and cleanly. In stance and in defence he reminded me of Phil Mead ... but he is by no means a purely defensive player, as the Australian bowlers soon found out.

Crossed out in his script then came the line: 'I have spent so much time describing this young left-hander because from today's showing he may well become one of England's regular Test batsmen.'

The spinners Pepper and Ellis came on for the opening bowlers, and Miller came on at the pavilion end just before lunch, as the fifth bowler tried in an hour. Robertson-Glasgow in *The Observer* the next day, like some others watching, was puzzled why Miller did not open the bowling. The under-bowling of Miller was now ending, however; for the remainder of the Tests Hassett would give Miller as many overs as anyone.

The crowd urged Miller to pitch the ball up when several of his deliveries bounced short of a length and flew about the batsman's shoulders. Suddenly Hutton and Dewes had to make their strokes very much quicker; Dewes took several sharp blows on the body. Dewes, like every other English batsman, had the bad fortune to face Keith Miller while the Australian was discovering that he was the fastest bowler in the land. Nobody really knew Miller as a bowler, Dewes recalled in 2009: 'He was learning and my word, he was good. And the other thing about him: if he bowled a good length ball, and if like me you weren't very tall, his good ball wasn't down here' – he pointed at his upper leg – 'it was up here'; and he pointed at his ribs. Dewes wore the best body protection that money could buy in 1945: a thigh pad and a towel under his trousers. Still, England made it to lunch in one piece, on 50 for one: Hutton 25 not out, Dewes 16 not out. Chester Wilmot told how Miller from the pavilion end had Dewes in difficulties after lunch:

> *Miller with his fine loose high action was sending down some real fast ones and they were swinging away just outside Dewes' off stump. Dewes swished rather wildly at a couple and drew a friendly warning from Hutton but in the next over, being a little anxious, he played rather late to a very fast inswinger and saw his off stump go flying.*

His 27 had good reviews. He had 'played very correctly and shown no sign of nerves', *The Cricketer* said. Also impressed was the *Sunday Express*, which reported that the stroke which got him out was his only bad one.

Dewes had played his part in a second wicket stand of 65. It would prove to be nearly the highest stand of the day. Miller was also troubling Hutton, and the new batsman Hammond, who had to endure two confident shouts against him for leg before. When Hammond ran his first single, Miller chased the ball from his own bowling, reached it ten yards past the wicket, threw on the turn and knocked a stump sideways. Hammond was just in his ground. Hammond was very cautious and in the *Yorkshire Evening Post*'s words 'refused to obey the crowd's injunctions to have a go'. He appeared to be settling down when he was stumped, on 13.

'Hammond's wicket was a triumph for Pepper,' said Chester Wilmot. 'He had been bowling a lot straight through but this one turned from the left just enough to beat his bat and go through into Sismey's hands while Hammond was still well outside his crease.'

Now with the score on 107 for three, the second debutant, White, came in. England plainly sought to partner a senior batsman with each youth if possible. Hutton, who as elder batsman had 'nursed' Dewes, did the same for White. Seeking to intimidate the young man, Hassett set four men around the bat. Hutton gave White so little of the bowling that spectators cheered ironically when Hutton hit a three and 'allowed the boy a chance', George Harrison reported in the next day's *News of the World*.

Hutton felt able to attack when he got to the batting end and the fielders were still set close in, as for White. James Freeman wrote in the *Daily Mail* that Miller ducked from a couple of Hutton drives quicker than any U-boat crash-dived in the Atlantic; military metaphors were still in vogue for the time being. Cristofani twice might have had Hutton caught in the 60s off a cleverly disguised slower ball. As close fielders Cristofani only had a silly mid-off (Miller) and short mid-on. Hutton let fly at a half volley, which just missed Miller's left ear. Elton Ede in the *Sunday Times* reported the next day: 'Miller had previously made Hutton duck twice to his fast bumpers and the crowd appreciating the jest to the full gave Lord's its biggest laugh of the day.'

'Hutton was going steadily on towards his hundred with the effortless style of the great craftsman that he is,' Chester Wilmot told Australian listeners the next day. 'None of the bowlers were worrying him and the crowd were delighted with his delicate cutting so late and sure, his crisp driving through the covers and his sharp punishment of anything loose on the leg side. Encouraged by Hutton, young White seemed to be settling down and it seemed that England would go to tea with seven wickets in hand and 160-odd on the board. But when White was 11 he made an agricultural swipe at a spinner from Cristofani and he was easily stumped by Sismey.'

Having played the junior part in a stand of 55, White left Hutton on 98. Not long after came tea with Hutton on 99. He reached his 100 with a pushed single off the first ball after the break. Next over Miller 'bowled another fizzer' and knocked out Hutton's off stump. It brought in the last of the debutants, Donald Carr, described on the score card as from 'Repton School'. He had to face some of the fastest bowling anyone of his generation was likely to encounter:

I remember Keith Miller was bowling terribly fast for the likes of me, who had only played at school practically to that time. When I walked in Len Hutton had just been out and he had made 100 and the clouds had come over – it really was quite darkish – and when Len got out, I was next man in, number seven. And I had to walk in; I thought, 'My God, if Hutton gets out like that, what can I be expected to get.' And as I walked by I had to go to the far end at Lord's and walk past Keith Miller as he was bowling from the pavilion end; as I passed him he said, 'Good luck, kid!' and I said 'Thank you, Mister Miller', and I thought perhaps he would give me one off the mark or something decent, but he bowled first ball [chuckles] and I never saw it and it was pretty dark; it thudded into the wicket-keeper's hands. I looked around and I clearly hadn't seen it so he laughed from the other end and then I decided I'd better play forward and hope for the best almost as soon as he started his run-up. And it hit the middle of the bat amazingly; it went for four. Past mid-off. He said, well played and all that. Two or three balls later [chuckles] hit the inside edge of my bat and went on to my middle stump and I thought to myself, 'quick enough for me', and I walked off.

Carr was bowled Miller for four; England had slid from a reasonable 162 for three to 175 for six. From the press box, Carr showed up well until he had the misfortune of receiving the third of Miller's 'blockbusters'. Bill Edrich and Billy Griffith now had the highest stand of the innings, 66. The new ball, taken by Williams, may have helped; Edrich hit a six to the pavilion. Cristofani, varying his pace and including an occasional fast one, took three wickets towards the very end of the day, to end as Australia's most successful bowler of the Test series so far with four wickets.

'After we had got Wally so cheaply I felt we would be all right,' Hassett told Chester Wilmot that evening. England had found the going hard against all of the bowlers, but Miller's aggression – or rather the fact that he alone was fast enough to upset the batsmen – stood out.

———————

England's experiment with youth began to unravel on the second day, the Monday after Sunday's rest day, though not through any fault of the three on debut. Hammond could not take the field because of lumbago, which 'pursued me like a remorseless shadow through half my cricket career', he wrote in *Cricket My World*. There was nothing for it but to apply hot towels and hot water bottles, and take bed rest. From the pavilion in the morning Hammond watched Griffith – the new captain and secretary of Sussex – act as captain. He gave the first over of Australia's innings, at the pavilion end, to Edrich. Hammond would have done the same because Edrich and Pollard were the only two faster bowlers he had. The *Manchester Guardian* called the arrangement 'ludicrous', while not blaming Edrich: 'If enthusiasm were all he would be good for he hurls himself at the bowling crease as though he had a personal grievance against it.'

According to Edrich, in Lancashire Pollard was known affectionately as 'tug boat Annie', 'because he is utterly reliable'. Edrich by contrast was one of the most spectacular bowlers of his time, because of the effort he made to 'sling 'em down'. John Arlott, writing after the 1947 season, summed up Edrich's action, in roughly the time it would take to see it: 'He ran up at a full and furious gallop, threw his body back so far that his cocked right hand almost brushed the ground, and then, with a furious heave, catapulted the ball down the pitch and followed through with a violence that threatened to tug him off his feet.' Surely few men shorter than the five foot six Edrich have opened the bowling for England. Bowling with the wind behind him, that first Edrich over of the day went for 11. An Australian spectator yelled to Griffith: 'Put Edrich on at the other end as well!'

Yet for a time all went well on the field. Edrich soon came off. Wright, flighting the ball cleverly, bowling into a blustery wind, beat Workman several times until the opening bat edged a turning ball to Edrich at short slip and was out for seven. Wickets fell steadily all morning. Pollard, having bowled Whitington for 19, came off after an hour for Roberts. Against Roberts' third ball Cheetham groped forward with his right leg, leaving his left behind on the crease, only to be bowled for five. Roberts, brought into the attack much sooner by Griffith, if only because England had fewer bowlers than in earlier

Tests, had taken his first wicket for England. Roberts beat the newcomer Miller; in earlier Tests some had queried if Miller was happy against slow bowling. Pollard dropped an easy chance off Wright, after juggling it, and in his disgust threw the ball away and gave away overthrows. Pollard came back for Roberts and in his first over bowled Miller for seven. Pepper came in at 71 for four, facing first a no-ball from Pollard. Next ball, Pollard had Pepper leg before without scoring: 72 for five.

Hassett and Carmody made it to lunch at 96 for five. After lunch, Edrich again opened the bowling, with Pollard, to more cheers from Australians in the crowd. While Australia still found the going hard – Hassett was missed before lunch at 27 and afterwards at 47 – England had more bad fortune when Washbrook hurt his right thumb trying to take that second catch, fielding behind the bowler Wright. He kept nursing it as best he could; he had to stay where he was, because the 12th man Robertson was fielding already for Hammond. The Australians, however, were falling well short in their first innings. White caught Carmody at mid-on, for 32. Hassett, after a stay of two hours for his side's top score of 68, was leg before to the persevering Pollard. Carr with the score at 171 for seven bowled for the first time, beginning with a maiden to Sismey. He and Cristofani added 34 for the eighth wicket before Australia were out just before 4pm. That gave England a handy lead of 60, given that batsmen were finding it difficult against fast and spin bowlers alike. Pollard as the only specialist fast bowler led the attack, taking six wickets.

Of England's first seven batsmen, three were the debutants, Hammond was doubtful to bat, and another experienced bat was injured. Much rested on Hutton and Edrich. Did England have enough batting to press their advantage? At first it looked so. Dewes, promoted to opener, because Washbrook's thumb was bothering him, played back to a real fast one from Miller 'and that was that', as the *Daily Telegraph* put it. Dewes' leg stump went flying and Dewes went without scoring. Hutton, however, was looking untroubled, and the lead looked formidable when Edrich, promoted to three, was bowled by Miller for 58, 20 minutes from the close. Griffith went in as night watchman, but was soon out without scoring, so Pollard as a second night watchman played out time. Hutton was anchoring his team on 49 not out; England were 118 for three; their lead was 178. Chester Wilmot, speaking overnight to Australia, predicted that Australia would probably be set at least 250 to win. Much would depend on Hutton: 'If he goes early, England's batting may collapse.' Wilmot was half-right.

Miller had opened the bowling in the second innings and he did so again on the third day, from the pavilion end, a further sign of his rise. Hutton kept Pollard away from the bowling until in the third over, Miller's second, Pollard was bowled, all ends up, for nine. White managed a single then an uppish couple through the slips, made 'two ineffectual flicks' at Miller, and was leg before to Cristofani, for four. Carr was quickly off the mark with a single but holed out simply, again to Cristofani; out for one. In no time England had slumped to 129 for six, with only three wickets to fall. Not for the first time the newspapers were likening Cristofani to the feared Australian (and fellow St George club) spinner Bill O'Reilly.

The word was that Hammond's lumbago was easier but he was still in no condition to bat. Washbrook had to go in at number eight, his thumb bandaged in something like a boxing glove. Hutton was scoring so slowly, adding only six in the first 40 minutes, that Australia seemed happy to bowl defensively at him and attack the other batsman.

Any stroke of power obviously hurt Washbrook. The last two senior batsmen were able to add 21 runs, mainly singles. To even things slightly, and possibly leave Australia weaker in batting, Miller in the middle of an over seemed to strain his back, and bowled the last three balls on a shorter run. The likely reason was a recent flying accident. It would be easy, but wrong, to see it as proof of Miller's dangerous, and therefore heroic, war. In truth it was typically impetuous of Miller, as he admitted in his memoirs, to make an unnecessary flight when his squadron had nothing to do – indeed, it disbanded in August. The squadron log book said for June 28: 'A small amount of practice flying carried out in the morning and afternoon. F/O [Flying Officer] KR Miller had starboard engine on fire and in making a single engine landing overshot. The aircraft was wrecked but fortunately no-one was hurt.' Stanford took Miller's place in the field.

At 150 Hutton tried to cut Cristofani, but snicked to Sismey; he was out for 69. Roberts was bowled without score by Ellis in no time, and Wright came in as last man. He pulled the first four of the day, off Cristofani. Washbrook did the same to Ellis, then Wright was caught at short leg by Hassett off Cristofani, for six. The innings had taken most of the morning to peter out, Washbrook making a mere 13 not out of the last 35.

England's second innings batting apart from Hutton and Edrich 'looked woefully weak' according to the Press Association. *The Cricketer* reported disapprovingly that there 'did not appear anything in the wicket to account for England's collapse'. All that said, Cristofani's figures for the third day were 14.3-5-17-4. By taking five wickets in the innings, out of the nine to fall, Cristofani bettered Australia's best bowling in the series for the second time in three days.

Australia were batting at 1pm, before lunch, and so had a good five hours, enough time to make the 225 to win. Given both teams' inconsistent batting all match, however, it would prove a contest between resilient batting – most of the Australians had scored some runs in the series so far – and what bowling England could offer. News of England's collapse must have spread through London quickly because crowds poured into Lord's to see a fighting finish.

They saw a sensational first over by Pollard. His first ball beat Whitington but missed the stumps. The second, Whitington snicked to the wicket-keeper. 'Stan Sismey joined Workman and Pollard's next ball went from the edge of Sismey's bat just short of Edrich, second slip,' Chester Wilmot told Australian listeners later. 'Playing forward to the fourth ball Sismey missed it and the crowd appealed as the ball went through to the keeper. The fifth was nearly a yorker but Sismey put the last one through the slips for a single. The crowd was fully roused.' Edrich, 'the human bullet', had to be the other opening bowler again. He like Pollard had five slips.

Sismey, promoted as the fourth batsman in six innings that Australia were trying as a number three, stole some cheeky singles with the blocker Workman. Australia lunched on 23 for one, needing 200, after the traditional spinner's last over before lunch by Wright. The news from the Australian dressing room was that Miller would bat if necessary; the masseur was busy on him. In the afternoon, Wilmot told Australia after it was all over: 'Workman was always comfortable but Sismey was full of confidence and scored all round the wicket, driving and pulling cleanly and powerfully. The bowlers were not getting as much help from the wicket as they had expected and for some unknown reason Wright was not turning them as much as Cristofani had been.'

Sismey and Workman ran a four off a tickle to leg off Wright and from the next ball took a single so sharp that the Australians in the crowd pleaded, 'Don't do that!' The minority of Australians watching, in army slouch hats or air force blue, were more vocal than the rest. They chorused of Pollard: 'Take him off!'

Roberts did replace Pollard, for an over, then made way for Wright. Sismey hit Roberts to leg for four; the match was swinging Australia's way. Wright beat Workman and Griffith caught the off stump as it flew out of the ground: 82 for two, Workman's share being 30. Pollard beat Sismey with a straight ball, and had him leg before for 51: 103 for three. Miller came in at number five to join Hassett. These two leading batsman, already halfway to victory, took tea needing only 89 to win.

England's only chance was to break the partnership. Then Hassett trying to drive Wright mistimed and sent the ball fairly hard, low and just beyond the reach of Edrich at silly point. Edrich dived and took a brilliant catch with his left hand. Australia were 151 for four. At 165, England might have had a fifth wicket, so Wilmot broadcast, 'when Miller hooked a short ball from Pollard over the square leg umpire's head and out towards Dewes. The crowd roared and the fieldsman ran towards it but the sun was in his eyes and he dropped the catch.'

Wickets kept falling – Pepper, after he hit a six into the members' stand; and Carmody, leaving Australia 193 for six. England had an outside chance if they could make good use of the new ball at 200. Runs only came quicker. After five runs came off a Pollard over, and seven off Edrich, Australia only needed 14.

Wanting 11 to win, Miller straight drove Pollard for three, Cheetham glanced the next for another three; Miller skied a no-ball for two and late cut the next for another couple, and the scores were level. Wilmot described the winning byes: 'Pollard ran up to deliver the last ball, banged it down almost at his feet, it flew head high, Miller ducked, Griffith ducked, and the ball sped on into regions once inhabited by the long stop. No one bothered to chase it.' Australia had won by four wickets. 'Batsmen, umpires, fieldsmen walked towards the pavilion while the crowd applauded and swarmed over the ground ... near the far sight board, a London policeman fielded the winning ball.'

Third Test, Lord's, July 14, 16 and 17

England won the toss

England first innings

L Hutton		b Miller	104
C Washbrook	ct Sismey	b Williams	8
JG Dewes		b Miller	27
*WR Hammond	st Sismey	b Pepper	13
LR White	st Sismey	b Cristofani	11
WJ Edrich	lbw	b Cristofani	38
DB Carr		b Miller	4
†SC Griffith	ct Pepper	b Cristofani	36
R Pollard	not out		1
WB Roberts		b Cristofani	1
DVP Wright	lbw	b Ellis	5
Extras (2 b, 1 lb, 3 nb)			6
Total (all out, 107.1 overs)			254

Fall of wickets: 1-11, 2-76, 3-107, 4-162, 5-169, 6-175, 7-241, 8-248, 9-249, 10-254

Bowling

Williams	19	6	45	1
Cheetham	19	5	47	0
Pepper	19	2	44	1
Ellis	19.1	6	25	1
Miller	18	3	44	3
Cristofani	13	1	43	4

The Victory Tests

Australian Services first innings

RS Whitington		b Pollard	19
JA Workman	ct Edrich	b Wright	7
AG Cheetham		b Roberts	5
*AL Hassett	lbw	b Pollard	68
KR Miller		b Pollard	7
CG Pepper	lbw	b Pollard	0
DK Carmody	ct White	b Pollard	32
DR Cristofani		b Roberts	32
†SG Sismey	ct Griffith	b Pollard	9
RG Williams		b Wright	4
RS Ellis	not out		0
Extras (4 lb, 7 nb)			11
Total (all out, 71.1 overs)			194

Fall of wickets: 1-29, 2-29, 3-50, 4-71, 5-72, 6-127, 7-149, 8-183, 9-184, 10-194

Bowling

Edrich	7	0	25	0
Pollard	23	4	75	6
Wright	24.1	3	49	2
Roberts	14	5	24	2
Carr	3	1	10	0

England second innings

L Hutton	ct Sismey	b Cristofani	69
JG Dewes		b Miller	0
WJ Edrich		b Miller	58
†SC Griffith	ct Pepper	b Cristofani	0
R Pollard		b Miller	9
LR White	lbw	b Cristofani	4
DB Carr	ct Pepper	b Cristofani	1
C Washbrook	not out		13
WB Roberts		b Ellis	0
DVP Wright	ct Hassett	b Cristofani	6
*WR Hammond absent hurt			
Extras (3 lb, 1 nb)			4
Total (all out, 77.3 overs)			164

Fall of wickets: 1-1, 2-106, 3-107, 4-122, 5-127, 6-129, 7-150, 8-151, 9-164

Bowling

Williams	3	0	10	0
Cheetham	4	0	7	0
Pepper	10	3	22	0
Ellis	14	1	29	1
Miller	16	2	42	3
Cristofani	29.3	8	49	5
Whitington	1	0	1	0

Australian Services second innings

RS Whitington	c Griffith	b Pollard	0
JA Workman		b Wright	30
†SG Sismey	lbw	b Pollard	51
*AL Hassett	ct Edrich	b Wright	24
KR Miller	not out		71
CG Pepper	lbw	b Edrich	18
DK Carmody	ct Edrich	b Roberts	1
AG Cheetham	not out		9

Cristofani, Williams and Ellis did not bat
Extras (1 b, 15 lb, 5 nb) 21
Total (six wickets, 77 overs) 225
Fall of wickets: 1-0, 2-82, 3-104, 4-151, 5-186, 6-193

Bowling

Edrich	12	1	37	1
Pollard	21	4	71	2
Wright	25	4	59	2
Roberts	13	4	24	1
Carr	6	2	13	0

Australian Services won by four wickets. Close of play, day one: England 254 all out. Close day two: England 118-3 (Hutton 49 not out, Pollard 7 not out).

That Australia led two games to one with two to play meant that the series was theirs to lose. Their win in the first match was not a fluke. Where had England gone wrong?

Many did not resist the temptation to blame the three teenagers. Sir Pelham Warner as editor of *The Cricketer* –

and one of the men who picked the team – had anticipated this in his magazine beforehand: 'Should they fail the selectors will no doubt be "caned". Should they come off they may expect a few bouquets but whatever is in store … we are certain that looking to the view to give youth every encouragement is the right policy to adopt.'

Understandably, after the failure, Sir Pelham tried to look elsewhere. To be fair, if Hammond had been able to bat, he may well have taken enough time and given England enough runs to force a draw. Though no-one said so in print at the time, surely the 'experiment' of picking youths was not wrong, merely that the selectors took it to extremes. One extra bowler – Pope – may have picked off Australia on the last day as England managed to do at Sheffield.

The Cricketer dispensed individual praise and blame. As for the bowlers, 'Wright bowled magnificently but fortune scowled on him. He kept a beautiful length, spun the ball and often beat the batsman … few bowlers can ever have bowled better with less tangible results.' Pollard, who took eight wickets in the match to Wright's four, was 'a bowler of high merit', particularly dangerous with a new ball: 'He is a striver and what CB Fry would call a hostile bowler. He has the right temperament and never gives in. All praise to him for a fine effort.'

Roberts, as at Sheffield, the least-used of the bowlers, had the merit of length but had to concentrate more on spin, and his batting. It was a somewhat damning verdict on a spinner.

As for the batsmen, Hutton was the 'mainstay'. 'You cannot fault his style for his method is correct in every essential. It is remarkable how finely he bats when it is recalled that he broke his left arm some three years ago and after it had been set had to have it re-broken and a piece of skin from his left calf grafted on to his arm … he is a great fighter with a cool head.'

Edrich, too, was in favour. 'He is a strong stroke player who is fond of the straight drive. He used to move his head before deciding on his stroke but we think he has now overcome this fault and fault it is for the head is a camera and if you move it too soon you lose the focus of the ball. He is also a brilliant fieldsman.'

The magazine came to the young men. 'Dewes played a plucky and good first innings. His style is unpolished but his defence is sound and practice and experience in good company should smooth out the rough edges.' White played too much on the back foot 'and must practice all he can against slow bowling'. And while of the three Carr had done least, he looked 'and is a cricketer all over. His style of batting is good, he fields smartly and he is a clever slow left handed bowler with an easy action and a good length.' Rather defensively, Sir Pelham summed up: 'Dewes, White and Carr are all under 19 and naturally lack experience and especially against fast bowling … a couple of years in county cricket would improve them immensely. That the ability is there is clear.'

Characteristically, Sir Pelham had kind words for the victors: 'The Australians are pleasant and sportsmanlike companions under their captain and fine batsmen Hassett and they are doing their own and our cricket good.'

For all the talk of giving youth 'every' encouragement, the three teenagers were not picked again in the series. Beating Australia, or at least drawing level, had to come first. That meant experienced players who could withstand Miller and get him out. Miller's 71 not out in the fourth innings was the second highest of the match, and, as much as Pepper's in the first Test, a match-winner. As important, Miller took six wickets quite cheaply in a low-scoring game, including what proved to be the crucial wicket of Edrich late on the second day when he and Hutton were at their best. Miller was making his name in the game. Lord Tennyson, as the grandson of the *Charge of the Light Brigade* poet, someone who could recognise a man with flair, wrote in the *News of the World* after the third Test: 'As for Keith Miller, in my opinion he is the best all-rounder now playing. He is splendidly alive as batsman, bowler and fielder. He really attacks when bowling and every now and then sends down a ball good enough to beat anyone.'

Miller was doing what he was good at, and enjoying the good life that came with cricket for a living; it would not get better than this.

Chapter Twelve

Sent to Coventry

We played all over England, even Scotland – Selkirk, Glasgow. We did a tour, played nine days' cricket in nine days and travelled 900 miles. The RAAF welfare officer organised us and that really frightened us.

Ross Stanford

The Australians had no rest all summer. Having taken the lead in the Victory Test series on the Tuesday, by the Saturday the airmen were going on tour.

Anyone who has been in the services, and in the hands of a 'welfare officer', will know what Stanford was talking about. 'Yeah,' he recalled in old age, 'we started off from Brighton in a coach, a blacked-out coach. We started at Coventry; Arthur Fagg made 100 against us there. Then we played a two-day game in Yorkshire, and Len Hutton played against us in that one. Then we went to Darlington, then from there to Selkirk. And then Greenock, that's out of Glasgow, isn't it? And of course the bus driver got lost once, and we went through the town of Hamilton three times. We arrived late at Greenock and Keith Carmody agreed to go on playing until eight o'clock that night.'

While the AIF and RAAF teams had each made forays to the north earlier, this was their furthest travelling of the summer. Otherwise, the Australians tended to play within a day's travelling to and from the capital. In an age when touring cricketers and tourists generally can sit in an air-conditioned coach and bypass most towns, and reach one end of England from the other within half a day, hardly noticing the motorway, it's worth spelling out how much of an adventure a northern tour by road was in 1945. While traffic was still light compared with before the war, let alone since, you headed north from London on much the same roads as the Romans; in the airmen's case on Saturday, July 21, the A5 to Coventry. Except that, as *The Observer* reported the next day, the RAAF arrived late because their motor coach broke down, they went without lunch, lost the toss, and were made to field for the rest of the day. As brief newspaper reports do sometimes, without even trying to, this gives a wrong impression of bad hospitality. The Coventry evening paper the day before told readers that the Australians were arriving at Coventry railway station at 12.43pm, to be welcomed by members of the Coventry cricket committee.

And while the Coventry eleven might sound a fairly minor team, big factories such as Courtaulds kept grounds, as part of their sports and welfare offerings to their workers, and they drew on unemployed county players – in Coventry's case, Warwickshire – and beyond. Arthur Fagg, for example, the Kent batsman, had played five Tests over the three years before the war, and had only just turned 30. Coventry's first four bowlers were county men – Grove (of Warwickshire), Herman (of Hampshire), Armstrong (of Derbyshire), who took seven for 52, and Jenkins (of Worcestershire).

So the hosts may have felt the large crowd – put at 3,000 on the Saturday and an enormous 6,000 on the Sunday – was there to see them as much as the Australians, and indeed Coventry had the best of the game. Play began on the Saturday at 3pm; rain made a delay for 45 minutes around 5pm, then stopped play for the day at 7.15pm. In between Fagg scored a 'faultless' 100 exactly, out of 215 for five. On the second day, Coventry declared at 273 for seven at 12.15pm. The Australians replied with 202, Staines and Cristofani (top scorer with 52, after taking five for 63) hitting well. Coventry closed the match on 96 for one.

That evening the Australians set off for Sheffield, where the next day, Monday, they faced Yorkshire for one day at Bramall Lane. The Australians put out the strongest side they could – including Miller and Sismey who sat out Coventry, and Hassett (as captain) and Pepper from the AIF side. In fact only Carmody, who did score 38 at Coventry but was not finding his form, played against Yorkshire and not in the fourth Test two weeks later.

The games in the far north did not stretch the Australians too much in the field, but they did ask a lot of their stamina for travel. On the Wednesday, under the RAAF banner at Sunderland they beat Durham easily – 305 for four declared (Stanford 101 not out, Cristofani 42 not out, Miller 75) to 160 (Roper five wickets, Miller and Ellis two each) – in front of another crowd of several thousand. By the next day, July 26, they were 80 miles further north and inside Scotland, playing at Philiphaugh outside Selkirk.

This was declaration day, when the general election results came out after the vote three weeks before, 'but amidst the glorious surroundings of forest and pasture lands of the Border hills few allowed their minds to wander from the cricket', Norman Preston wrote in *The Cricketer.* Another crowd of thousands saw opener Hartley Craig make a 'brilliant' 74 in two and a half hours; otherwise, as the local paper the *Southern Reporter* ungallantly put it, the Australian batsmen were 'slow and unenterprising'. Miller walked in to an ovation but was soon out.

Hartley Craig's score was all the more impressive by comparison with the previous big game at Philiphaugh, in August 1944. Sismey as captain and three other Australians – Stocks, Cristofani and Roper – had played a Scottish eleven on what the *Reporter* had called a 'somewhat tricky wicket'. The Scots made 77 and the combined services 100. A year on in reply to the Australians' 176 the Scottish Services team slumped to 18 for five and you suspect that the Australians let the hosts rally to 143.

These games far from the centres of cricket were partly about flying the flag – Sismey as captain planted a cypress (still standing in 2009, in a corner beside the rugby club). Margaret Smith, a later stalwart of the club, recalled how her father, who brought her up to love cricket, took her to that 1945 match, her first. Asked in 2009 what she remembered of the day, she answered: 'I was told to keep quiet!' Spectators on such occasions wanted to concentrate on the players they otherwise only read about.

The Scottish team had an odd mix of England Test players such as Hopper Levett of Kent and the Welshman Austin Matthews – Ames and Robins were invited but could not make it; and the likes of the captain, Colonel JGW Davies, whose claim to fame was bowling Bradman for nought while at university; and Viscount French, whose claims to fame were playing for his school, Winchester, and being a viscount.

The airmen stayed two nights in Selkirk and left Friday morning for an afternoon game in Greenock. Unfortunately their air force coach 'partially broke down', as Norman Preston put it, and another large crowd put at 4,000 did not see play begin at Glen Park until 3.30pm. Workman, without big-match cares or feeling able to play freely against lesser bowlers, drove cleanly, and Carmody showed some of his 1944 form. John Kerr, described as the 'GOM' (Grand Old Man) of Scottish cricket, who first played against Australia in 1909, was in this Scots team at the age of 60. This was not the airmen's only encounter with that era. In 1944, the great left-handed batsman Frank Woolley, then aged 57, and not that long retired from Kent, pulled a muscle bowling his first ball for the Birmingham Festival XI against the RAAF. Woolley had played Test matches in 1909 against Australia including Trumper, Noble and Gregory: a remarkable link with the Edwardian past.

At Glasgow on Saturday, July 28, the RAAF had the all-important first innings at Hamilton Crescent, Partick, home of the West of Scotland club. What Norman Preston called a 'sporty' pitch cut up by the time Scotland went in. The Australians made 149 (Workman 42, Stanford 25, Pettiford 33) to Scotland's 90 (RG Williams three for 43, Roper six for 29, Cristofani one for 14).

The Australian Army and air force halves were combining only for the Tests and other most prestigious matches, and when playing separately were finding it ever harder to manage. On July 28, for instance, at Chalkwell Park, Westcliff-on-Sea, the Metropolitan Police were 'little troubled' by the AIF bowling – Hassett and Whitington having to do a share – and declared on 208 for six before dismissing the Australians for 134. Only Pepper and Price were other Victory Test-class players that day, and Price was still recovering from an injured bowling finger. Their ranks were thinning: Cheetham for example returned home after the third Test. Senior players had to take the strain still more, as Hassett did the following Wednesday, against the Royal Navy and Royal Marines at the United Services Officers' Recreation Ground, Portsmouth, not many stones' throw from the docks and the Solent. He hit the Australians' highest score of the season, 189 out of 267, in no time – three and three-quarter hours – hitting one six, and 18 fours, until he was caught from a skier at fine leg. Replying to the Australians' 331 the Navy – including opener Cadet Dewes – were one for none overnight. On the Thursday, the Navy fell to 46 for five before Sub-Lieutenant Kenneth Cranston, of Lancashire and later of England, made runs. The Navy followed on and saved the game.

The following Monday, August 6, the fourth Test began at Lord's. Worryingly for any Australian player wanting at least the prospect of an end, the South African Cricket Association cabled requesting a visit from the Australians. It was beginning to look as if Hassett and his men were too popular for their own good.

Chapter Thirteen

What is bright cricket?

> *Great institutions – churches, armies, political parties,*
> *and the MCC – abandon, after a time, the objects for*
> *which they were formed, and devote all their energies*
> *and other people's money to trying to maintain*
> *unaltered the structure that served well enough once,*
> *but has long ago lost its usefulness.*
>
> Learie Constantine, *Cricketers' Cricket* (1949)

In a little 1945 book titled *English Cricket*, Neville Cardus recalled how, after the 1914–18 war, cricket 'as a sensitive plant' responded to the English mood. It was an 'age of disillusionment' and 'safety first'; 'beautiful and bold stroke play gave way to a sort of trench warfare ...' English cricket in the 1920s was like the country as a whole, 'psychologically ill'. The more popular newspapers, so Cardus hinted, praised huge numbers of runs for the sake of them; as a reporter for the *Manchester Guardian*, Cardus rated himself above such vulgarity. The question after the 1939–45 war (leaving aside that the Japanese had yet to surrender): would the country be any healthier after a second war?

In arguably the most praised cricket book of all time, *Beyond a Boundary*, the West Indian CLR James played the same note: 'Luckily the war put an abrupt end to cricket as it was being played in the 1930s.' Writing some 15 years after the war's end, he knew the answer to Cardus' question, and indeed said so: 'The relief was only temporary.'

Though very different men, both saw that something was wrong with top-class cricket until interrupted by Hitler. The two had something else in common; each had put ocean between themselves and the war, and hence were not in England, nor even professionally concerned with cricket, in 1945. As with so much else in this story, then, we have to go beyond the usual sources.

Just as wartime demanded that the state and its people worked harder and in industries not needed in peacetime, so wartime forced a more carefree and loose style of cricket. Nothing was at stake except your own pride. You could make the most beautiful runs and be killed by a bomb before the next game; you were thrown into a team you hardly knew, just as you had been thrown into an army or air force of strangers; so why not do as you pleased? Indeed, why bother at all?

Set against man's natural selfishness is the equally natural wish of men in a group to not let the others down, or those watching. A game of cricket or any other sport was a reminder of normal life, to be cherished while it lasted. Even if a player found it hard to rouse himself – understandable if he had just flown a ten-hour mission to Berlin – and even if the pitch was rotten, once a batsman was taking guard, the next ball would have his full attention.

So it was at Burton upon Trent at the end of August 1943, when the town cricket club – set on an island between two arms of the River Trent – hosted 'a galaxy of stars' according to the *Burton Daily Mail*. It was not the first nor the last newspaper to exaggerate to its readers. A Services XI included some English county players; Keith Campbell; and Reg Ellis, who had just announced himself by taking eight wickets for an air force team against Derbyshire club and ground at Derby. (Donald Carr took six wickets for Derbyshire; Carr and Ellis took each other's wickets. They were not to know they would meet at Lord's two years later.)

The other team, Charles Leatherbarrow's XI, came largely from Lancashire, county players such as the wicket-keeper Bill Farrimond, and batsmen Eddie Paynter, Charlie Hallows and Winston Place; and league men – the West Indians EA (Manny) Martindale, Edwin St Hill and Ellis Achong, and George Pope of Derbyshire. They were far too strong for a scratch team, let alone on a pitch that the *Mail* politely termed 'sporting' and 'tricky'. On the first of two days, Leatherbarrow's XI was all out for 115 (Ellis five for 35), only for the Services to be out for 77. Next day, Pope's 85 not out gave the crowd some batting to enjoy. Set 203 in three hours, the Services got nowhere near – all out for 98. Campbell top scored, caught and bowled Achong for 21.

Probably because the field had been let for grazing for at least one season, the ball had overpowered the bat. Keith Campbell's sole recollection of the game was as a fielder being impressed by how well Paynter, when batting, kept down the rising deliveries. The game was not a financial success, so the *Burton Mail* afterwards reported. It was, the newspaper insisted, good entertainment: 'They are trying to find something like this to increase the popularity of county cricket after the war. The secret of the game was of course that men went in either to get on or get out. Those were the instructions given by both captains ... the holiday spirit was always paramount.' Burton and other towns ran similar games in 1944 and 1945.

By the middle of the war, every town was competing for cricket and other attractions to fill what the authorities called 'holidays at home' weeks. Instead of people wasting time at the seaside – much of it behind barbed wire in case of invasion anyway – people with time and money on their hands could listen to bands or watch cricket, and any money went to war causes. This was largely what seaside resorts such as Scarborough and Hastings offered at the end of each peacetime season: festival cricket. Much as the holiday-maker could relax, so could the festival cricketer.

An unnamed reporter on the *Birmingham Post* best defined the sort of cricket that pleased spectators. He was describing the June 1945 match at Edgbaston between the RAAF and West Indies: 'Play was always interesting on Saturday because it was progressive. The batsmen, without indulging in slogging, continually sought runs and fulfilled their mission so satisfactorily that … their score of 275 averaged a run a minute, and the bowlers courageously and consistently tried to capture wickets, never merely to keep runs down.'

Or as Ken Newitt, an RAAF wireless operator from Victoria, recalled Lord's at his Melbourne home in 1998: 'We had an area for Australians reserved. The banter between each one … good-humoured, banter between one another. Miller, Pepper; and it was cricket, not just –' here he played an imaginary defensive stroke – 'but this –' and he made an imaginary big hit.

So bright cricket that was appreciated by spectators – who after all chose to pay to watch, rather than sit in a park – did not necessarily need the biggest names, only basic proficiency. As that Birmingham reporter hinted, both sides had to take risks. For every winner there had to be a loser; for every high-scoring batsman, a high-scored-off bowler. If both sides entered into the spirit of it, the better side would win. The batting side had to hit for runs, rather than merely pat the ball or let it go; the bowlers had to toss the ball wider or slower or with more spin, to tempt the batsman into maybe giving a catch, rather than merely denying a batsman the room or time to play a stroke. There had to be a contest.

What sort of contest? Between batsman trying to hit every ball as hard as he could, or straining every time to survive against the turning or rising ball? Despite Ken Newitt or any spectator's wish to see sixes, a batsman could not hit a six every ball, or at least could not try to do so and expect to last for long. Sometimes the pitch or the quality of bowling called for defence. The RAAF, and the Services teams under Hassett, each sometimes found themselves batting at two an over, or even less. The Australian Services playing Yorkshire at Bradford on July 11 were all out for 204 after 103.1 overs. This may have been due to the slow outfield – a Hassett drive to the sightscreen was the first boundary of the day, at 3.30pm – or the accurate bowling by men playing their first county game since 1939 and wanting to impress. Bill Bowes' 21 overs went for 35, Alec Coxon's 41 overs for 66. The normally hard-hitting Cec Pepper was top scorer with 51.

A decently-prepared pitch was necessary, then, one that neither favoured batsmen nor bowlers. The groundsmen at Bramall Lane and Old Trafford were suspiciously and similarly defensive when asked before their Victory Tests. Both denied that their pitch was 'doped', that is, chemically deadened so it gave no hope to the bowler. Harry Williams, the groundsman at Old Trafford, promised that his pitch would be as good as 1939, though sheep had grazed on it during the war. 'Water and the rollers are the secrets but the final treatment will be dependent on the weather,' he said before the fifth Victory Test.

No matter how determined a cricketer or team were to play brightly, a viciously untrue pitch made bright cricket impossible. Indeed, it could put off youths for life. True pitches took rolling, and someone had to pull the roller – in other words, it took time and money. And too much or too little rain could always spoil the work.

Hammond had his say in July 1945 in his weekly column. Naturally a groundsman had pride in making perfect pitches. In that case, a batsman would take fewer risks because, again naturally, he would want to make as many runs as he could, while the going was good. If a pitch was 'sporting', it was no use for a batsman to wait for bowlers to tire. A pitch, though, could be too dangerous. Hammond doubted if a groundsman could suit all 22 players. In other words, the groundsman had 'a thankless task'.

Pitches mattered to every cricketer, as tools did to a carpenter and his rifle to an infantryman. Hence the informal discussion on the northern tour, as listened to by Norman Preston, between the Australians and Scottish players and officials on the way Australia fostered young cricketers, compared with the British Isles.

'The Australians are great believers in the value of the concrete pitches in their municipal parks and other sports fields where boys and young players are also provided with equipment so that they can practise whenever they like. I feel inclined to agree with the Australians, particularly as far as the ordinary school and minor club cricketers are concerned, that we would produce many better players and retain them if only they could begin the game on a true surface.' As Preston added, many playing fields had become allotments during the war; could they be laid with concrete pitches?

Some Australians did not recognise this description of their country. An airman, WJ Leggatt, had a letter

What is bright cricket?

printed in the *Daily Mail* of August 3 after a claim by Sir Pelham Warner that Australian boys had better pitches. 'I have played much cricket during my four years in England and have found to my amazement how well catered for are your schoolboys – good wickets prepared by competent groundsmen, batting gloves, always two pads, not to mention cricket coaches. These conditions prevail in Australia only in first class colleges. Elsewhere boys get difficult, often unplayable wickets. But these tend to sharpen their eye and footwork so that when they come to play on better wickets they have already formed a natural not a textbook or copied style. Nor are they molly-coddled.' Surely Leggatt was talking about English private schools; one wonders how many state schools in cities he had seen.

Tellingly, it was difficult to ask how to make brighter cricket without straying into what made the game, and society, tick, and how the Australians compared to the English. And as Preston and Leggatt's very different opinions suggested, you could never make everyone agree. Whether you were a conservative, who felt that cricket was fine if only players played brightly – a suspiciously vague term – or someone who sought change to keep the game alive, you could not avoid change, if only the change between playing generations, and, as Cardus and CLR James were clever enough to weave into their writing, wider social and world events. Whose idea of change was right, and how to manage the pace of change?

Football and rugby had descended from the all-day, all-village, anything-goes ball games of the Middle Ages into 80 or 90-minute affairs. Cricket alone kept the option of altering the length of a game. English county cricket prided itself on starting one-day, fixed-overs cricket in the 1960s and inventing Twenty20 cricket in the 2000s although in truth there was nothing new under the sun. Men free only at weekends or evenings had played one-day and 20-over-a-side cricket for generations. How else could busy men spare the time to play? The Chauntry Cup and similar single-innings games on airfields between squadrons was the first cricket in England for Australians like Ross Stanford. For weekend club players, this was nothing new. What was radical about the war was that the county grounds and players, even Lord's, embraced the single-innings game, decided (or left drawn) in a day.

In the regions and parts of counties where the county club seldom reached, festivals were not only popular; they made sense to spectators and were good business. Take the Parkhead week at Sheffield in June 1945, a Twenty20 festival in all but name. Three of the five teams batting first lost, with totals of 134, 172 and 180. In such a shortened game, on an admittedly small ground, a batsman had to try to score off every ball. The festival was an occasion for a handful of paid professionals – such as the West Indian Martindale; and Bowes, Arthur Mitchell and Wilf Barber of Yorkshire – to please the crowd with big hits. Usually they succeeded: on the first night Mitchell made 111 not out and Martindale 35 (five sixes, one four) out of Parkhead's winning 176 for four in 20 overs.

Such cricket had its place; so did other sorts. The 20-over-a-side cricket could easily become too one-sided in favour of the batsman, or quickly boring if the bowlers took several wickets suddenly. While administrators and know-alls could argue over how to tinker with the rules or hours of play – as if something they alone could do would make cricket more appealing – the truth was that brighter cricket would only come if the cricketers made the effort. The official appeal for brighter cricket, and blame on the professionals for playing for safety, was hypocritical because the grinding length of the peacetime season fixed by the authorities made bright cricket impossible.

Keith Miller spelt it out in an article for Cyril Washbrook's 1949 *Annual*. Whereas Australians played in moderation, English county professionals had to play six days a week: 'My idea of cricket is that it should be something which makes one forget the cares of the world, and at the same time provides relaxation and exercise. As it is, in England the county player is like a farmer who ploughs his fields – it is a hard grind, and he is glad when the day is done.' If the English county first-class season ran solid from the start of May until the end of August, you could hardly expect every week to be a harvest festival.

Unfortunately, the authorities misread the reasons for the crowds for the Victory Tests. After the first Test, *The Cricketer* said: 'It was a triumph for the three day match and at a time when there are many pessimists in the land will do an immense amount of good and send people flocking to cricket.' This was the complacent and self-congratulatory voice of authority: '... we are convinced that in future cricket will flourish as never before in all its long and splendid history. It is not only an institution but a part and a great part of the life of the English people.' The authorities saw the Victory summer as proof that they did not have to change things – indeed, ought not to. In contrast, reformers said that now was the time to modernise, while the going was good, to bring in one-day county cricket and to build a new, larger Lord's and other stadia.

Lord's had to turn away thousands for the same reasons that horse racing, boxing and athletics meetings drew huge crowds. After years of restrictions, people wanted a treat, and had money to afford it. The Saturday after the first Victory Test, came a Victory football international between England and France at Wembley – a two-all draw ('we were almost beaten at our own game,' wrote a shaken Frank Butler in the *Sunday Express*).

Other sports were not the only competition. People flocked to the nearest seaside. Some Londoners had to sleep on the beach at Brighton because the hotels and the trains home were full. Once the novelty wore off, would cricket keep hold of people? The likes of Learie Constantine feared not. In a midsummer series of newspaper articles, in *The People*, he said: 'I don't want to see it [cricket] die out under competition from the cinemas and speedways and greyhound tracks. But it will have to brighten up if it is to live … things that do not move do not live.'

Constantine suggested three cricket divisions and a national cricket cup; and once every five years, instead of the county game, an 'international cricket carnival year'. All Constantine's ideas came true: a cup competition from 1963, an 'international carnival', or World Cup, every four years from 1975; and a two-division county championship from 2000. Similarly, Constantine had the right idea about competing attractions squeezing the life – or rather money – out of cricket. He had no way of knowing that entirely new and affordable pleasures – cheap foreign holidays, family cars and television – would make cinemas, cricket, and much else, seem old-fashioned. As the reformers and conservatives alike feared, cricket was forced into change just to stay in business.

What is bright cricket?

So many of the calls for brighter cricket were like appeals for more obedient children, or more church-going on Sundays; if the conditions that made people do (or not do) something did not alter, nor would their behaviour. Not that people stopped making the appeals. In the 1952 edition of *Wisden*, the new editor Norman Preston quoted a Captain WA Powell's list of rival attractions such as golf, tennis, sailing and flying clubs, private cars and motorcycles, even ice rinks, all showing huge increases since 1900 (especially flying, as it had not been invented in 1900). In a letter to the *Manchester Guardian* on August 18, 1945, the same (presumably) Captain WA Powell proposed making the wickets lower and narrower. He suggested an extra run for every ball scored off, and an extra deducted for every ball not scored off, 'in view of the safety first tactics so prevalent in first class cricket today'. This might only have reinforced the safety first mentality – by the fielding side, which could penalise the batting side for not scoring runs. As Powell admitted in his letter, he was proposing merely a tactic, something that the other side could negate. Constantine was on surer ground – and ironically the conservatives at Lord's could agree with him – when he argued that there was nothing wrong with the tools and rules of cricket. The conservatives, according to Constantine, were the problem: 'There is plenty of life in cricket yet, if only it is not stifled by too many grey parties.'

The trouble was not only that you would never get agreement on what was bright cricket, or what would make it brighter. Some people cherished cricket's rituals, even its dull routines – because how else could you appreciate the occasional excitements? In that same August 18 *Manchester Guardian*, a special correspondent at Blackpool deplored what he called the 'loudspeaker menace'. The reporter grumbled that the announcer did not say anything that listeners could learn from the scorecard, or scoreboard. And the 'canned music given forth during the intervals was regrettable'. In a fast-changing, bewildering and too often brutal world, some people clung to something unthreatening that stayed the same: 'Cricket is almost the only game which retains some measure of peace and dignity ...'

Yet the game at Blackpool sounds as bright as any. A strong North of England side out-batted then out-bowled a strong Australian team that was much the same as the side about to play the fifth and final Victory Test at nearby Manchester a couple of days later. Norman Preston saw Hassett 'in holiday mood ... and his 103 out of 132 in 77 minutes will live long in my memory'. Pollard and Pope were on top when Hassett went in, 'but ... he hooked delightfully besides driving superbly'.

During the first day's play, according to the *Manchester Guardian* man, the Australians took the new ball at 400, only the umpires did not have one; hence a delay: '... but the sun was shining and no-one seemed particularly worried about it'.

That was one of the rarer two-innings games the Australians played in their years in England. Much more usual was the one-day, single-innings game, more to the taste of the reformers. The purpose of the day was to show as many of the visitors batting or bowling as possible, who when not on the field would sign autographs. For their own esteem both sides wanted to do well; it was just that the stakes did not demand that men went for each other's throats. Take the one-day game on Sunday, July 1, between a combined Australian Services and air forces XI and an Oxfordshire and district XI, on the Christ Church ground, Iffley Road, Oxford. Hassett won the toss, 'and so far as Oxfordshire were concerned,' the *Oxford Times* reported the following week, 'everything depended on whether their bowlers could keep the Australian batsmen quiet as it is a well-known fact that the visitors' main objective was to get runs quickly'.

The opening bowlers did the bulk of the work: Oswald Herman of Hampshire (born in Oxford) and Frank Rist of Essex (serving at RAF Abingdon in the county). After 50 overs in two and a quarter hours, Hassett declared on 142 for five, himself top scoring with 45 not out. Because of an hour lost to rain, Oxfordshire had a mere hour and three-quarters to bat, and in 35.1 overs they made 104 for five. Hassett spread the bowling between nine. A dinner at the Angel restaurant, and speeches by the captains and mayor, followed.

One man's meat is another man's poison; what to you is brighter cricket is to me a farce. The gossip column of the *Bradford Telegraph & Argus* newspaper during the third Test at Lord's – albeit hardly a first-hand observer – deplored impatient spectators for shouting 'have a go' at England's batsmen on the second ball of the match. The Australian Services at Lord's had a 'reserved enclosure' like the 'Sydney Hill'. There, at least at some distance from the rest of the crowd, the Australian supporters could make what the T&A termed 'good humoured barracking'. For example, when Griffith walked out to bat in the second innings late on the second day, while the Australian fielders were throwing the ball to each other, to keep on their toes, waiting for the new batsman, one fielder missed, and the ball rolled towards Griffith who picked it up. 'How's that!' yelled the 'Hillites', claiming handled the ball. In fairness, the barrackers mocked failings of their own men, too: when Williams missed

White in the second innings, the shout was, 'You are for the next draft home!'

To many English watchers, Australian wise-cracking on the lines of Are you paid by the hour, Hutton?' was simply unfunny, and unwelcome. In his memoir of Bodyline, Jardine had written that 'the behaviour of Australian crowds at its best, when judged by the standards accepted by the rest of the world, is not naturally good'.

It was one thing for English Test cricketers in the outfield to endure earache from behind on the other side of the world; it was another matter to hear it as a paying customer. This was the first time that an English sports ground had to host any appreciable number of visiting supporters.

One of them was Garth Tattersall, a bomb-aimer who survived a tour of operations with 462 Squadron in Driffield in east Yorkshire in the winter of 1944–5. In Adelaide in 1998 he recalled how he roamed the country in the summer of 1945, and saw a Lord's Test:

> *Plenty of booze. There would be Australians on one side of the oval and another mob over the other side, I think air force one side and army the other, fellers back from the prisoner of war camps in Germany, and yelling at each other, and this was unheard-of at Lord's; and the more they drank the louder they got. I remember the headline: This hooliganism at Lord's must stop!*

(Two Australian-English terms need explaining: 'oval' means any sports ground, and 'mob' any group, not a riot.) Newspapers were, as always, prone to exaggerate. As with any body of men near beer, you had some larrikins or what Bob Crisp during the third Test described as 'a few score oafs'. The *Sydney Morning Herald* did describe the hush between balls in Australia's second innings – as victory beckoned – as 'cathedral-like'. There is evidence that the native crowd entered into the colonial guests' carnival spirit. John Graham, an RAAF 460 Squadron wireless operator from the Western Australian wheat belt, who went to the Sheffield Test, saw a couple of mates on the outfield in an interval – 'They had been on the grog I think, they had got hold of a ball' – and the crowd shouted 'not out!' or whatever else the impromptu play suggested. Besides, the Yorkshire crowd barracked Pepper the batsman for appealing so often as a bowler; and when Miller hit Washbrook, let alone the Yorkshireman Hutton.

The fact was, idle men made mischief, and the authorities were shipping the Australians (and, separately, Canadians) home as soon as they could. The *Hampstead News* of June 28 reported the court case of an Australian private, waiting to go home after four years as a prisoner of war. He fired a souvenir revolver at the Duke of York – a pub in St Ann's Terrace, St John's Wood, not an aristocrat! The target was a Canadian soldier who, the Australian suspected, had stolen £40 from his wallet. The court sentenced him to one day in prison, which suggested that the magistrates just wanted to see the back of the man. The newspaper did not mention cricket, and the pub is around the corner from a barracks to this day, but the guilty man's address was given as a club in London W1, so it's tempting to place the man in NW8 because he had gone to Lord's, or had tried to.

This all foreshadowed West Indians, and later other immigrant minorities, who cheered on 'their' overseas team, rather than England. It did show that even if you wanted to keep cricket or anything the same as it always had been, you could not, if only because the rest of the world changed around you. In any case, someone would always pioneer change.

To return to loudspeakers, the organiser of the wartime cricket festivals at Edgbaston, Colonel RI Scorer, broadcast to the crowd during intervals. He took the view that he made things more intimate between players and spectators. After the first Test CB Fry in *The Cricketer*, while showing his distaste, admitted that you had to move with newspaper and public opinion: 'We have burned our canoes on the further shore of democracy and we must all of us pay meticulous attention to the importance of what people think ...'

Between the third and fourth Test came what the people thought: the general election result. Despite the newspapers one-sidedly championing the Conservative war prime minister Churchill, Labour won. Yet as with cricket, it was hard to be sure what people wanted in politics. Had people voted for change? If so, what change? Or were people happy, and voting not to change? Was the fact that Britain, for all its faults, had won another world war a sign that the country changed a thing at its peril?

Looking back a dozen years later on the fourth Test, Hammond wrote: 'The pitch was perfect for runs, the light good after some early rain clouds cleared away and there was a feeling of peace and happiness in the air that was very delightful to me. It seemed as though after years in the shadows, England was marching into sunshine again ...'

In truth the Victory Tests were a brief respite before the game, like the country, worked out where to go next.

Interlude: Chester Wilmot

For the Australian war reporter Chester Wilmot, the third and fourth Tests were a welcome rest. Broadcasting for

What is bright cricket?

BBC radio by day and working late editing a summary for Australia, he earned ten guineas a day, which as he wrote to his wife was 'not to be sneezed at'. (It made him probably the best-paid man in the ground – certainly better paid than the players.) It gave him a break from house-hunting around London. He and his family could settle after his remarkable five years of war-reporting: first in North Africa, then New Guinea, where he jeopardised his career by warning the authorities of Australian Army shortcomings. The BBC invited him to England in time to crash-land in a British paratrooper glider at 3.32am on D-Day; then he followed the Allied armies for nearly a year, pushing the heavy and by later standards primitive radio recording equipment to its limits. 'I was really very played out at the end of the campaign …' he wrote to his parents from north Yorkshire, between the third and fourth Tests.

More work followed. A dozen days after the fourth Test, Wilmot was in Berlin, touring Hitler's former chancellery: 'The whole place stank of death and filth and we were quite glad to get out.' The unexpectedly early end to the war against Japan thanks to the atom bombs ended his plan to report on the fighting in the Pacific. Instead he was starting to collect material for what became his history of the war from D-Day to VE Day, *The Struggle for Europe.*

Though a serious and hard-working man of affairs, he knew and liked his cricket. From 1937 to 1939 he had led a Melbourne University debating team around the Far East, North America and Europe; their time in England happened to coincide with the 1938 tour led by Bradman. Wilmot's pocket diary shows he went to all the Tests, even the four days at Manchester, famously ruined by rain without a ball bowled. With characteristic energy, the next day Wilmot went by train to Dublin.

By 1953, his *Struggle for Europe* printed and acclaimed, he turned out at prestigious London cricket matches such as the Authors versus Publishers. As an early member of the jet-set he was returning from Australia to England, when one of the first Comet airliners crashed in January 1954, killing everyone inside. Michael Davie of *The Observer* praised Wilmot as a 'truly lovable character' and described the newspaper's Monday cricket games: 'He was not a very good cricketer; it was not a very good team. But he really liked to play. He used to wear rather tight trousers and did not run very fast. From the slips where he usually fielded he used to boom out comments on the play to fielders, umpires, batsmen. One detected the qualities which had had him thrown out of New Guinea after he formed the impression and expressed it that General Blamey was incompetent.'

He was 42.

Chapter Fourteen

Fourth Test, Lord's, August 6, 7, and 8, 1945

*Cricket never was and never can be a game of continuous
excitement or of great achievements every day.*
JM Kilburn, *Cricket Decade:
England v Australia 1946 to 1956* (1959)

Elton Ede, previewing the fourth Test in the *Sunday
Times*, told young cricketers to watch Keith Miller's
bowling action. 'His body rotates freely from the hips so
that his right shoulder travels a long way down the pitch
giving width to his swing as he delivers or catapults the
ball.' Ede made the unflattering yet valid point that the
previous, 1938 Australians owed their success – because
they kept the Ashes – to half a dozen great cricketers
(not named); the others, apart from their fielding, were
'just useful'. Ede might have been hinting the same of
the present Australians. Miller as an all-rounder was
an asset that Australia and indeed England had lacked
for years. A fortnight before the Test, against Yorkshire
at Bramall Lane, Miller top scored with 111 out of 232.
Hutton too scored 111 in two hours 45 minutes, which
was 40 minutes less than Miller. In other words, to be
sure his side had runs, Miller was ready and able to bat
with fewer risks, to bat slower than Hutton – who was
inaccurately stereotyped as a slow opener.

The Australians made two changes, one batting and voluntary, one bowling and enforced. Stanford returned for Carmody. Though Carmody had made some important runs in the second and third Tests, and was named in the 12, he felt he had not found his true form and asked to stand down. In the chapter devoted to him in their 1950 book *Cricket Caravan*, the sympathetic Whitington and Miller said that Carmody when batting at this time was handicapped by recurring lapses in concentration, 'so common to ex-PoWs'.

In place of Cheetham, who was going home, was Jack Pettiford, making his first-class debut. The 26-year-old clerk from the Sydney suburb of Gordon was a flying officer. *The Cricketer* had praised his bowling for the RAAF against the South of England in June: 'slow to medium leg breaks with accuracy of length'. Another clue to the Australians' thinking was that Pettiford had form as a slow scorer; for RAAF versus RAF at Lord's in June, he took an hour to score 13.

England went from one extreme of bringing on youth to the other. Pope and Robertson returned; and new for England was Laurie Fishlock, the Surrey left-hand batsman. The south Londoner, who toured Australia in 1936–7, had turned 38 'but,' said *The Cricketer*, 'he is a very fit and active man and speeds about the field in a manner which some of this generation may well note and take heed'. Fishlock, having trained as an engineer before he took up cricket, worked in London making aircraft gauges throughout the war, and taught physical training to Home Guards. George Pope was available; presumably the Monday start would not interfere with his weekend job. A Derbyshire butcher paid Pope's league expenses so Pope could play for England.

Lord's had to lock out thousands, and the crowd sat 12 deep on the turf. Britain's most famous soldier of the

Second World War was an afternoon guest in the MCC president's box. Bernard Montgomery at El Alamein in 1942, before his first battle as an army general, had told his mix of Indians, New Zealanders, South Africans, Australians and Britons something they could all understand: 'Hit the enemy for six'. (What did Monty's Greek troops make of it?!) He was home on a visit from Germany. 'As his car entered the Members' Gate he was at once recognised, and on his way to the Committee Room he was cheered to the echo, the pavilion standing up to welcome him,' Sir Pelham Warner, never one to leave a famous name unsaid, wrote the year after in his history of Lord's.

Pope set his leg trap: three short legs, Wright, Pollard and Hutton; one slip, Hammond; and a gulley, Edrich. Pope opened from the pavilion end, Pollard from the Nursery end. Whitington cut Pollard for the first boundary, while Workman played out two maidens. The openers seemed under orders to blunt the bowlers. To the last ball of Pollard's third over, however, Workman was leg before wicket: 15 for one. Hassett sent in Sismey at first wicket again as his first-class best of 51 had set up Miller to win the previous Test. Sismey was at once completely beaten by Pope's in-swinger but the ball just missed his pads and stumps. Wright took over from Pollard; and after 45 minutes, Pollard relieved Pope, whose figures were 7-3-5-0. After the first hour, Australia stood at 35 for one.

A storm stopped play soon after. In his review for Australian listeners, Chester Wilmot called it 'almost a tropical squall. One flash of lightning seemed to strike at the wicket itself and the claps of thunder reminded us of the cricket played last year in the days of the buzz bomb'. Some plaster fell from the bomb-damaged ceiling of the press box. So close together were all the spectators, the groundsmen had trouble pulling out the covers to both ends of the wicket. The wicket and outfield (and people not under cover) were drenched, 'and yet in half an hour it was clear and play was resumed with eight minutes to go before lunch'.

The day, and the match, were already set. Whitington and Sismey were, *The Times* reported, 'unadventurous in strokes', but it was essential, the report admitted, that a batsman be 'well dug in' to partner Miller. The limitations of the English medium pace bowling were obvious. England were as negative as Australia. Bowlers like Pope relied on aiming at leg stump, and only Hammond stood in the slips as he did not expect the ball at pace to reach slip catchers. Australia lunched on 65 for one: Whitington 43, Sismey nine.

Whitington was out soon after. In came Hassett, who went for shots over Pope's ring of legside fieldsmen, Pope making them swing late. After a late cut for four, Hassett went to glance, 'but it flew from the edge of his bat, fine, hard and high, past the keeper, but not past Doug Wright at short fine leg,' said Wilmot: 'Wright shot out his right hand wide and high and the ball stuck … Hassett out for 20 but his innings was worth three times as many; he and Sismey carried the side through a tricky period when the wicket might well have yielded three quick wickets.'

Miller came in at 108 for three. As the only Australian who had passed 80 so far in the Tests, his side needed him to stay, and make runs. And the others had to stay with Miller. Sismey was often beaten by Wright and several times by the other bowlers. The *Yorkshire Evening Post* reported: 'On a perfect batting wicket the batting was well below standard and the vast crowd was very quiet.'

Wilmot showed more sympathy for the batsmen. Miller was almost out in his first over. A ball from Pope snicked his bat, rapped his pads, shaved his wicket and went past the keeper for four. As Miller said later, 'if I hadn't hit it, I would have been lbw, and if it hadn't hit my pads, I would have been bowled.' Hammond set the field to save runs but Miller found a way by good placing or stole singles by quick running.

At tea Australia were 175 for three; Sismey's half century came at 202 for three. His 50 thus came out of 187 and had taken three hours and 35 minutes. England took the new ball at 214. Sismey was unmoved, even by slow-handclapping from some of the crowd. Bob Crisp wrote the next day in the *Express* how, late in the afternoon, an Australian voice rang out from the crowd, 'Why don't you play cricket?!'

'That is how bad it was,' Crisp commented. On 59, Sismey took a blow on the right hand from Pollard and had to retire. Ross Stanford took his place. In old age, he said that he played his best innings with Miller; this day was not one of them. Stanford was all at sea to the fast bowlers and Miller kept him away from the bowling as much as he could. After what the newspapers merely called 'half an hour of Stanford for two', Sismey returned, only to be caught by Fishlock off Pollard. He had defended for four and a half hours.

Bad light ended the first day early with Australia on 273 for five: Miller 107 not out, Pepper three. The first editions of the next day's evening daily papers, taking agency reports, accused Australia of 'playing timeless cricket', 'clearly showing that although they lead England by two wins to one in this Victory series they possess an inferiority complex', so the *Nottinghamshire Guardian* and others reckoned. 'Often this season the Lord's crowd has been accused of being noisy and unappreciative but yesterday the packed house watched Australia's crawl with scarcely a murmur.'

Whereas the first day had been frocks and shirt-sleeve weather, England took to the field for the second day in sweaters. Despite the overcast skies and chill, the threat of more rain, and the previous day's slow cricket, the Lord's gates closed again with a crowd of 30,000 inside. The queues before play had been half a mile. Everyone at this holiday time wanted to see the spectacle. That day's guest in the MCC president's box was the new Labour Prime Minister, Clement Attlee.

Pepper, not one to hang around, hit a ball so hard that Miller had to jump out of the way and knocked two of the stumps flat. According to *The Cricketer*, Miller never settled to take Australia to a commanding total: 'At no time had he looked as safe as Hassett. In fact he seemed in a different mood.' Miller was sixth out, at 301, bowled by Pope. Some said it was a ball that kept low and broke back from leg to off stump. Some said it was a slower ball. Either way, it was the first time in the Tests that Pope – or indeed any bowler apart from Pollard – had dismissed him.

That may have prompted Miller, batting the week after at Blackpool, to ask Pope about bowling grips during the pause of a minute or two at the fall of a wicket. As Miller told the story in his memoir *Cricket Crossfire*: 'He showed me the middle finger of his right hand. On each side of it was a corn caused through the wear and tear of bowling cutters.' Miller realised that day in, day out cricketers like Pope were lifelong learners and, if Miller wanted to make his living as a cricketer too – evidently his unstated ambition at that time – 'I realised I too, would have to pay more attention to the tricks of the trade.' Talent and athleticism would not be enough even for him, Miller saw.

The 'tricks' included breaking the rules: 'I also noticed that every time Pope went on to bowl he took off his cap and rubbed the ball in it. Despite the fact that he hadn't a hair on his head, his cap was greasier than any I have known! He used to help shine the ball with it! I caught on. Now when I play cricket I put a lot of grease on my hair!' More brazenly still Miller then admitted that he used to lift the ball's seam with his nail.

Ross Stanford recalled something similar:

> *George Pope, he was a big in-swing bowler. He was bald, but he had Brylcreem in his cap and of course in between bowling he would rub one side of the ball in his cap with this grease, to get it to swing. But it depended on the atmosphere, actually, as to whether he could swing it, because I batted against him. He would swing them a yard in the right atmosphere, and yet if he never had the right atmosphere he didn't swing it at all.*

'That's illegal!'

> *Probably is now! Lifting the seam, which a lot of bowlers have done.*

The crowd gave Miller an ovation as he returned to the pavilion. Passing him by was Pettiford, on his debut. If Pettiford soon proved to be 'strictly on the defensive', 'and for all the imploring of the barrackers resolutely played a dead bat to all the bowling', as the agencies reported, the morning papers had warned what to expect. Only 44 runs came in an hour, mainly from Pepper. Pettiford's first run, after more than 30 minutes – and that a single – earned an ironic cheer from Australians in the crowd. Wilmot, once more, was sympathetic to the Australian.

'It was a trying ordeal for a young player and Pettiford came through it well.' When Roberts offered a no-ball, Pettiford pulled it for four: '... it was his first aggressive shot and the crowd roared their approval. That set Pettiford going and encouraged him to use the strokes he undoubtedly has.'

Pepper was caught off a no-ball on 48. Once he passed 50, he had a few words with Pettiford, presumably about policy, and hit a six into the Tavern side, off Pollard, who joined in the crowd's applause. Pepper tried again, and was caught by the other bowler, Roberts. At 359 for seven, Australia were almost where they wanted to be: safe. Cristofani hit 12 in an over then was well caught by Edrich, at deep square leg, off Pollard. It was enough to earn an ovation. Williams was soon caught, by Fishlock, off Roberts, and when Ellis as last man came in, Pettiford hit out at Pollard but Wright caught him in the covers. The fall of the last four wickets for 29 rather flattered some of the bowlers. While Roberts had taken two wickets, and Wright none in 28 overs, and Pollard went for more than three an over, George Pope had dismissed four of the first six men. Hammond had trusted him with far more overs than anyone else – 43 – and he went for less than two an over.

Hutton and Fishlock went in at 2.10pm. Edrich wrote in his memoir *Cricket Heritage* of how, when Australia scored their 388, '... we got together in the pavilion and promised each other that we would take no risks until that total was passed ... it was merciless tactics but it paid.'

As one of Australia's only two at all fast bowlers, Miller bowled first but with a shortened run and at reduced pace 'in view of his doubtful back', the *Yorkshire Evening Post* explained. Still, his length was, in the view of the London *Evening Standard*, 'erratic'; he bounced one right over the batsman's head and hit Fishlock and Hutton on the body. Workman, the substitute wicket-keeper because Sismey was still injured, had difficulty catching Miller. Nine of the first 15 runs were byes. Hutton was leg before to Williams, for 35; Robertson played himself in then edged Pettiford to Miller at second slip for 25. After tea Fishlock took ten off an over of Pettiford, but the bowler had revenge with a ball that turned and took middle stump. Fishlock, out for 69, left England 173 for three. The Australian bowlers tired and the new ball at 200 made no difference.

Wilmot reported Miller's competitiveness: 'The crowd was drifting away but suddenly it was roused by a spectacular incident. At 243 Hammond, batting to Miller, blocked a rising ball and it rolled two or three yards up the pitch. The field was well back and Hammond called Washbrook for the run. Washbrook dashed down the pitch with Miller hard at his heels racing for the ball. As Washbrook neared the crease, Miller reached the ball and kicked it straight and true to the stumps. As it hit Miller shouted an appeal but Washbrook had just got his bat down in time. It was a lucky escape and a brilliant piece of work by Miller.'

Just before 6pm, Washbrook appealed against the light, though it looked no worse than on the first day. By giving up half an hour of batting time England made it clear that they expected a draw, and were well placed, on 249 for three, Hammond 38, Washbrook 31.

The last day 'offered cricket in the true sense of the word after first day austerity', so *The Times* judged. It took England until near the end of the match to gain a lead on first innings and so put Australia under pressure.

The newspapers credited Hammond with a sporting suggestion. As Stanford recalled:

> *It was the most enjoyable cricket I ever played in my life, because it was played in a great spirit. There was*

no antagonism between the players, and at times we tried to help one another. Was it the fourth Test? I think it was, our wicket-keeper Stan Sismey got hit under the chin and had a loose piece of skin, and he had to go off and have stitches. And Lindsay Hassett put Jimmy Workman behind the wicket. He didn't know how to keep wicket at all. So next morning; Keith Carmody was 12th man. I had got a game, and somehow or other – Wally Hammond had a great knowledge of cricket. When he arrived at the ground, he poked his head in our dressing room and he said to Lindsay Hassett, 'Do you know, Lindsay, that if you asked me I can let Keith Carmody keep wicket?' And Lindsay said, 'Well, I didn't know that, and thanks very much Wally'. And that was one of the fine sporting gestures that happened.

As *The Cricketer* put it matter-of-factly, Carmody was allowed to keep wicket 'in accordance with law 37', which allowed substitutes. Perhaps someone had passed the idea to Hammond overnight; or, he felt able to make the offer once England seemed in little danger, having passed the follow-on total so easily. It looked as if Hammond had only to choose if or when to declare.

Hassett set a run-saving field and in the first hour England could manage only 52 and might have lost Washbrook. Late cutting Ellis, he edged low and straight to Pepper, the lone slip, who missed and the batsmen took a single.

As Wilmot told Australia later, Ellis 'was most persistent pitching ball after ball well up on the off stump and turning away just enough, beating the bat. A couple of times Hammond drove him aggressively … but then Ellis bowled one that dropped a little shorter and turned a little more. Hammond did not quite get to it and the ball flew from the edge of his bat towards Workman in the gully. Workman dived forward and took a good catch with his hands touching the grass … it was the only wicket Ellis got all day but it was he more than anyone else who foiled England's attempt to get a quick and commanding lead.'

Hammond 'walked', out for 83; Workman, ironically, had given up the wicket-keeper's gloves. Hammond admitted later to exasperation at missing a century that he thought was 'a certainty'. Hammond and Washbrook's stand of 157 was the highest of the series so far.

Bill Edrich, the last of six experienced specialist batsmen – a contrast with the previous Test – came in at 330 for four and set about overtaking the Australian total. At 350, Miller returned, and Carmody and the two slips wisely stood well back. Miller in his second over hit Edrich on the body.

Still, Edrich and Washbrook overtook Australia in five and three-quarter hours, in other words an hour and a quarter faster than Australia. Washbrook was out at 435 for five after a chanceless 112. Pope and Pollard did not take long and Hammond declared on 468 for seven, 80 in front. It was enough of a lead to make it worthwhile for Hammond to set an attacking field and the match briefly came to life. The usual openers Whitington and Workman fell to Pope, and Hassett to Pollard, for seven, nine and seven. Miller survived a leg before appeal first ball.

The promoted Pettiford made 39, until bowled by Wright. Wilmot described it as 'a first-rate innings. He was not overawed by the close set field and he hit hard and well. Above all he showed that he has the temperament for really big cricket.'

Even so Australia were only level at 80 for four with a possible 80 minutes left. If the rest of the Australians fell

The Victory Tests

as fast, or faster, England might have a few overs to chase a target smaller than the one set Australia in the first Test. Because of that faint chance, Hammond placed eight fielders around the bat. Miller and the incoming Stanford, however, stood firm and the teams agreed to abandon the match as a draw at 6.30pm. Apart from that hour towards the end, it was the dullest Test of the five by far.

Fourth Test, Lord's, August 6, 7 and 8

Australian Services won the toss

Australian Services first innings

RS Whitington	ct Hutton	b Pope	46
JA Workman	lbw	b Pollard	6
†SG Sismey	ct Fishlock	b Pollard	59
*AL Hassett	ct Wright	b Pope	20
KR Miller		b Pope	118
RM Stanford		b Pope	2
CG Pepper	ct and	b Roberts	57
J Pettiford	ct Wright	b Pollard	32
DR Cristofani	ct Edrich	b Pollard	14
RG Williams	ct Fishlock	b Roberts	1
RS Ellis	not out		0
Extras (16 b, 8 lb, 9 nb)			33
Total (all out, 130.3 overs)			388

Fall of wickets: 1-15, 2-70, 3-108, 4-262, 5-265, 6-301, 7-359, 8-374, 9-380, 10-388

Bowling

Pope	43	11	83	4
Pollard	37.3	7	145	4
Wright	28	5	75	0
Edrich	6	0	13	0
Roberts	16	4	39	2

England first innings

LB Fishlock		b Pettiford	69
L Hutton	lbw	b Williams	35
JDB Robertson	ct Miller	b Pettiford	25
*WR Hammond	ct Workman	b Ellis	83
C Washbrook	ct sub	b Williams	112

Fourth Test, Lord's

WJ Edrich	not out		73
GH Pope	ct Hassett	b Williams	5
†SC Griffith	ct Stanford	b Pettiford	7
R Pollard	not out		2

Wright, Roberts did not bat

Extras (27 b, 12 lb, 4 nb, 14 w) 57
Total (seven wickets declared, 147 overs) 468
Fall of wickets: 1-73, 2-136, 3-173, 4-330, 5-435, 6-443, 7-464

Bowling

Miller	23	5	49	0
Williams	39	9	109	3
Pepper	18	3	63	0
Cristofani	12	3	41	0
Pettiford	18	2	62	3
Ellis	36	9	80	1
Whitington	1	0	7	0

Australian Services second innings

RS Whitington	lbw	b Pope	7
JA Workman	ct Fishlock	b Pope	9
J Pettiford		b Wright	39
*AL Hassett		b Pollard	7
KR Miller	not out		35
RM Stanford	not out		33

Extras (5 b, 5 nb) 10
Total (four wickets, 38 overs) 140
†Sismey, Pepper, Cristofani, Williams and Ellis did not bat
Fall of wickets: 1-12, 2-30, 3-54, 4-80

Bowling

Pope	12	3	42	2
Pollard	13	2	58	1
Wright	7	1	23	1
Roberts	6	2	7	0

Match drawn. Close of play, day one: Australian Services 273-5 (Miller 106 not out, Pepper 3 not out). Close, day two: England 249-3 (Hammond 38 not out, Washbrook 31 not out).

In the *Manchester Evening News,* a columnist named Gaius managed to combine a northern dig at the south with a stereotypical northerner's complaint about poor value for money: 'This week at cricket's principal shrine a Test match has dragged out its weary length and on two of the three days an appeal against the light has led to a record crowd being deprived of several bobs' worth of play. Small wonder that there are people who think that the return of village cricket to Old Trafford would be a most satisfying spectacle.'

Bob Crisp complained that Australia set the tempo (such as it was) seeking a draw, to stay two Tests to one ahead – so that Australia could go to Manchester and not lose the series. In the time left after the first two innings, England lacked the time to win the fourth Test.

Anyone writing for *The People* was hard to please. The Sunday before the game, Stanley Nelson made one of the meanest comments of the summer: 'Somehow these Tests seem to lack glamour in spite of the crowds which are flocking to see them.' Apart, perhaps, from Hammond, Nelson claimed there were no outstanding personalities in the sides. Nor did Nelson like Miller's 'schoolboy mannerism of throwing his hair back all the time'. The Sunday afterwards, Nelson deplored the Test as 'a travesty of cricket'. Wiser and more forgiving by far was Robertson-Glasgow, who in a recent essay had reminded *Observer* readers that on the village green, to stay in was the first thing; to make runs second.

Hammond did not mind either, partly perhaps because critics could blame his bowlers for failing to knock over the stone-wallers, like Sismey, who could (and did) answer that passive English bowling and field placing sought to keep the runs down.

In his next *Yorkshire Evening News* column, Hammond said of the drawn Test: 'In the circumstances Australia rightly took their time to make the runs. They were on top when the match began and by winning the toss they were in a position to dictate the policy. We had to find the answer to that policy and the answer was not to throw the game away, but to attempt to save it.'

The Australian tactics at Lord's, though a success, perhaps also showed a failure of daring that had allowed the Australians to over-achieve so far. Or, the Australians were admitting that they were tiring: not only of cricket, but all that came with it: the travelling, the packing and unpacking, the speeches and, in Hassett's case, giving of speeches. We can assume the fourth Test go-slow stemmed from Hassett because, as Whitington and Miller put it later: 'Hassett played to win, to the last inch and the last second. If he could not do that, he set out to prevent the other fellows from winning.'

After the fourth Test ended on the Wednesday, the RAAF and AIF halves briefly went their own ways again. On the Saturday, the AIF lost to Northamptonshire, traditionally one of the weakest counties. Hassett had to open the bowling, before the spinners did most, as usual. Pepper and Gordon Carlton each took four wickets. Carlton was the son of Percy Charlton, who played two Tests for WL Murdoch's tourists in 1890 – and lost the 'h' in the surname. The hosts, at Spinney Hill, made 189. Though the last Australian was only out five minutes before time, again the Test men starred: Price made 44, and Hassett 49, out of 165 all out.

On the Sunday, the Australians were at High Wycombe again, where in the words of the local *Bucks Free Press* they 'overwhelmed' GO Allen's XI.

Wycombe's captain ST Theed had to deputise for the 43-year-old Allen, who had reportedly snapped a calf muscle. Against no more than a good club side with the likes of the wicket-keeper elder brother of Bill Edrich, Eric, who was working in nearby Northamptonshire as a farm bailiff, the Australians declared on 306 for four.

Hassett helped himself. His 119 not out included 18 fours and four sixes, including one that landed in the scorebox, and a straight one to reach his 100. According to the scorecard in the paper, Hassett made three stumpings as the local team was all out for 161. Mick Roper, though an airman, helped out as an opening bowler.

Meanwhile down the road, a combined services side including Stanford and Pettiford beat Beaconsfield just as easily. Pettiford made 54 and took seven for 31. This weekend cricket was the sort that most of the Australians were used to. What was beginning to be beyond them was the longer game, against professional players who showed not only skill but more stamina. The following Thursday, for example, the regular Victory Test team came together, plus reserves, at Stanley Park, Blackpool, for a two-day game against the North.

Whitington and Miller (and later biographers) incorrectly placed a story set in Blackpool on Victory in Europe night, when in fact it happened in mid-August, at Victory over Japan time. As everywhere else, the town was in carnival for the proper end of the war. As the pair told it:

> The mayor of Blackpool made an official speech of welcome to the Australian side on the steps of the Town Hall. Being in uniform, we were all heroes. Then Warrant Officer Hassett began his reply. 'Never have I seen such an ugly lot of men in all my life,' he declared. The silence which followed seemed interminable. Then the boos and jeers started. A section of the crowd was hostile. Lindsay held up his hand for them to be quiet. When the noise subsided he went on: 'But never have I seen such a crowd of pretty women.' The jeers became cheers – especially from the ladies. Lindsay was made. He stood there with that wicked, twisted little grin of his, hugely enjoying the situation of his own making.

While it did show the man's endearing sense of mischief, it's always a risk telling any man in Blackpool that they are ugly. The tale could suggest someone tired of caring about the impression he made.

At the resort, the Australians put out their strongest possible team – apart from, arguably, Mick Roper and the reserve wicket-keeper Bremner, as Sismey was newly wed in Scotland – and yet were on the wrong end of a thrashing by a stronger side. Despite their name, the North were arguably as good an eleven as any in England, and they wanted to prove it. First, the North made 438 – mainly through 109 by Denis Smith of Derbyshire, and 171 by Norman Oldfield of Lancashire. The *Manchester Guardian* rated the Australian bowling as 'seldom better than moderate', though the ground fielding was good and Bremner was 'obviously a wicket-keeper of great ability', who did not give a bye away in 125 overs. As the *Guardian* noted, the Australians were spoiled for choice for wicket-keepers, but otherwise lacked depth in batting or bowling.

On the Friday, the Australians were twice out, for 202 and 147, Pollard and Pope taking ten wickets between them and Hollies eight. The following day, the RAAF lost easily to another strong RAF side. The RAF – whose first four batsmen were Washbrook, top scorer with 66; Squires; Bill Edrich and Ames – declared on 213 for five and the Australian airmen were all out for 169, Stanford 79 not out.

Other Australian cricketers sought to make the most of the last weeks of summer, as any sportsmen do as any summer fades. Some men took chances to turn out for minor and first-class counties, who were starting to play each other, before many Englishmen had come home from the armed forces. For instance Lance Corporal Bennett, a native of Kalgoorie, came to England in 1938, joined London Fire Service on the outbreak of war, and served throughout the blitz; and played regularly for the LFS team. He played once for Northamptonshire against Warwickshire at the True Form ground, Northampton, in July. And two regularly-playing Australian airmen turned out for Northamptonshire in a two-day draw against Buckinghamshire at Agars Plough, Eton, on August 8 and 9. Gordon Carlton took eight for 122 in the match; and Eddie Williams opened the bowling.

Other Australian veterans seized the chance to compete at swimming, or tennis; demonstrated surf lifesaving to holiday-makers at Eastbourne; or took part in a surfing gala at Newquay. An RAAF eight lost in the final at the first Henley regatta in six years in July. Australians had won at Henley in 1919.

As with so much sport so soon after the war, sportsmen were out of practice and to be able to take part was, truly, the main thing. The 20 or so Australians in and around the Victory Test team, however, were tiring like any cricketers towards the end of an English season when even rain did not allow much respite. Every team tried their hardest against the Australians, and the top teams were outplaying them. On the eve of the fifth Test, Bob Crisp reckoned that several recent setbacks suggested that Australians were 'pretty stale and probably rather sick of cricket'. As a tourist once, Crisp could spot the signs. Could the Australians make one last effort against England, to go home as victors?

Chapter Fifteen

Fifth Test, Old Trafford, August 20, 21 and 22 1945

There was no avidity to see England win. They were just hungry to see big cricket. Big cricket they certainly saw ... indeed I doubt whether any set of big matches in England has ever been so much enjoyed by so many.
CB Fry, radio broadcast to Australia, September 1945

Day one

This fifth, deciding Test, set for Monday to Wednesday, was taking the place of a two-day Lancashire versus Australian services match. From mid-July, some 60 German prisoners of war, paid the pittance of three farthings an hour, 'transformed the shambles of the Lancashire Cricket Club ground at Old Trafford into a state of orderliness ...' as the *Manchester Evening News* put it in the days before the match. 'Many of the scars caused by the blitz of 1940 have been temporarily disguised.'

The city and its cricket ground had suffered like most. An oil bomb had burned out the Old Trafford members' dining room. The ground had had six years of weathering and wear. The RAAF all-rounder Eddie Williams had, for instance, knocked paint off the top of the sightscreen, when hitting the only six of a one-day game against the North in July 1944.

A German sign writer painted the words and figures on the scoreboard; and other German PoWs painted all the stands and scoreboard. Understandably after the second war started by Germany well within a lifetime, the newspapers were quick to tell readers if German prisoners had at all an easy time. The *Daily Express* told how some of the PoWs at Old Trafford had orders to wash 5,000 dishes and teapots, sat under the pavilion since the last Test in 1938. Because, under article 6 of The Hague convention, PoWs could not work 'excessively hard', the Germans stopped work at 4.30pm, leaving hundreds of dishes unwashed. Five men and four women from a local brewery finished the job, voluntarily on the Sunday evening.

Other reports suggested the 60 prisoners were Italian, who had done 'a splendid job'. Whatever the rights and wrongs, or nationalities, Old Trafford was freshly painted green and white. The club expected a capacity crowd or more. Two circles ran around the boundary: the inner ring marked the boundary, an outer ring the limit for the crowd sitting on the grass. The idea was to give the fielders a chance to chase the ball without fear of falling into the spectators. Such was the crowd on the day, however, that after half an hour some people advanced from the outer to the inner line 'and in an instant thousands followed their example'.

Police orders, printed in newspapers beforehand, warned that vehicles could not stand outside the Old Trafford ground during the Test. Parking for private cars would be at the athletics ground by Warwick Road, and coaches were to park outside nearby Manchester United Football Club. Through traffic could not pass the ground along Talbot Road.

The Australians hoped Sismey would be fit in time, though he had yet to rejoin the side from his honeymoon. Carmody came in for Workman. Hammond left out one Lancashire man, Roberts, for another, Eddie Phillipson, a pace bowler, twice selected earlier in the summer, but unable to play because of injury. Vainly, as they always did, newspapers beforehand put up other batsmen: Norman Oldfield (still), Charles Palmer, the 26-year-old Worcestershire amateur, and WGA (Gilbert) Parkhouse, then 19, of Wycliffe College and Swansea, who as a Glamorgan batsman did play some Tests for England in the 1950s.

First in the queue was 14-year-old Graham Brown, who left his home in Hillberry Crescent, Warrington, at 5.30am and reached the turnstile at 7.30 am. By 10am, crowds were flocking to the ground, with rugs, knapsacks and raincoats to join a 200-yard file outside Old Trafford's high wall. A police loudspeaker van controlled traffic on the road. Dozens of omnibuses marked 'Cricket ground' passed. On the pavement was a sea of people, as for the earlier Victory Tests: men in blazers and jackets, ties and jumpers; raincoats over shoulders and arms, in case; in some mouths, a pipe. Some wore flat caps or other hats; most were bare-headed. Some boys wore school caps and their school uniform, whether because their families could not afford other clothes or that was what they wore for occasions.

In another, less orderly, era, so many people wanting to enter one sports stadium might have led to a crush. Red-capped military police worked beside civilian police to marshal a good-humoured crowd. The men on the gates let in so many, it was doubtful if everyone would see the play. A policeman at the turnstile directed people to the less crowded parts. Thousands had to turn away.

Inside, inevitably, some of the finer distinctions broke down; some five shillings spectators 'invaded' a dearer part of the ground. Those in the members' stand and the ladies' marquee could lunch on salmon, chicken and beef, and ice cream, so the *Manchester Evening Chronicle* reported; such food was remarkable enough to write about after years of rationing. The *Chronicle* the next day went into more detail: in an outbuilding, a cook prepared 16 turkeys and more than a dozen salmon. Each day, spectators were consuming 180 four-pound (by weight) loaves, several thousand meat pies, hundredweights of vegetables, 3,000 dozen bottles of beer, more than 30 36-gallon barrels of beer, and mineral water and ice cream.

Hammond tossed and Hassett called. A broad grin spread across Hammond's face; Hassett kept his customary poker face. Having won the toss, Hassett decided to bat on a pitch described beforehand as easier than usual. 'Groundsman Williams called it full of runs and likely to play well throughout the game,' John Kay reported in the *Manchester Evening News*. As the outfield had not felt a heavy roller for six years, the turf resembled a 'thick pile carpet' which slowed the ball.

Whitington and his new opening partner Pettiford walked out in shirt sleeves rolled to the elbow. Phillipson opened the bowling. Whitington pulled his second ball, a long hop, to leg for four. Pope set his usual leg trap of four fielders on top of the batsmen. After half an hour, Pollard came on for Pope and bowled a maiden; and in his next over Whitington made one tentative shot too many and Hammond caught him at second slip, for 19. Pollard hit Pettiford in the ribs. Carmody took one on the hip off Pope. Pettiford called Carmody for a quick single, too quick for Carmody who sent Pettiford back, who had to dive head first for his crease.

Hammond took a second, more spectacular catch from an edge by Carmody, diving and rolling over with the ball safe in two hands, gone for seven. Sismey did not last long, bowled Phillipson for five, and Pollard bowled Pettiford for 28, leaving Australia 66 for four. Miller joined Hassett, knowing that though there was batting to come, they had to pull their side around. Miller hit three fours off Pollard, gave a near chance to Pope in the slips, and was beaten next ball. He kept hitting the ball hard. When they took a short single, Miller seemed to impede Pollard, who was ready to receive Washbrook's throw. The batsman refused to run any overthrows, to the cheers of the crowd. This goodwill extended to the players' wives, sitting on benches together, Mrs Workman and the new Mrs Sismey next to Mrs Wright and Mrs Edrich.

Hassett had only made six when he fell to an attempted pull off Pope 15 minutes before lunch. Phillipson had four slips and a gully to the newcomer Pepper. As at Sheffield, northern fast-medium bowlers were making the most of the conditions. Australia at lunch were 104 for five. Miller's first 33 had come 'in classical style … with off drives and pulls', John Kay wrote approvingly. More severely he wrote: 'Hassett could safely have left the ball alone and must take full responsibility for an act which may mean a great deal before this match is over.'

Phillipson began to Miller after lunch and with his fourth ball struck Miller a 'hard blow in the ribs from a fast short-pitched ball. The batsman resumed after attention and played the remaining balls with care,' John Kay wrote. Pollard at the Warwick Road end made it an all-Lancashire attack. Phillipson, swinging the ball away, hit Miller in the chest and beat Miller and Pepper repeatedly. The batsmen took singles, apart from a couple of twos by Pepper off Pollard. Two avoidable decisions now ruined the Australia innings. At 116, Pepper tried for a second run off a Pollard no-ball. 'Little John', John Bapty for the *Yorkshire Evening Post*, told how, from deep third man, 'Hutton swooped on the ball and with a deadly throw from more than 40 yards out knocked the leg stump down to beat Pepper comfortably'. Pepper was run out for nine.

Stanford came next and was lucky to see a ball from Pollard flash dangerously past his off stump. Spectators had by now sat in front of both sightscreens; the batsmen did not protest. More on their mind was that both Phillipson and Pollard were swinging the ball and the Australians were struggling on what was proving a fast wicket. Ross Stanford recalled more than 50 years later:

> *Keith Miller was in and when I came in he said: Eddie Phillipson, he would swing them a yard and he thought it would be better if he played Eddie Phillipson rather than me. So I hit one down to third man straight away, and Len Hutton was fielding at third man and I thought I could get back for two, trying to do what Miller requested and of course I couldn't make it. So I got run out. That was a disaster, because if Miller and I had stuck together it might have made a big difference to the result of that game.*

To add some detail: from his cut Stanford turned for a second, only to find Miller 'staying at home'. Miller did have his back to Stanford and no doubt recalled how Hutton's quick fielding had already run one man out. Miller did send him back but before Stanford could make it Hutton's return reached the wicket-keeper Griffith, who rolled it to Pollard. Stanford was out for one; Australia were 125 for seven.The next man in, Cristofani, was so at sea against Pollard he was beaten four times in an over. Phillipson bowled a first maiden to Miller, something unusual enough to note. Cristofani on eight was soon well held in the gulley by Edrich: 138 for eight. Miller, who had been batting quite quickly in the circumstances, closed down as Williams could only scrape.

A four from a Pollard no-ball did take Miller to 51 after a chanceless hour and a quarter. RC Robertson-Glasgow in *The Observer* ahead of this Test wrote that he feared Miller the most: 'Not even CG Macartney exceeded this Miller in gay [meaning, in those days, carefree] and almost insolent confidence.'

Miller by now was making every effort to keep the bowling to himself, but at 149 was missed at third man by Phillipson. He got only his right hand to a fast-moving ball, and the batsmen took a single. Phillipson had bowled unchanged with Pollard for more than an hour after lunch, and finished the job: Williams was caught behind for five. After Miller scored all 18 of the last wicket stand, Ellis had to play two balls from Pollard – only to pull the second to short leg for his first duck of the series. Miller's 77 not out of 173 was 'a magnificent forceful innings', John Kay reported. Hammond likewise wrote in praise of Miller: '… he defended his weaker teammates and like a lion looked all around the field to see where he could send his boundaries'.

Hutton and Fishlock began England's reply at 3.50pm. Miller opened from the Stretford end to the left-handed Fishlock, who brilliantly cut the third ball for four. Hutton meanwhile left the opening deliveries from Williams 'severely alone', wrote John Kay, taking a leg bye off the fifth ball. Hutton's first runs were two off Miller, who was, according to Kay, 'making the new ball swing and lift dangerously'. Miller soon had Fishlock leg before for nine with a cleverly disguised slow yorker, that dropped on the batsman's toe. Pepper as the first change bowler had Robertson caught for 13, then Hammond and Hutton added 97. Williams had Hutton caught behind for 64 by Sismey, and Cristofani had Hammond caught by Pettiford for 57. Cristofani, who had had an ineffective time in the previous Test, did more good work. Pollard, sent in as a night watchman, half did his job; he was out leg before, for nought, which ended the day.

Again Miller had kept Australia in the game with the bat. The match was still uncertain: much would depend on whether England could bat much beyond their close of play 162 for five. On a pitch friendly so far to bowlers, even a small lead could prove decisive.

Day two

Compared with the 30,000 or more on the first day, only about 15,000 watched the second afternoon. Rain took the two hours before lunch. Cristofani began the day at 2.15pm, by finishing his over to the new batsman, Washbrook. In Williams' first over, Pepper showed he was quicker than a man of his size might seem. When Edrich played a ball to leg, Pepper fielded and threw and hit the stumps from square leg. Edrich was in his ground and ran an overthrow.

Pepper took Williams' place. Some felt that the soaking had taken the pace out of the pitch; others saw a bright sun shining on a wet wicket. Again the outfield seemed slow. England went ahead until at 198 Edrich gave a dolly – a simple caught and bowled for Pepper; out for 23. Pope came and went.

Despite Pope's reputation as a hitter, Cristofani placed a short mid-off and mid-on. Cristofani's first bad ball, a long hop, brought Pope's wicket. He played forward to Cristofani almost on his hands and knees and the ball seemed to come off the shoulder of his bat, or a glove, for Pepper to hold close to the ground at first slip. Cristofani and Pepper bowled for more than an hour. Cristofani showed style and imagination, so John Kay reported: 'His accuracy and length troubled all the English batsmen. Pepper lent admirable support.'

Later *The Cricketer* gave its view: 'Cristofani made the most of the drying wicket and he had a rare duel with Washbrook ...' A Cristofani full toss – that is, another bad ball – picked up Washbrook at 213, well caught on the square leg boundary for 38, by Carmody. Griffith was soon out without scoring at 221, caught low down at cover by Ellis, although, according to John Kay, the Australian pick-ups and throws compared unfavourably with England's of the day before. Phillipson, opening out with what Kay termed 'shots of doubtful origin' gave a simple chance off Cristofani that Pettiford put on the floor. Wright swept Cristofani to leg for three, which brought the usual crowd cheers for a last bat. Wright had reached nine, his highest score of the series, when Hassett brought on Pettiford, and Sismey stumped Wright second ball. It meant that Australia would have to bat better, and for longer, than they did the day before if they were to set England many runs to win.

Australia did not have the pitch rolled before their second innings. Phillipson opened again at the Stretford end to Whitington, Pope at the town end to Pettiford, at 4pm. Both bowlers made the ball fly. Pettiford, 'completely deceived' by Phillipson according to Bob Crisp, gave a dolly to Robertson at silly mid-on and was out for eight. Sismey after several scoreless overs suddenly tried a hook and missed; leg before to Phillipson for four. Of Australia's 37 in their first hour and a quarter, the opener Whitington made eight singles. He appealed against the light; after what he later termed 'an annoyingly brief conference' the umpires said no.

Whitington faced Phillipson again: 'For four balls he probed forward like a man descending into a dark cellar,' he recalled later. 'The fifth ball he stroked straight into

George Pope's unprepared lap at first slip and thence to fine leg for the only two-run stroke of his innings.' Just then rain began to fall really heavily. After he had scored ten Whitington was caught by Griffith high and wide on the leg side with his left hand at full stretch above his head; like a football goalkeeper, said some; 'as fine a catch of its kind as ever seen', in the *Daily Telegraph*'s view.

Years later, with feeling (though writing in the third person), Whitington recalled how he had stood negatively 'taking balls on his chest, neck, upper arms and thighs and keeping his bat out of the road. Not one deliberate attempt did he make to score runs.' He knew his job: to suffer, so that better batsmen than he did not have to. When caught, for a hard-earned ten, he 'strode disconsolately from the ground to the accompaniment of organised hooting from the Old Trafford members, who had formed a "guard of dishonour" to usher him off'.

Rain drove the players in at 5.35pm. Whitington wrote that he was 'prouder of that innings of ten scored in 90 minutes of self-discipline and self-denial than of any of the few centuries he made in first-class cricket'. *Wisden* agreed, calling it 'a praiseworthy effort for usually a fluent player'. Though feeling misunderstood by the crowd and the next day's English press – as a newspaper journalist himself, he could hardly complain – Whitington had done what he set out to do: Hassett and Miller were safe for the final day.

Day three

Wednesday began in sunshine. A short ball from Pollard hit Stanford on the fingers, who resumed after attention. As all along, the bowlers were dominating. Miller snicked Phillipson towards Hammond at first slip, but the ball fell short. The next ball, short and rising, head high, Miller tried to hook but got only an edge. Miller took a few steps towards the pavilion as if he expected to be caught, but no-one was standing at short leg. Edrich, the nearest in the slips, ran over to field.

Hassett was unlucky, according to Bob Crisp: 'He made a split-second decision to leave a suddenly rising ball alone and it flicked his glove as he dropped his hand.' Out, in any case, for one; and the other major batsman Miller was caught behind off Phillipson for four: Australia were 46 for five. Stanford hung on while Pepper snicked one dangerously through the slips for two off Pollard, and again off Pollard took a four to leg for only the second boundary of the innings. Only 30 runs came in the first hour. 'Stanford's fondness for drawing away from Pollard earned him another rap on the fingers and he was far from impressive,' John Kay wrote. Wright and Pope replaced Phillipson and Pollard. With one run still needed to wipe off arrears, Stanford was caught behind off a top spinner off Wright, Griffith's fourth catch of the innings. The Sussex amateur 'was giving a wicket-keeping display in the style of Duckworth', wrote Kay. A Manchester journalist could not give a finer compliment!

Whereas Stanford defended nearly two hours for his 23, Cristofani the incoming batsmen went for his strokes. So did Pepper still. He put Australia in front by opening his shoulders to Pope and hitting a four to leg. Pope was difficult to get away, bowling at the batsman's legs or wide of the leg stump with his 'leg trap' of fielders. Warner later praised Pope in *The Cricketer* as 'that admirable and persevering bowler' while criticising him for 'persistently making use of the extreme width of the crease'.

It hardly seemed to matter when Pepper tried to hit Wright across the line and was bowled middle stump for 23 by a shortish leg break: 87 for seven. Carmody on three gave another catch to Griffith, off Pollard: Australia were 105 for eight, and Crisp ordered a taxi for 3.45pm. Williams, leaving alone everything off the wickets, and Cristofani went to lunch on 120 for eight, a lead of merely 50. Heavy rain clouds came nearer then the afternoon had sun, as Australia's outlook brightened too.

Pollard bowled Williams, with a no-ball. Williams sought only to stay in while Cristofani reached 50 with a cut for four. On seeing him for the first time in the third Test, Chester Wilmot had judged that Cristofani had plenty of strokes but needed more patience. With nothing to lose, Cristofani could go for his shots – such as cuts to third man, as the faster bowlers, kept on mostly by Hammond, found lift. Cristofani, trying to unsettle the faster bowlers, stood outside the batting crease except when Griffith, who normally stood back to Pope and Pollard, came up to the wicket in response.

Cristofani was as open to ideas as a bowler: for the RAAF against Sussex at Hove just before the fourth Test, he took the new ball for want of alternatives and at medium pace took the first two wickets; then with the shine off the ball and at his usual pace, bowled several times from five yards behind the crease.

In the half an hour after lunch, Australia added 35. For the first time in the match, Australia were making runs at such a rate that if England did not take the last two wickets soon, they might struggle with a fourth innings target, so Kay, for one, feared.

Hammond brought on Edrich for the first time in the match, who opened with a maiden to Williams. Cristofani played a maiden to Pope, then hit the first six of the match, 'a huge one off Pope'. Australia were 104 ahead.

In a Thai village on the edge of jungle, the English cricket writer EW Swanton was free after three and a half years as a prisoner of the Japanese. 'In a little café our hostess delightedly turned on the English programme,'

Swanton wrote in the next year's *Wisden*. 'Yes, we were at Old Trafford and a gentleman called Cristofani was getting a hundred.'

In his later autobiography, he wrote slightly, significantly differently – 'dammit a fellow unknown to me called Cristofani was about to get a hundred'. The former journalist had spotted at once that he was out of touch with the game. He would have to hurry and apply himself to regain his pre-war occupation; as indeed he was doing with that article in the 1946 *Wisden*. The glory of cricket played only for the love of it, without thought of making money or a living out of it, was passing, if it had ever completely existed.

Cristofani reached a 'brilliant century', Kay reported, 'with a lofty drive off Wright. Hutton could not take a running catch.' Clouds were gathering and an England victory was beginning to look doubtful. Cristofani's 100 came out of 125. He took less than two hours and hit one six and 12 fours. At 196 the umpires Chester and Elliott refused a hopeful Australian appeal for bad light. At 200 Williams gave Griffith his sixth catch of the innings, and was cheered off by the crowd. Though his 12 had taken more than 90 minutes, his effort had given Cristofani time. The crowd had the pleasurable prospect of more cricket for their money, while – they hoped – not too difficult a target for England to reach. Phillipson ended the innings at 210 by having Reg Ellis caught, to give him bowling figures of six for 58; England's best of the series. England needed 141.

Fishlock again fell early, bowled by Williams for four. That was the first and only second innings wicket Williams took all series, perhaps a sign that this former prisoner of war had not become fully fit. Miller bounced the ball but gave away runs. Pepper as first change bowler was spinning the ball a lot 'and bringing the occasional ball straight through very quickly', the *Manchester Guardian* reported. Pepper had Hutton leg before for 29 and Robertson for 37, which critics would point to as another in-between sort of score.

Edrich, coming in at 70 for three, and a 'subdued' Hammond took England towards victory with a stand of 54. Hammond was on 16 when he jumped out to Ellis, and hit straight for what seemed a six, but substitute Eddie Williams, on the boundary to the right of the sightscreen, caught the ball high above his head with both hands. Washbrook made 11 of the last 17 runs wanted, though Edrich made the winning hit at 6.15pm, off Hassett's first ball. The captain, admitting defeat, had brought himself on. Edrich, on 42 not out, had made useful runs in every Test except at Sheffield. He felt satisfied, writing later: '... for one thing it was such delightful cricket marked by a mood of good temper, challenge, excitement, and a thoroughly happy spirit'. Edrich pipped Washbrook to head England's batting averages, '... and that I felt was my answer to the Selectors for leaving me out of the side against the West Indies in 1939'.

Fifth Test, Old Trafford, Manchester, August 20, 21 and 22

Australian Services won the toss.

Australian Services first innings

RS Whitington	ct Hammond	b Pollard	19
J Pettiford		b Pollard	28
DK Carmody	ct Hammond	b Pollard	7
†SG Sismey		b Phillipson	5
*AL Hassett	ct Pollard	b Pope	6
KR Miller	not out		77
CG Pepper	run out		9
RM Stanford	run out		1
DR Cristofani	ct Edrich	b Pollard	8
RG Williams	ct Griffith	b Phillipson	5
RS Ellis	ct Pollard	b Phillipson	0

Fifth Test, Old Trafford

Extras (2 lb, 6 nb)   8
Total (all out, 59 overs)   173
Fall of wickets: 1-41, 2-59, 3-64, 4-66, 5-102, 6-117, 7-125, 8-138, 9-155, 10-173

Bowling

Phillipson	27	4	72	3
Pope	10	3	15	1
Pollard	22	3	78	4

England first innings

LB Fishlock	lbw	b Miller	9
L Hutton	ct Sismey	b Williams	64
JDB Robertson	ct Williams	b Pepper	13
*WR Hammond	ct Pettiford	b Cristofani	57
WJ Edrich	ct and	b Pepper	23
R Pollard	lbw	b Cristofani	0
C Washbrook	ct Carmody	b Cristofani	38
GH Pope	ct Pepper	b Cristofani	1
WE Phillipson	not out		18
†SC Griffith	ct Ellis	b Cristofani	0
DVP Wright	st Sismey	b Pettiford	9

Extras (3 b, 6 lb, 1 nb, 1 w)   11
Total (all out, 86.2 overs)   243
Fall of wickets: 1-14, 2-46, 3-143, 4-159, 5-162, 6-198, 7-201, 8-218, 9-221, 10-243

Bowling

Miller	9	0	20	1
Williams	18	7	40	1
Pepper	24	3	74	2
Ellis	7	0	21	0
Pettiford	6.2	0	22	1
Cristofani	22	3	55	5

Australian Services second innings

RS Whitington	ct Griffith	b Phillipson	10
J Pettiford	ct Robertson	b Phillipson	8
†SG Sismey	lbw	b Phillipson	4
RM Stanford	ct Griffith	b Wright	23
KR Miller	ct Griffith	b Phillipson	4
*AL Hassett	ct Griffith	b Pollard	1

The Victory Tests

CG Pepper		b Wright	23
DR Cristofani	not out		110
DK Carmody	ct Griffith	b Pollard	3
RG Williams	ct Griffith	b Phillipson	12
RS Ellis	ct Pollard	b Phillipson	3
Extras (1 b, 5 lb, 3 nb)			9
Total (all out, 87 overs)			210

Fall of wickets: 1-13, 2-17, 3-37, 4-41, 5-46, 6-69, 7-87, 8-105, 9-200, 10-210

Bowling

Phillipson	29	12	58	6
Pope	19	6	49	0
Pollard	23	11	46	2
Wright	13	3	44	2
Edrich	3	1	4	0

England second innings

LB Fishlock		b Williams	4
L Hutton	lbw	b Pepper	29
JDB Robertson	lbw	b Pepper	37
*WR Hammond	ct sub	b Ellis	16
WJ Edrich	not out		42
C Washbrook	not out		11
Extras (2 b)			2
Total (four wickets, 45.1 overs)			141

Pollard, Pope, Phillipson, †Griffith and Wright did not bat
Fall of wickets: 1-5, 2-69, 3-70, 4-124

Bowling

Miller	11	1	41	0
Williams	8	0	41	1
Pepper	12	5	18	2
Ellis	7	2	13	1
Cristofani	7	0	25	0
Hassett	0.1	0	1	0

England won by six wickets and drew the series two-all.
Close of play, day one: England 162-5 (Edrich 9 not out).
Close day two, Australian Services 37-3 (Stanford 12 not out).

Fifth Test, Old Trafford

In the next day's *Manchester Evening Chronicle*, Hassett asked rhetorically, and generously: 'Who said English cricket was dying? We at least have seen no evidence of its decease. All the matches have attracted great crowds and judging by the enthusiasm the cricket public have enjoyed every minute. So too have the players. The games have been played in fine sporting spirit and have provided a tonic after the grimness of war. There is no need to appeal for brighter cricket when games provide such excitement as at Sheffield and Manchester.'

In his first *Yorkshire Evening News* column after the last Test, Hammond said something similar. He called it the best pitch for a Test: 'If the Old Trafford type wicket could be produced for Tests in this country there is no doubt in my mind that the authorities would have great difficulty in finding accommodation for all the public who would want to see the matches.'

John Kay called it a 'brilliant finale to the season', 'but more important still it has in my opinion pointed the way to a new cricket era. Manchester and the North supported the match splendidly and cricket's public is still legion providing the game remains attractive as this last Test match proved to be. The first and most important lesson to be learned from the match is that given a natural and lively wicket bowlers can still control a game that in pre-war days was becoming a paradise for batsmen.'

Kay, as much as Swanton, was looking ahead already. 'The RAF did the game a great service when they requisitioned Old Trafford's heavy roller for the more important job of levelling airfields in the Middle East. Their powers of requisitioning are now no doubt less important and I do not suppose the heavy monsters will disappear from Lord's, Nottingham and Headingley, but let the cricketing powers take to heart the lesson of the Manchester Victory Test and instruct their groundsmen to prepare wickets without the use of marl and heavy rollers.' In other words, Kay was against deadening a pitch too much in favour of batting as in the 1930s.

The Australians and their manager, Flight Lieutenant Keith Johnson, left Manchester by train; satisfied like most people. Ross Stanford recalled in old age: 'Yes, we had two wins each and a draw, which both sides thought was a very fit result. We were very pleased to do that, because we wondered how we would do against all these English cricketers we had to play against.' Maybe Whitington was right about the 'stunned mullets' of May.

The overall result hid some narrow margins. Bill Bowes, at Manchester as a reporter, recalled that when Cristofani put Australia 100 runs ahead, 'there was a huge black cloud looming over the skyline and it was small wonder that Hammond rang the changes on his bowlers continually and that the Australian players on the balcony showed great enthusiasm'.

The Sunday before the last Test, RC Robertson-Glasgow had written in praise of Hassett as captain: '... his cricketers move into their necessary places as if drawn by invisible wires of his arranging'. Robertson-Glasgow concluded with his customary nobility: 'In the Victory Tests ... Hassett has captained Australia with a judgement that has remained unshaken either by the voices of the critics or the variety of his opponents and we take leave to honour him not only as an enemy in the best of all games but as a companion in the greatest of all Wars.'

Opinion varied, as in all things. John Kay felt that Hassett did little with the bat and his leadership did not impress: 'Judged from every angle his side was just good but definitely not great.' Kay did give credit to Cristofani, 'the stockily built all-rounder', 'and we shall no doubt see him again along with Miller and Sismey' ... 'From the playing point of view England can reap very little satisfaction from these Victory matches because the Australian team contained no more than three men who can be regarded as up to that country's first class standard.' As for England, Hammond was 'still majestic in style and courage', and 'Hutton, Phillipson and Pollard were the only players to produce form that entitled one to think them any better than the majority of county cricketers, although Griffith, much criticised for his earlier displays, did nothing wrong in this match and his six catches in the second innings will no doubt guarantee his place in the next representative games. England's attack when the two Lancashire men were resting was decidedly poor in quality and lacked aggressiveness. Pope disappointed and Wright does not flight the ball in the manner of good leg spinners.' Leaving out Roberts was a mistake, and Kay advised the selectors 'to seek out left-arm spinners until the new Verity appears'.

Meanwhile in London, *The Cricketer* felt that Pope and Pollard bowled really well; and Wright was 'seldom fortunate but first class' (again). The magazine, like most, felt a lack of bowlers: someone genuinely fast; a 'Maurice Tate' medium pacer, and a slow left-hander. Hammond for instance recalled later: 'The series left me and I expect a good many other people with an unpleasant awareness of England's bowling weakness especially in the fast division.'

Cristofani – the last three syllables pronounced short, so Robertson-Glasgow said in an end of season sketch in *The Observer* – was instructed in New South Wales by the feared and admired spinner Bill O'Reilly. Cristofani's face was 'innocent of those furrows which slow spin bowlers like to regard as the penalty of thought'. He did not play in the first two Tests because Hassett could call on 'an impressively large Magic Circle' of slow bowlers. As for Cristofani's 110 at Manchester, the only Australian

Victory Test hundred apart from Miller's two, 'it was England's victory but the match belonged to Cristofani'.

Likewise in a broadcast to Australia on September 3, CB Fry devoted much of his talk to Cristofani. Fry called Old Trafford 'the finest cricket match for sustained and dramatic interest I have ever seen', and Cristofani's century 'one of the best I have ever seen in a big game'. 'Had that innings been played by Victor Trumper or Charlie Macartney it could not have been better played. This cheerful rosy youth played his defensive strokes with complete certainty and among other feats he stopped four balls that were as good as shooters. He drove with perfect timings and great force ... He hooked beautifully and with curious precision. He cut beautifully. He made no mistakes. I am not exaggerating ... so you had better take care of Cristofani.'

Fry went on: 'Of course Keith Miller is in our eyes your star turn. We know very well we have been watching one who is already a great batsman and who is likely later on to challenge the feats of your champions of the past ... Apart from his technical excellence Keith Miller has something of the dash and generous abandon that were part of Victor Trumper's charm.'

When asked about batting with Keith Miller, Ross Stanford said: 'He would help you if he saw you were doing something wrong. He said, "Don't do that any more, do it this way". He helped me on a lot of occasions when I was with him. He was a beautiful batsman in England. He batted better in England than he did in Australia.'

I asked: 'I have read he was a gifted cricketer but unlike Bradman he wouldn't always concentrate.'

'Yes,' Stanford said, 'if he reckoned the side had enough, he would windy-woof and get out.'

Miller seldom felt he could 'windy-woof' in the Victory Tests. Whitington gave his opinion in his 1950 book *Cricket Caravan*: 'It is a tragedy that Australians have never quite seen the Miller of 1945. He has only rarely been the same classic clean-striking swordsman-like batsman that he was that first peacetime English summer.'

Miller carried the Australians' 1945 batting, showing self-discipline besides flair. Miller, not disagreeing, told Whitington for his 1981 biography: 'I just loved playing cricket, it was fun to be in the game all the time. If you missed out say with the bat you tried harder to contribute with the ball.'

Watchers admired Miller not only for what he did, but the way he did it, batting bare-headed, and the top couple of buttons of his shirt undone. For a man with what seemed such a simple approach to life, Miller already had paradoxes. Like many Australians, and indeed other young men, he had volunteered to serve in the war yet had no time for the bullshit of the armed forces – indeed, as Miller told it, he was set on becoming a stoker in the Navy, but because the friend he was joining with could not get in, they went for the air force instead.

Stanford recalled that Miller began as an airman at Victor Harbour, south of Adelaide. Miller was captain of an air force team that played the Army at Adelaide Oval: 'He was an AC2 [a low rank] and he really enjoyed ordering the flight lieutenants around – "Change positions!"'

A revealing little story. The opposite, being ordered around by men just because they had a higher rank on their uniform than you, annoyed Miller. Somehow Miller never settled as a free man, when civilians, too, could order you around even though they did not have your respect. The 1945 season alone was a time when Miller could excel and excite crowds while – thanks to the air force – he was free of the cares of finding meals and shelter for himself, and the 101 other tedious yet necessary things of everyday life.

By Saturday, August 25 – that is, only two clear days after the last Victory Test – Miller and seven other Australians made the bulk of the Dominions team in another three-day match, against England, at Lord's.

'It was cricket in excelsis,' wrote a thrilled Sir Pelham Warner. 'A joie de vivre in the batting sparkled through a game which fulfilled any known axiom as to how cricket should be played.'

Arguably the greatest event came before any of the 1,241 runs and 40 wickets. On the morning, Hassett, who was supposed to be captain of the Dominions, was 'ill and could not play', according to Warner. One wonders if Hassett was diplomatically ill, or whether he was simply resting. It left the captaincy open to the man who, with 18 Tests played in 11 years before the war, was in any case most qualified to lead: Learie Constantine. It was quite a step, though, for ten white men to play under a black man. In his 1951 memoir *Long Innings*, Warner began the story by denying colour prejudice in Britain:

> *It was, however, necessary to secure both the consent and the co-operation of the rest of the Dominions side, and I went to their dressing-room. I chose my words with care, referring to his seniority and position in the cricket world. I think I sensed that for a moment there was some slight hesitation, but after a very prominent member of the side had agreed that it was a proper choice one and all fell into line. On leading his side into the field Constantine had a great reception.*

In the *Daily Mail* at the time, Ronald Symond spelt it out: '... it is pleasing to see that no prejudice either racial or economic prevents the best man from getting the distinction which belongs to his experience and abilities.' As Symond explained, not only was Constantine coloured, he was the only professional playing for the Dominions, and indeed, was arguably the best-paid cricketer in the world.

The Dominions were six Australians who had played at Manchester in the week – Miller, who may have been the 'very prominent' one who led agreement for Constantine; Pettiford, Pepper, Cristofani, RG Williams and Ellis – two reserves, Hartley Craig and Colin Bremner; the South African DR Fell; the New Zealander Martin Donnelly; and Constantine. Similarly England kept Fishlock, Robertson, Hammond, Edrich, Griffith, Phillipson and Wright from Manchester, and brought in able men: James Langridge, Harold Gimblett, JGW Davies and Eric Hollies.

Briefly: Hartley Craig once again showed how those Australians on the fringe of the Victory team could rise to an occasion, opening with 56. Donnelly made a 'splendid' 133 and Pepper down the order 51. The Dominions made 307 at near exactly three an over. England replied with 287 at better than three an over, thanks largely to Hammond (121) and Edrich (78). Though he hardly bowled because of back trouble, Miller then made his best score of the summer and arguably of his career, 185 out of the second innings 336; the next highest scorer was Constantine, with 40. Hammond in his next column wrote: 'Miller's hitting was the finest I have seen for a long time, it was not just slogging. He hit the ball cleanly and his drives were well controlled.'

England wanted 357 to win; despite 102 by Hammond, they were all out for 311. Giving an interesting clue as to what in his official opinion made good cricket, according to Warner all three parts of the game had a share in the greatness, besides the record 16 sixes: 'Under all this heavy punishment the bowlers never wilted, and the fielding remained at a high standard.' Constantine bowled 21 overs for the Dominions; Australians bowled the other 169.

By August 31, that is, only two clear days later, several of the Australians were in the field again, for their Services two-day game against Nottinghamshire at Trent Bridge. On the Thursday evening before the Friday and Saturday play, the city's cricketing and other worthies hosted the Australians at the Council House. One sentence of the Lord Mayor of Nottingham's speech can give a flavour of the occasion (that the Australians had been through many times): 'We thank you for all you have done in service during the war and for your efforts to bring the British people and the people of your country together in affectionate friendship through the medium of sport.'

Flight Lieutenant Keith Johnson, as the Australians' tour manager, responded in a similar spirit: 'We felt it was our duty to help to protect this beautiful country which we regard as our Motherland. A land which has a ground like Trent Bridge on which we hope generations to follow will play is worth fighting for. Thank goodness when England is in danger in future it will be only when playing a Test match against Australia!'

The next day, Johnson was telling the local press that Hassett, Carmody, Sismey, Workman, Pettiford, Cristofani and Stanford had 'stomach trouble'. Was it something they ate; or was that a polite way of saying they were all hung over?!

Another sign might be the way the Australians collapsed the morning after, admittedly on a rain-affected pitch and against Bill Voce, left arm over the wicket from the pavilion end. Like all professional cricketers, even the most famous ones, he had a point to prove that he was still worth his wages.

The Nottinghamshire county cricket club minutes of the time show Voce tried to hold out for more than £390 a year, as offered to several other professionals, by hinting he had other offers. Voce took five for 32 in 15 overs. It's a moot point, though seldom aired, how many great individual feats in cricket or any other sport are due to a player trying to get a pay rise (or another contract) out of his employers.

The Australians, sent in, were 100 for eight at lunch. Price and Roper counter-attacked in a stand of 61 in 40 minutes until Price, on 44, skied to Nottinghamshire captain George Heane at cover point. The last wicket put on 51 until Roper was out for the top score of 58.

Australia, 194 all out in 58.3 overs, then bowled Nottinghamshire for 130 in 54.3 overs, to end the first day. Pepper took seven for 40 and only Voce, with 45 not out, denied him.

For their second innings, in front of a crowd of 10,000, Hassett promoted those who had been a success on the first day. Price opened and Williams went in first down. Was Hassett trying to freshen his men or was this another sign of hung-over players?! Miller pulled Jepson for a 'glorious six', reached 50 in as many minutes, and with Hassett took the score to 185 for five at lunch. Australia were 215 all out inside two and a half hours. What Nottingham's *Evening Post* called Miller's 'majestic' 81 not out included two sixes and six fours. It left Nottinghamshire three and a quarter hours to get 280. Keeton and CB Harris put on 50 in 45 minutes, until Roper caught Harris brilliantly at square leg off Cristofani, who took six for 59. Pepper supported him with four for 71, as Nottinghamshire folded for 176. Voce set about the bowling late on, making 35 out of 51 in 35 minutes including one six and six fours.

That gave Voce match figures of 11 for 113 and 80 with the bat for once out.

By the Wednesday, September 5, the Australians were at Scarborough, to play HDG Leveson-Gower's XI. The first Scarborough festival for six years began on the previous Wednesday, when Yorkshire won the toss against RAF. Rain turned worse before the players could take the field, and the majority of the 2,000 spectators not lucky enough to be in the pavilion raced for shelter. Over the weekend, Leveson-Gower's team out-batted a New Zealand Services team, only for the Australians to do the same to them. Whitington and Price began cautiously against Austin Matthews at the scorebox end and Coxon. Runs soon came. Pettiford hit the first six of the day, off Matthews to deep square leg. Pettiford drove Hollies hard to Edrich, making it 72 for two. Miller drove his first six; the second went to the spectators' enclosure at the Trafalgar Square end; and the third, off Hollies, over the enclosure roof, resulting in a lost ball. After a single, he skied Robins to Coxon: 181 for three. Miller's 71 came in 65 minutes. That only let in Pepper to do something historic, and incredible to the seaside visitor today who takes a bed and breakfast in Trafalgar Square, and makes the short walk to the ground.

Pepper had already hit the slow bowlers for two sixes, the first off Hollies, the second off Robins, through the bedroom window of an unoccupied house in Trafalgar Square. Arthur Wood, the wicket-keeper, said to Pepper, helpfully though inaccurately, 'You want to put one over there, it's about 150 years since it was done'. 'There' was over the roofs of a row of four-storey lodging houses, a feat managed by the amateur CI Thornton in 1886. Little John of the *Yorkshire Evening Post* gave the fullest account:

Fifth Test, Old Trafford

The ball passed between the second and third chimneys above the Trafalgar Square gap and it was recovered by an official of the Scarborough Club who was helped in his search by a man from the houses over which it passed. They found it on the grass on the island around which motors are parked when cricket is played on the North Marine ground ... Hollies the bowler says it pitched middle stump and was just short of half volley length and was magnificently hit on the rise. He watched its flight interestedly, thought at first it was booked for the green painted roof window between the second and third chimneys but saw it climb over the tiles. Emmott Robinson the umpire says it cleared the rooftop by two or three yards, a view supported by AB Sellers and Arthur Wood.

JM Kilburn, at Scarborough for the *Yorkshire Post*, told how Pepper eventually hit the first five balls of an over of Hutton's leg-spin for 20 – three fours to leg, an off drive for two, and a straight six – and was stumped by Wood off the last ball: 'His cricketing immortality is in this one day assured.' Pepper's 168 came in two hours and 20 minutes out of 284; he had given a catching chance to Fishlock on the leg boundary at 33. The Australians closed the first day on 477 for eight and next morning were all out for 506. Already the ball was turning, too sharply even for the wicket-keeper at times.

The openers Hutton and Fishlock gave the English side a start – Hutton had made 55, 73 and 188 at the festival so far – until Reg Ellis came on at 160 for one. He recalled in 2009: 'It was just a wicket that suited me.' He remembered one batsman but not his name:

I could see he was going to have a go at me; you could tell by his attitude. So I got in ahead of him, bowled a

wide one on the leg side and Stan stumped him. Got
him out of the way quickly.

The one batsman stumped by Sismey was Walter Robins
in the first innings; such batting was in character.

Reg Ellis took five wickets in each innings, the
Englishmen were all out for 258 and 140, and Australia
won by an innings and 108 runs. Kilburn summed up:
'There is no need for further explanation of the event than
that one side was enormously superior to the other and
anyone wishing for more entertaining all round cricket
than the Australians have shown must indeed be beyond
pleasing.'

That day in his latest column Hammond said farewell
to the Australian servicemen, the 'Good Companions of
cricket': 'I think some of them will not be sorry to say
goodbye to cricket for a few weeks for although I am sure
they have thoroughly enjoyed their matches over here
they have probably found the long programme made
possible by VE Day coming early in the season something
of a strain; they have been playing nearly every day for
some weeks. Before the war most of them were only
Saturday afternoon cricketers ...'

'It would not be fair to compare the XI with previous
Australian teams,' he added, maybe because he did not
rate the servicemen with the touring teams of before the
war, and did not want to hurt them; 'but I will say that few
Australian teams have proved themselves better visitors
than these soldiers and airmen ... they have been grand
companions on the field and very pleasant companions
individually and collectively off the field; I have enjoyed
playing against them and have also enjoyed their com-
panionship. They have been at all times a happy bunch.'

That happiness came partly thanks to their individual
and team success, as the end of season first-class averages

(mostly the Victory Tests, Scarborough and the Dominions game) proved. While Pollard took most wickets, 28 at 24.24, Pepper took 27 at 27.44, and Ellis 25 at 19.92. Hutton scored the most first-class runs in 1945: 782 in 16 innings, at an average of 48.89. Next came Miller, whose 13 innings, including three not outs, brought 725 runs at 72.5. Other England batsmen excelled: Washbrook made 637 runs in 15 innings, average 49; Edrich, 602 in 16 innings, at an average of 46.3; and Hammond 592 runs in ten innings at 59.2. Donnelly of New Zealand topped the averages, with 348 runs in four innings, average 87.

Most of the Australian batsmen had much less to show: Hassett 296 runs in 11 innings, average 26.9; Whitington, 11 innings, 294 runs at 26.72, Sismey, 260 runs in nine innings, at 28.88. In other words a lower-order, merely stickable batsman like Sismey did nearly as well as those two specialists.

Still the Australians' summer was not quite over. On the Sunday, September 9, they played Surrey at Kingston upon Thames in a low-scoring, two-day game. On the Wednesday, they said farewell to Sussex by beating the county by three wickets in the last over, hailed by the *Brighton Evening Argus* as 'some of the most thrilling and most sporting cricket that has been witnessed on the historic Hove ground for many a day'. On the Saturday, September 15, they thrashed a combined counties XI at Middlesbrough, declaring on 268 for five (Price 120, Stanford 40, Papayanni, the reserve for the reserve wicket-keeper, 66 not out – another example of how some fringe players kept doing well, whenever given a chance).

The mainly northern team only managed 77. Gilbert Parkhouse, of Glamorgan, top scored with 25; Pettiford took six for 20.

On the Sunday, at Darlington, drawing a crowd put at 4,000, the Australians lost by 28 runs to a North

Yorkshire and South Durham league eleven. That same day, Northamptonshire 'soundly beat' RAAF Brighton at Hastings central ground: 'This was partly due to the inability of the Australians to send over a team that they had originally intended to field; in fact only five of the 11 players named on the scorecard were able to appear,' according to the local paper. Dennis Brookes made 119 not out of 189 for seven; the airmen folded for 95. It was a bad sign.

Chapter Sixteen

The Way Home

If I am to have any standing with the Australians later on I must have shared their experiences in the Pacific war.

Chester Wilmot in England, in a typed letter to
his parents in Australia, July 1945

There is something melancholy about the end of any season, whatever the weather. You know you have to go through autumn and winter before you can play or watch cricket again. You can feel sad even at festivals such as Scarborough. Besides the ache of leaving another summer behind, you can never be sure that everything will be the same after the winter. At Scarborough in 1945, Fattorini, the groundsman for 33 years, told Little John of the *Yorkshire Evening Post* the story of a dozen festival regulars who stood at a tree at the corner of the pavilion. Whenever a wicket fell, they turned sharply into the bar for a drink. 'The tree went, a piece of concrete was put down where the tree used to be. But they still assembled although their numbers gradually declined. At the festival of 1938 only one was left. He took his stand at the old place. This year I have not seen him.'

The Australian airmen felt the pull of home after a year, perhaps two, three or five – an intense, dangerous time, yet often novel and always in places they could never have hoped to see but for the wartime shaking of routine. Like other veterans of other wars, some would find that peacetime never quite matched the comradeship between men facing the prospect of violent and sudden death. The survivors were leaving behind the physical remains of those killed in the fighting.

In a telling article in June 1945, the *Yorkshire Evening Post* told of how sometimes 15 to 20 men a day were visiting the Dominions air force cemetery at Harrogate. Quoted were two unnamed airmen from New South Wales, there to visit the grave 'of a cobber of ours'.

'The three went to school together. One was killed when a Wellington crashed. The other two are back to England from prison camps in Germany and each carries the caterpillar badge of the men who have baled out.'

Roses had only just begun to grow between the hundreds of white crosses. Greenery would soften the cemetery in time. The airmen who went home would never be able to deny the feeling that they had the rest of their lives to enjoy while men no less than them were in a foreign field forever England. Some veterans got on with their lives and only felt the silent tug of their dead cobbers in old age; Miller seemed never to free cricket, as he played it, from its wartime associations. Sir Home Gordon, a fan of Miller from first sight in 1943, wrote with foresight in 1944: 'I want to emphasise that he possesses far more defence than he cares to display and it is permissible to conjecture whether his light-hearted happiness in the game will ever be toned down to the earnestness with which Australians play Test Matches.'

As Whitington admitted as early as 1950 in *Cricket Caravan*, Miller's batting after 1945 was blunted by the cares of marriage and being a father; and 'a certain amount of postwar disillusionment'.

Disillusionment set in even before they reached Australia. If the Services tour had a turning point, it was the sudden end of the war in mid-August. A reason to linger in Britain had gone. As Miller put it frankly in later life, '... one thing I didn't really get too worked up about the end of the war in Europe was the fact we could still be pushed out into the Far East.' After the fifth Test, they had even less keeping them in England. Their magnificent thrashing of a strong invitation team at Scarborough may have been mere end of term relief.

Dr HV Evatt, the Australian foreign minister on a visit to London, gave a farewell lunch to the cricketers at Claridges Hotel. Lords and leading men attended. The cricketers left Liverpool on October 3, sailing via Gibraltar and the Suez Canal, bare-chested in the heat, arriving in Bombay on October 22.

Prince Duleepsinhji, 'Duleep', an England batsman between the wars, now chairman of Bombay cricket association, welcomed them with garlands. They faced nine matches and 29 days' cricket in 43 days, beginning in Lahore on October 28, taking in Delhi, two games at Bombay, then Poona; two games in Calcutta, then two games at Madras, ending on December 10. It was as demanding a schedule as any ever given to Australian cricketers.

From Lahore to New Delhi players faced Indian railway travel at its most uncomfortable. At the last minute a coach set aside for the team had a shunting engine crash into it. Fortunately the players were not on board. Players had to take pot luck on a crowded train, some in second-class compartments. They froze on the 300-mile night journey across the Punjab plain. In Delhi, the team were guests of honour at a cocktail party given by Sir Iven Mackay, Australian High Commissioner for India. Hassett was quoted as saying (diplomatically!): 'We thoroughly enjoyed our visit to Lahore and greatly appreciate the kindness and hospitality accorded to us during our five-day stay. We had a good match and we are looking forward to our other fixtures in this country.'

At Delhi, Hassett and Pepper had to deny remarks credited to them by an Indian newspaper. They talked casually to an Indian reporter travelling with the team and (so they said) had no idea it would be published and (in any case) denied they said anything as reported. Pepper made violent statements against the umpires at Lahore. They were hardly the first or last sportsmen – or anyone else – to speak their mind and have to take it back when they saw it in print.

His teammates said Hassett never revealed his true form with the services in England. Now enjoying the easier pitches, Hassett made 187 and 124 not out in the drawn game against a Princes' XI at New Delhi.

Like other touring teams before and after, they experienced that country's bewildering cricketing and other differences. Already they were agape when they spoke of Indian hospitality. Whitington and Miller, when they wrote about it years later, treated it all whimsically, as a colourful experience – the 'wildly enthusiastic' and noisy crowds, the elephants, the circling vultures, the stinks, and the amusing patches of western civilisation – such as the Indian luncheon marquee bands and orchestras playing classics from Wagner to Sousa and Lili Marlene.

Miller and Compton had a joke in common for life when Compton was batting for East Zone in Calcutta. The Australians were fielding and student rioters were marching onto the field. One told 'Mr Compton': 'You very good player, but you must go!'

The reality was stickier, stranger and unhealthier. Even before the Australians sailed for Asia, the English newspapers were reporting that Bombay was under curfew after days of rioting between Hindus and Muslims. Reg Ellis recalled a colony of monkeys at Madhopur:

> *They invaded the train, took sandwiches out of your hands and all sorts. They were oh, about that high [four or five feet] and you could see some of them were vicious. So you kept well clear of them. There was one big old male monkey sitting up on the station who did nothing and there was about oh, at least one hundred females and he ruled the colony and any males he used to kill them; so they told us.*

Most players soon came down with something. While playing at Lahore, Roper went to hospital with a temperature. Hearing of the rapid fall of Australian wickets, he leapt from his bed and had a turbaned, bearded Sikh drive him to Lahore cricket ground. But by the time he arrived, Cristofani and Miller had stopped the rot. At Bombay, versus West Zone, Bremner took the place of Stanford, who was 'suffering from a touch of the sun and a mysterious affliction called "curry tummy"'. Bremner himself retired with a strained thigh and Hassett took his place. Miller had been acting captain while Hassett rested.

Against West Zone, so William Marien, a *Sydney Morning Herald* staff reporter travelling with the Australian team, wrote: 'Whitington had to lie down beside the wicket for a few moments. He was suffering from a hangover after an attack of dengue fever. After five minutes he resumed batting confidently.' And days after his hospitalisation Roper had, according to Marien, 'intermittent fever and irregular pulse'.

The first day of the first unofficial Test came on November 11. At 11am, players stood still for the two-minute

227

armistice day silence, 'but the vast crowd in ignorance of what was meant whistled and cheered impatiently at the delay', Marien reported.

Australia closed on 336 for six. While Carmody, 'the dashing cavalier', made 113, Pettiford was 'the footslogger who in spite of stomach and arm cramps kept going with a dogged persistence'. During his 124, he became so exhausted he slumped down to rest on his bat for the next ball. When India replied, the Australian bowlers had to struggle against an easy pitch and, reading between the lines, biased umpires. Fortified by curry for lunch, Keith Miller 'sent them down with terrific speed, extracting from a lackadaisical pitch a certain amount of devilment'. Pepper, after failing to get a leg before, 'gave an unnecessary display of petulance, kicking the ball towards Miller to be fielded. The batsman ran a single whereupon Pepper bumped the last ball of the over viciously head high to the batsman. This demeanour should be unnecessary to a service side touring largely for goodwill. Pepper who is really a very fine cricketer is unsuited to actions of this sort,' Marien wrote. Worse was to come.

A two-day 'picnic game' followed at Poona, against Indian Universities. Australia made 300 and 85 for three, the students 385 for one. Those scores suggest what Reg Ellis said in 2009: 'But it was hard in India. It was in the 90s, dry pitches. Ball didn't turn much ...'

Another developing gripe was the hundreds of miles of travel between games, or rather the bad organisation. The Australians arrived in Bombay from Poona by air, giving them time to attend the races in Bombay. The team then flew by an RAF Dakota transport aircraft to Calcutta for a match against East Zone. Stanford was reportedly 'definitely not playing any more matches in India', as he had suffered a 'breakdown' in Poona. Presumably by breakdown Marien meant physical rather than mental collapse, for as Stanford recalled it in 1998: 'I didn't play many games in India. I got dengue fever and ended up in hospital.' Cristofani, injured rather than unwell – he sprained his groin, reportedly, at the nets on arrival in Bombay – was reported 'better'.

Reg Ellis had a rare rest in Calcutta:

> When I got up it was about 10 o'clock. I went to go out to get a rickshaw, of course, instead of taxis. And they wouldn't take me, this feller wouldn't take me, he said no, too dangerous. Anyhow I went back again and I went out again and I told the rickshaw driver, another chap, that I would give him double the money if he took me out to the ground. He said all right, so I got aboard and we had only gone about 100 yards and this mob caught up with us and they tipped the rickshaw upside down and I was on the ground and while there was a mob deciding what they were going to do with me, I crawled out, crawled between their legs and went for my life back to the hotel and later on I had to get another [rickshaw]. And he took me, I had to pay double for that too. When I got out there the mob had stopped the cricket.

The Australians were simply caught in nationalist riots against the ruling British. India, in politics as in cricket, wanted independence, and equal treatment, and to that end welcomed the servicemen. Ellis, when looking back, stressed how interesting a time it was. Each man had an orderly: 'While we were in India we paid him sixpence a week and that was enough for him to live on with rice but we gave him more than that, but that's all we had to pay. And he did all our clothes; if you had dirty clothes he would wash them overnight and press them. Like having a butler.'

For the second unofficial Test at the end of November, yet more players were in the wars and the fit men had to fill in. Workman replaced Sismey, who was recovering from an operation to remove shrapnel from his back. Carmody, the stand-in wicket-keeper, missed several chances. At least the batsmen did enough on the easy pitches. Whitington hit a five-hour 155 including 15 fours; Carmody, according to Marien, had 'developed into a run making machine'. Pettiford was 'outstanding' in India and made runs when really needed, in the first two unofficial Tests. Thanks to Cristofani's 'hurricane' 54 not out in half an hour, the Australians beat South Zone by six wickets on December 4, their first win in India. That was not so much a sign of Australian weakness as of the dead pitches made to insure the Indians against losing.

It was a group of poorly men, weakened by long batting and fielding stints – an unwelcome change from England – now protesting against their scheduled Australian tour. The men wanted only to play in five mainland state capitals, not Canberra and Hobart. To play in Perth, Adelaide, Melbourne, Sydney and Brisbane with only three days between matches meant, the organisers in Australia were assuming, travel by air rather than train. By the standards of the 1940s that was a rush; and 1940s flights between Australian cities were rough affairs, not the bus-like routine of the 2000s. And to fit in the planned games in Ceylon and Perth, the RAF arranged to fly the Australians from Colombo to Perth – that is, a body nothing to do with the Australian Board of Control (ABC), the supposed managers of team affairs.

Marien was reporting on December 10 that the players asked Johnson to cable their complaints to the ABC. The players objected to playing in Perth on Christmas Day and to four state games of four days, not three. 'The men feel that they have already played more continuous cricket than any combination previously; that the Indian tour has been more than strenuous; that if the Indian tour is followed by an equally laborious Australian tour their cricket will suffer as well as their health.'

They were not to know that the papers at home were full of news of strikes by coal miners and iron workers. Just as the authorities showed no sympathy to strikers – alleging they were communist – it looked as if the cricketers were likewise on the wrong side of authority.

In a December 17 article Sismey took the role of shop steward, the public face of a team unhappy with its workload. He spoke of 'disappointment' at the Australian authorities' misapprehension of the real state of affairs. He admitted it was 'difficult to envision cricket in Ceylon in heat and mugginess' for 'stale, tired, dejected and weary' men.

The team arranged air travel to Australia by itself, through the RAF. The Skymaster due to take them across the Indian Ocean was unserviceable so they had to go to the top – Louis Mountbatten, at South East Asia Command – for permission to use two operational Liberators.

'If it had been left to the Australian authorities, I believe we would never have been home in time for the Western Australia game at Christmas,' said Sismey. Many of the players had been away for more than five years. They were not able to play their best cricket. Ceylon, less advanced in cricket than India, offered a respite. Ellis took eight wickets in a day, as they beat Ceylon by an innings. They left Colombo on December 17 by air and landed at Guildford airport near Perth three days later.

Their first act on home soil was to make long-distance telephone calls to their families. Then they toured the city of Perth and its beaches. The Adelaide men, Ellis, Workman and Stanford, left for their home city.

While the authorities did not give in to the players – the game against Western Australia began on December 25, the hosts on 70 for no wicket when rain stopped play after 43 minutes – at least you could say the states were paying the servicemen a compliment by being so keen to see them. WA, particularly, had an agenda. The *West Australian* newspaper quoted Hassett, who beforehand said the state should compete in the Sheffield Shield. The newspaper agreed. 'With air travel bringing Perth within probably no more than a day's journey from Brisbane, the most distant venue of Sheffield Shield games, participation by West Australian teams may be brought closer to realisation.'

However, even the *West Australian* called the Services team jaded. The *Sydney Morning Herald* reported the bowlers were erratic and fielders dropped easy catches. The headline 'Dull batting by services' ran below reports of inter-state cricket. Already the servicemen were becoming yesterday's news.

By this time, Reg Ellis was feeling hard done by and 'run down'. He had more overs to bowl, and he was not even allowed home: 'We played South Australia and I wasn't allowed to come home here, I had to stay with the team at the hotel; they allowed my wife to come and stay with us. That's the first I had seen of her for just over five years. And we had one daughter and I hadn't seen her at all.'

Cheetham re-joined the Services in Adelaide for a draw that saw what Keith Miller in one of his memoirs called 'the Cec Pepper incident':

At that time Cec Pepper was, in my opinion, the best all-rounder in the world. Pepper deceived Bradman with his 'flipper', a kind of leg break which scarcely turned but made a lot of pace off the pitch. Most of the players on the field believed that Bradman failed to stop the flipper and was plumb leg before. Stan Sismey, the wicket-keeper, as fair a man as you could wish to meet, said there was no doubt that Bradman was out. There was a terrific appeal, but umpire Jack Scott did not grant it. In the heat of the moment Pepper turned to Scott and said something.

As Miller added diplomatically, he was not playing so he did not hear it, but Miller did read the report Scott made, 'and it finished Pepper. He should have been a cast-iron certainty but was not picked for the tour of New Zealand ... it would be a poor look-out for all of us if our careers were held forfeit for one remark said in temper ... a potentially great player was lost to Australia.'

Stan Sismey's cynical-sounding view was outlined in his obituary in the *Sydney Morning Herald* in 2009: 'Don made 112 against our Australian Services XI, and he was a sick man in all the war years, but he walked out there and batted just like Bradman always batted ... getting runs, hundreds of them.'

Either man might have added that it would have taken a brave umpire to cut short Bradman's comeback.

As in England, each state wanted to prove themselves against the famous Victory Test team. Victoria thrashed them in Melbourne, by an innings. Miller, acting captain, top scored in both Services innings. New South Wales did the same at the Sydney Cricket Ground. Here Ray Lindwall and Miller first came face to face on a first-class cricket field. Bill O'Reilly, as NSW captain, declared at 551 for seven after the first day. O'Reilly, Ernie Toshack and

Lindwall then took all but two of the Services wickets. While the Services bowlers were evidently wilting – except, according to reports, Ellis – those NSW bowlers were Australia's main three in the single Test in New Zealand that March. Miller's 105 not out was the first hundred off NSW that season.

The servicemen had their pride, or merely the wish not to be the one to let themselves and their mates down. As they saw the end, they rallied. They drew with Queensland after Hassett sportingly declared and set 190 in 96 minutes. Queensland needed 13 off the last over bowled by Cristofani. The local *Courier Mail* newspaper hailed it as one of the most spectacular batting efforts in Australian first-class cricket.

Lastly in Hobart at the end of January 1946, the Services almost beat Tasmania, albeit the weakest state. It is touching to read the accounts in *The Mercury*, the Hobart daily paper, both for the servicemen's resilience and the Tasmanian pride as hosts. The Services batsmen enjoyed themselves on the first day, making 440 for seven by 5pm, when rain stopped play.

Stanford top scored with 153 in four hours, including 13 fours. Hassett dominated a stand of 70 for the third wicket with Stanford; then Miller made 56 (six fours, one six) in a stand of 111 for the fourth wicket in an hour. Finally Cristofani hit 72 not out in 43 minutes as the bowlers tired.

The visitors threw the bat in their second innings, declared, and the match ended with Tasmania nine wickets down; the last pair defended 11 balls in the last five minutes from Cristofani, then Pepper, while all the fielders stood around the bat. Hassett nearly took a winning catch; a leg before appeal was turned down. Pepper's last ball fizzed off the pitch and beat the bat and the wicket-keeper Bremner. It was a fair ending; the

Services had done well, trying to win one game back home; and the hosts were pleased too.

––––––––––––––

Speaking to the press as they landed at Cambridge airport by air force 'plane from Melbourne, only the day before the Tasmania game, it was time to reflect. England had said in October that they would tour the next Australian season, now only seven months away. Hassett believed Australia might have a 'slight edge'. Both sides would be strong in batting but a little weak in bowling and big scores appeared almost certain, Hassett predicted. Plainly he did not spot the potential of Miller and Lindwall as a pair. The team did praise Lindwall as the fastest bowler they had encountered. Loyally, the players backed Miller who spoke of a 'dislike' for bowling; his comrades felt that by bowling, his batting would suffer.

That said, Miller had bowled only 363 overs in all since May, compared with Ellis' 957 and Pepper's 1,157: so wrote Whitington in an article placed in *The Mercury* while the team was in Hobart. Partly, he was putting on record the averages for all the 1945 Services matches; though he did add that the bowling figures of Pepper and Price were incomplete 'owing to unfortunate and mysterious loss of second AIF team scoring book in a little inn near the White Cliffs of Dover'. Partly, as the headline suggested, 'Services XI measures up well to first AIF team', Whitington was pleading for his team's place in history. At times his effort made sad reading. He admitted the team's 'disappointing' form in Australia. Both sides, in 1919 and 1945, 'performed beyond expectations' and there was little to choose between them, so he argued.

The first AIF finished in Australia in a 'blaze of glory' because the men of 1919 had several weeks' rest after games in England and South Africa. The later services team, after a 6,000-miles tour of India, started their Australian tour after only six days' rest. 'Sismey, Carmody, Hassett, Stanford, Price, Roper and Pettiford have never at any stage of the Australian tour been fit and well.'

Australians have no more time for excuses than anyone else. In separate and unnecessary shows of disrespect, *The Melbourne Age* and *Sydney Morning Herald* reporters of the Melbourne and Sydney matches printed unfunny military puns at the Services team's expense. In truth, it's impossible to know quite how many overs Ellis and Pepper, the airmen's and Army's stock bowlers respectively, bowled between May 1945 and January 1946 – 1,500 each? While unheard-of by 21st-century standards, it was a heavy but not incredible load then. An English county spinner might bowl 1,200 a summer, an Australian or English Ashes tourist several hundred. Ellis, though, had sailed to England to fly, not to bowl month after month.

As presented to the world by Whitington, the final statistics needed some explaining, as any do. Whitington and above all Hassett emerged as the batting successes. Hassett in 56 innings, six times not out, made 2,565 runs, at an average of 51.3. Next came Miller – 2,266 runs at 48.2 – Whitington himself, 2,076 at 35.9, and Pepper, 1,541 at 30.2. Everyone else was well behind such as Stanford, 819 runs at 23.89; and Workman, 952 runs at 21.6. Whitington did not say so but the figures flattered him; and made Miller's look all the more outstanding. Whitington and the other Army men had made plenty of their runs in England against mere strong club teams, while Stanford and the airmen had fewer easier games outside the Victory Tests.

The servicemen had something left at the end – something that did not show in any averages or scorecard.

The Way Home

You can see it in a striking picture in *The Mercury* of the Tasmania and Services teams together. The Tasmanians, obviously less used to being photographed, put on neutral expressions for the camera, while Hassett, Price and Ellis managed smiles. The servicemen had long lost any stage nerves and although grossly overworked by the authorities, they still had sunny temperaments; they were doing something they enjoyed. Individually, then as a team, they had done things they would never have dreamed of. Between them they had seen every inhabited continent. They had met rajahs of India; they visited 'those lush green hills' of Kandy in Ceylon, where Dick Whitington 'bought a huge and still-treasured topaz for the mother of my sons', as he put it the year before he died; and they stayed overnight on an island between Ceylon and home, where, Reg Ellis recalled, 'the beds were all high and all made of iron, iron piping, and at night no sooner had we put all the lights out the place was invaded by crabs'. Now the work for a living began again.

Chapter Seventeen

A New Era

Time takes more spin than nineteen thirty-four.
Drummond Allison, *Verity* (1943)

The Last Enemy, published in 1942, is Richard Hillary's memoir as a Battle of Britain pilot and, as memorably, someone recovering from a burned and repaired face. Early on he recalls how before the war in Germany he and fellow amateur, carefree, Oxford student rowers beat an efficient, nasty German team, once the Englishmen were roused by the Germans' hatred and plain bad manners – someone spat at them.

The moral of Hillary's story: the English, because of their love of peace, began the war at a disadvantage to the warlike, well-drilled Germans. Once Englishmen applied themselves, their very freedom of thought helped them to better the Germans at their own game. Hillary never lived to see the victory. He died in 1943, like so many others, in a training air crash. His story implied that once the English won the war, they wanted to return to how they were before the war, or at least to try to.

War did make some change inevitable. At the start of the summer of 1945 Hammond, with remarkable honesty, recalled the year before: 'When I returned from overseas duty with the RAF I was asked to captain a side at Lord's. I accepted but had not realised that time had marched on. When I walked on to the field with my team I suddenly felt that something was wrong. I realised at once that I did not know more than half the players or who were the bowlers and who the batsmen. It was a queer feeling and for a time I felt lost.'

Hammond must have felt stranger than most because, as one of the longest-serving players around, he expected to know everyone: 'Most of us who were taking part in first-class cricket before the war had become used to playing with the same team mates week in and week out. Over a period of years we came to know each other's virtues and faults and were able to make allowances and to look at the coming season's fixtures list. Weeks ahead we knew almost exactly what to expect ... And every ground where we were due to play we would look forward to meeting old friends and acquaintances.'

That summer Hammond spoke privately of calling it a day. The authorities were keen for him to play on, while the English game formed again, even if Hammond would not be around for long to enjoy it as a player.

Sadly, out of duty, Hammond stayed in cricket long enough to show his age. In the next Ashes series in 1946–7 the Australian hosts thrashed England. The Australians on their tour in 1948, led by Don Bradman for the last time, were, famously, the Invincibles – never beaten by England or anyone else. England's 1950–1 tour was much the same and only in 1953, the Coronation year of Queen Elizabeth II, did England win the Ashes again, the beginning of yet another new era that did not last.

At the time, it's important to say, it was not obvious at first that Australia would dominate. Writing in *The Cricketer* in spring 1944, Jack Fingleton in Australia worried that England 'might well repay Australia the drubbings which Australia inflicted' after the First World War. Writing just before the 1946–7 tour, in the third edition of their *History of Cricket*, the English authorities HS Altham and EW Swanton wrote how England's batting promised to be 'transcendentally good': 'The outlook for the bowling is however less reassuring. History shows that to beat Australia we need pace, flight and the ability to bowl accurately to the field.' So it proved. Bill Bowes, touring as a Yorkshire journalist, admitted to hoping beforehand that England might beat the Australians. Afterwards, in his book *Express Deliveries*, Bowes made a wide-ranging confession that could apply to most decades since:

> *Let us face the facts about the present-day superiority of the Australians. Are they better fed? Do they study and play the game more keenly? Are they superior or should I say psychologically tougher in the war of nerves? Any or none of these reasons may be the answer. The fact remains that they are too good for us.*

Of the Victory Test Australians, only Miller and Hassett remained, and Hassett had made his name before the war; only Miller was a Victory Test graduate. In part this showed how many talented cricketers Australia could choose from.

Another English journalist following the 1946–7 tour, Bruce Harris, made the point that even in minor matches, the English bumped into capable young players who could make a show in the best company. Writing early in 1948, Bill Edrich said something similar: that 'Australian second and third XIs today could give an England first XI very hard games'.

That was one way of looking at the Victory Tests. Selecting cricketers, or any sportsmen, or indeed workers to fill any jobs, is like so much in life a matter of opinion. Did the Australian state and national selectors give the Victory players 'a fair go', something that Australia likes to believe it is all about? In sport and life generally

Australians took some convincing that something done well abroad was as well done as at home. Or was it plain jealousy? Chester Wilmot told his parents in a letter from England in July 1945: 'In Australia people are going to forget the German war very quickly and they are not going to count service over here as being of much importance compared with the Pacific.'

Did the authorities have a bias against men who had made a name for themselves in England? Or did the Victory Test men at the least have to prove themselves all over again? In the case of Pepper, were those in authority determined to show who was boss? As Miller wrote: surely Bradman could have saved Pepper with a word? Miller made sure in his 1981 interview that he put his view of Bradman on record: he was 'a great admirer' … but … Miller plainly still did not like the control that Bradman, 'Mr Cricket', had over selections.

We can see that the only difference between Miller and Pepper had been that Miller as a fast bowler to partner Lindwall was too valuable to ignore, whereas Australia had alternatives for everyone else. Why put up with the temper of Pepper – a spinner who could bat – when you could pick McCool? Or Toshack? Or Ian Johnson? Or Doug Ring? Australia, despite its self-image as a land for the independent and plain-speaking, was as bad as England for leaving out the men with minds of their own.

Not that it seemed to hold Australia back. In 49 Tests between the world wars, England won 15 to Australia's 22. In the first 20 years after the Second World War, England did worse, winning ten Tests of 55 to Australia's 22. In the 40 years after, England won 32 to Australia's 52, out of 118. That masked a rally by England in the 1970s and 1980s. In the 20 years of Tests from 1989, England won eleven to Australia's 35, 12 drawn. Australia dominated so much that they could re-write their history, as Steve

Waugh did as captain, claiming that they were playing the Australian way, scoring faster, more open to ideas, unlike the English stuck with tradition.

That was in fact a double rewriting of history because if any country gave up tradition – to play on a Sunday, for instance – it was England; and after Miller, for much of the 1960s, Australia played defensively, to draw, rather than take risks to win. In truth, Australia were the same as any other country. When they had great batsmen and above all bowlers, they played aggressively, to win, because they could; when they couldn't, they drew or lost. In the Victory series the Australians batted as best they could; apart from Miller, and Hassett, they were defiant rather than flamboyant; like Stanford, they went to the extreme of their ability, even beyond, liberated of the stress of combat flying.

The goodwill seen in the Victory Tests, with Miller as a leaven, could have led to, if not a new era of brilliant cricket, at least a few years of sportsmanship led by the generation that had a shared experience of combat and the joy of being alive. Bradman either ignored this possibility or did not even see it, and re-imposed the pre-war ruthlessness.

Even had Bradman been a war hero, and more receptive to the war generation, others in authority, who had stayed at home in the war, set the tone – business as normal, as if the war had meant nothing. To be fair, it happened in England too. In August 1945, the Nondescripts beat 51 MU – the maintenance unit at RAF Lichfield – for the Chauntry Cup. 'It is good to see the cup once more in the hands of a local team,' the *Lichfield Mercury* wrote, though a couple of years earlier that newspaper had been glad enough of overseas visitors while they were dying over Germany.

A New Era

Settled back in Australia, Miller wrote remarkably in *Cyril Washbrook's Cricket Annual 1949*: 'Given good weather, I would prefer playing in England to any other cricketing country. Having spent three wartime years with the RAAF I find, above all, that Englishmen are unsurpassed as a "people".'

What sort of Australian or any foreigner, let alone someone famous and admired by his countrymen, would admit to preferring England to their own country? (Reg Ellis showed a similar attitude, when, recalling his bomber crew, he said he wouldn't have Australians 'because they weren't reliable enough'.) Miller was saying, in other words, that English people surpassed Australians!

Bradman said diplomatically kind words in England, and became Sir Donald in 1949; but whatever the diplomat says, he is always putting his country first. Two veterans were the next Ashes captains in 1950–1 – Hassett and the former prisoner of war Freddie Brown. They improved relations.

Sir Michael Parkinson as a boy saw Keith Miller and wrote of him as his hero, but Parkinson was above all an able journalist who teased out, and printed, the contradictions and sadness inside the man he met, grown old and infirm. In 1994 Parkinson reported an interesting story from Miller – interesting, because it was not quite complete, and yet gave a clue to the man. It dated from the first Ashes Test proper after the war – at Brisbane in 1946. Australia made 645 then caught England on a wet pitch.

> *My old mate Bill Edrich was playing. He had a serious war and he survived and I thought: 'He's my old Services mate. The last thing he wants after five years in the war is to be flattened by a cricket ball', so I eased up. Bradman came up to me and said: 'Don't slow*

down, Keith. Bowl quicker'. Do you know, that remark put me off Test cricket? Never felt the same way about it after that.

No doubt Miller identified sincerely with his fellow veteran and not with war-dodger Bradman. The fact is, as Miller did admit in print, he hit Edrich eight times that day in Brisbane. Edrich ended with a 'mass of bruises'. Miller had, incidentally, hit Edrich in the Victory Tests, too. Edrich, in his memoirs, did not resent being hit – indeed, he wrote that 'for all our spirited [!] play on the field Miller, Lindwall, Compton and myself were always the greatest pals off it'. Edrich did claim that Lindwall and Miller overdid the bouncer in 1948, though not in 1946–7.

Miller's story of Bradman telling him what to do, 'like an erring schoolboy', as Miller put it another time, told, like many stories we tell, the truth according to the teller. His new captain Bradman, and the authorities that Bradman represented (and as a cricket administrator later led) did not listen to combat veterans. This disillusioned Miller. And yet he *did as he was told*, this rebel who, 'you felt', according to the admiring Sir Michael Parkinson, 'didn't give a damn about anyone or anything'. Miller wanted to get on, the same as everyone else.

Not that Miller's compromises ever quite satisfied the authorities. Just as Edrich captained Middlesex but not England, Miller became captain of New South Wales, but not of Australia. Here lay Miller's unresolved, and unresolvable, sadnesses. The great athlete could not stop thinking.

Reg Ellis compromised, too. He played once for South Australia at the end of the 1945–6 season, taking six wickets, then became the chief flying instructor of the Royal Aero Club of South Australia for about 12 years. As he explained in 2009: 'Flying was my first love.' It meant he had to give up cricket, because most pupils flew at weekends.

Chapter Eighteen

Adelaide Two

The short semi-humorous comedies we live, our long certain tragedies, and our springtime lyrics and limericks make up most of what we are.
Norman Maclean, *Young Men and Fire* (1992)

Of all the Australian Victory Test players, it was fitting that Reg Ellis was the last one alive; partly because he was the team's regular number eleven. As the last batsman, he had been used to watching the others leave the dressing room and come back, dead in a batting sense, if you like, while he was always the very last to return, out or not.

I knocked on his back door early, so early in fact that he had a bowl of cereal on a table, beside his glasses and pen on that day's – Thursday, June 25, 2009 – *Adelaide Advertiser* crossword. He invited me to sit across from him and said: what did I want to ask?

Hoping to show I knew what I was talking about, I quoted Hammond's praise of him, before the first Victory Test: 'The more I played against him … the less I liked it.'

Reg Ellis answered: 'I got him out quite a few times but he also made a lot of runs against me.'

I recognised this as a line from a 2006 ABC South Australia interview with him and (separately) the ailing Ross Stanford. Had I come so far, I wondered, only to get brief answers? Had my over-eagerness put him off? To make me even more uncomfortable, he asked about Stan

Adelaide Two

Sismey and I had to say that I was sorry, but he had only just died; I had read his obituary in the *Sydney Morning Herald* that Monday.

I understood, later, that in those first minutes he was sizing me up, as he had his pupils as an instructor, to work out how best to treat them, strictly or easily. This was the other reason he was fitted to be a last man; if I live to 91, I hope I am like him. He had a hearing aid, but his blue-eyed stare was firm. He still drove. He was still a justice of the peace, though he no longer sat in court. And, like other bomber veterans, he had a strong sense of his *luck*: he had never found any sport hard; he had good health; and he had survived.

One of his wartime photographs is of him and three men in shorts and their pilots' helmets, during initial training at Deniliquin. The other three were killed: 'I am lucky to be alive.' His brother, too, gained his 'wings' but was killed in training at Mildura when he collided with another aircraft.

It took me much thought to put his character into words – which was a sort of tribute: because he was a precise man, comfortable with the study necessary to reach precision, whether as a slow bowler or pilot. He was self-reliant, something on which Australian men pride themselves, yet not the supposedly typical rugged Australian; not someone who would rather have two drinks than one, and certainly not someone who would wave away trouble with those magic Australian words, 'She'll be right.' That was not the attitude of a flying instructor or the safety and security manager of an oil refinery – another of his later jobs.

He was one of the few bomber veterans I have met to deny fear in combat: 'You just did what you had to do of course, that's the way you were taught. And that's how you didn't have nerves, you were taught that way' –

again, that trust in teaching – 'but,' he added, 'once you got going and got near the target that's a different matter.' Then he did admit to nerves, at the most dangerous time of all, when you had to fly straight no matter what, to drop the bombs and take a flash-photograph, to prove back at base you had done what you were supposed to. He had kept one picture all this time, of a hit right on target. Similarly, while he conquered his nerves as a bowler, he recalled (ironically?) the bombed-out stands at Sheffield, and how he had felt, trying to save first the follow-on, and in the second innings the match: 'Batting, I was nervous there. Couldn't help it.'

This man who did not fit Australian stereotypes was a free-willed Australian for all that. He told stories of rickshaw races at Durban – paying the drivers well – while ashore on the voyage to England; and visiting St Paul's Cathedral with a mate who convinced the authorities to let him play the organ, until he played the popular tune *Show Me the Way to Go Home* and was ejected.

One time – the English and Australian players used to travel to matches by the same train – the Aussies tied a sleeping English player's shoelaces together and yelled out 'Fire!' in the carriage. Most extraordinary of all: he bumped into a former fellow instructor who was a test pilot for the Meteor jet fighter. He invited Reg to try it, solo, because the cockpit could only fit one. The pilot talked Reg through the controls – 'Don't open the throttle too quickly or you'll put the fire out' – and Reg taxied around to get the hang of it before take-off: '…ah, it was entirely different to flying an engined aircraft because there was no noise or anything, only the swish of wind, it was just like flying a big glider and it was fantastic. It was quite simple to fly and I was rather lucky because it didn't matter what the aircraft was, I could fly it.'

Adelaide Two

Again: that feeling of good fortune. Reg Ellis was plainly trustworthy, but what if the air force knew its most important and secret 'plane got borrowed?!

My questions answered, Reg put on a videotape – to hand, naturally – of that 2006 ABC interview. I felt sad to see Ross Stanford after his stroke. Here, then, was the end of the innings. Yet does not a run at the end, however made, count the same as at the beginning, however glorious?

In the back garden on my way out I remarked on the orange tree; Reg let me have a couple of the riper fruits. As soon as I was out of sight I peeled and ate one; how I marvelled at this, and many things the Australians take for granted. Just as they may marvel at what England takes for granted: Stonehenge, Lord's, St Paul's. The first chance I had on my return, I went inside the cathedral – only so far, because they charge so much to enter (and what would wartime Australian airmen have said to that!?). I hummed *Show Me the Way to Go Home,* to myself; and not loud. I am English.

Chapter Nineteen

The Last Enemy

Yet question we always must, even though the answers might dismay us, even though we find it impossible to reach a conclusion.

Don Charlwood

It would take a brave man to cross Bradman while he was alive. Only someone with a war record had the authority to question Bradman's war-dodging. Even when the man was dead, few obituary writers dared rock the boat. One told me, in conversation: 'If he [Bradman] had wanted to go [to war], he could have.' Significantly, only EW Swanton, a man who did go to war, dwelt on Bradman's war in his obituary, printed in *Wisden* in 2002 after Swanton's own death in 2000.

Miller could have said something more, except always at the back of his mind lay the self-knowledge that he had not had the chance to pass the test of combat. It is a credit to the man that he did not 'shoot a line' (air force slang for boasting), when everyone assumed he, their sporting hero, was a war hero too. Miller said, in one of the longest interviews to dwell on his war, for the National Library of Australia in 1981, '... as far as I am concerned my war was very modest compared to some of the other things that I have done'.

What if Bradman had gone to Bomber Command? He would have given Britain heart until he died in some otherwise anonymous raid over Germany. His Test average of 99.94 would have left him statistically as far ahead of everyone else, but he might not have been quite so obviously the greatest batsman ever. More on a par with Victor Trumper, perhaps. Indeed in 1978, aged 70, Jack Fingleton brought out a biography of Trumper that doubled as an effort to bring Bradman down to size; aided by a Bill O'Reilly foreword.

There are two war-dodging charges against Bradman. First, his switch from the air force, with the prospect of front-line service, to the safety of Army PT; second, his release through ill-health. On the first, more serious, charge, it may be that Bradman took the offer from higher-ups of a safer job; certainly few men ever had the choice of swapping branches of the armed forces. On the second, as any employer knows, who can tell whether a man truly has back trouble, or is shamming? Only Bradman could answer either charge.

So? Wouldn't the world have been poorer, if Bradman had not lived to bat again? To answer, stand in one of the regional cemeteries in Britain, at Cambridge or Harrogate or Chester, that hold some of the Australian and other foreign air force dead. The rows of headstones do not voice opinions. Still, the least man there had a mother the same as Bradman.

And if there had been no war? Reg Ellis might never have learned to fly, because of the expense. Instead, he might have made the Ashes tour of 1942. Bradman might have retired younger with a better average than 99.94. How else would the world have been different? I know that but for the war I would not be here; or at least, I would not be me.

Cricket mirrored society, as usual. The English public's enthusiasm and goodwill for the game at the war's end ran out in the 1950s. The cricket authorities took the money at the gate yet were too short-sighted or stupid to see that the crowds would peter out unless the authorities met at least halfway the demands for a spectacle worth watching. It was the old human story: the reformers were the ones not in power; the ones in power were not reformers. So when change came, in the 1960s – an end to Gentlemen versus Players and amateurs; the embrace of sponsors in one-day knock-out cricket; above all, foreign players and a Sunday league – there was never the sense that the authorities were at ease with commerce. By then the men who stamped their names on the Victory Tests – Hutton, Edrich and Miller – had long retired with 12,000 Test runs and 32 Test hundreds between them. Pettiford and Pepper batted together for a Commonwealth XI during the Hastings festival against an England XI (including Donald Carr) in September 1957; and 1958.

The 1959 season saw the last of some of the longer-lasting characters of 1945: Pettiford had a benefit at Kent, and Robertson at Middlesex; Washbrook retired at Lancashire. Keith Miller played once for Nottinghamshire, scoring 62 and 102 not out against Cambridge University, who included the future broadcaster Henry Blofeld. In 1961, Donald Carr, captain of Derbyshire, played for the Gentlemen against the Players at Scarborough alongside a teenage Cambridge University wicket-keeper-batsman by the name of JM Brearley. Twenty years later, as the returned captain of England, Mike Brearley would win the Ashes.

So, when we look back, one generation shades into another. The year 1963 was the last that Ted Blagg was a professional for Steetley Works in his native Nottinghamshire, two decades after he and the Australians of RAF Lichfield swept aside all-comers. Or, we can even stretch a thread to September 17, 1983, when the West Indian Bertie Clarke, aged 65, batted and bowled for an Old World eleven against an Old England eleven at the Oval.

The players of 1945 were dying before then: William Roberts first, in 1951; Pettiford, back in Sydney, in 1964; Hammond, only just 62, in 1965; Workman, on a London bus, in 1970. Most lived to attend a 40th anniversary dinner in London. When the Australians gathered for a 50th anniversary dinner in Sydney, Miller was too ill to attend. Gradually, the telephones fell silent. Griffith, Hassett, Pepper and Pope died in 1993; Charles Price, down the road from Miller, at Avalon on the far north shore of Sydney, in 1997; Doug Wright in 1998, Cyril Washbrook in 1999; Cristofani, in Hampshire, in 2002; Miller, not quite 85, in 2004; Ross Stanford in 2006, not long after that ABC interview, aged 88.

The English cricket grounds of 1945, like the rest of the country, so glad to survive Hitler, changed almost past recognising. As late as the 1980s at Trent Bridge, you went to the gents against a brick wall, the same as a century before. Now as elsewhere there are proper toilets, and floodlights, adverts for 'official beer of England', and plastic seats and plastic hats; and plastic cricket to match.

The old Hastings cricket ground – where I watched a game one weekday afternoon in 1990, to put off revising for a journalism exam – is a shopping centre. In the piazza, a statue of a batsman hooking on one leg, unveiled by the Queen in 1997, is called, without irony, *The Spirit of Cricket*. The wartime Lichfield cricket ground is but a green on the edge of a housing estate. The runways of RAF Lichfield went under houses and the aircraft hangars became prized warehouse space for such necessities as chocolate Easter eggs. The same happened to many other bomber airfields. Reg Ellis' RAF Burnaston is now a Toyota car factory. As he drove me in 2009 around south suburban

Adelaide, I could not believe that all the streets we passed were, in his boyhood, fields and vineyards. Even while the Second World War was within living memory, it had become difficult to point to anything in cricket or life – buildings, clothing, belongings, attitudes, even language – that was like the war years.

For a while after the war, bomber service was something to be proud of. When he stood, unsuccessfully, for the Liberal Party in the 1966 federal election in Adelaide, Ross Stanford included his war record in his biography, as something of merit. Bomber airmen, unfairly, alone of the veterans of 1939–45 became labelled as criminal by liberals, frightened of the nuclear war they were powerless to prevent. Campaigners against nuclear war turned their fear and anger on the ageing, ever weaker, men who did the nearest Second World War equivalent. Such was the gratitude of some for not being slaves of Germany or Japan. Australia came to regard its bomber veterans not with disgust but with indifference.

Fighting a European war seemed ever more irrelevant to a land now turning to eastern Asia and the United States rather than the Old Country, which itself was turning to America or continental Europe rather than the English-speaking Commonwealth.

Some bomber veterans were not the first or last to find they had more in common with the men who once tried to kill them. A Western Australia bomber veteran I met in 1998, Angus Belford, recalled a 1975 gathering between German and Allied air force veterans: 'The fact that they were Germans was like after a footy match – there was nothing personal in it.'

Belford has a link with this story. His 1995 memoir, *Born to Fly*, centred on the mission he flew on the night of March 5, 1945. Flak over the target wounded his two gunners and damaged his Lancaster. He crash-landed in

France. The following night, when Belford returned to 463 Squadron, Reg Ellis was surely among the unnamed crews who heard the extraordinary tale of survival. Ellis was a fellow pilot, but new on squadron, while Belford was one of the longest-serving – aged 21 the next month! Even if men are able to speak of such times, when death was so close and so easy, it is hard to bridge the gap to understanding. For bombing is in no way like a footy match. Football of whatever code does not flatten cities or kill half its players. Veterans of sport do not have nightmares that wake them in sweat, with memories too upsetting to ever share.

As every Test-playing country has been part of the British Empire and never gone to war with another (leaving aside the Boer War; and any fighting when Britain brought the countries into the empire), we are at least spared lazy and insulting comparisons between cricket and war, as when England play Germany or Argentina at football.

John Dewes did speak of a difference between *competition*, when all men on a sports field compete, because they want to do well, as in 1945 – and *malice*, as he felt, aimed at him in later Ashes matches. By way of explaining the Australian way of beating the 'Poms', he punched his clenched left fist into his open right hand. And while the utter difference between sport and war holds good, on hearing John Dewes' flesh smack flesh there was no mistaking his strength of feeling, even a lifetime later. Reg Ellis said something similar: 'We all got on well. Even the batsmen you were trying to get out, you were all friends once that's finished; cricket was totally different then.'

That said, it was to Steve Waugh's credit that as captain of Australia he took his men to the battlefield of Gallipoli before the 2001 Ashes in England. Waugh and his team posed for photographs where Australians did play cricket in 1915, seeking to fool the Turks as the Allies sought to leave. Waugh was both honouring the past and drawing strength from the Anzac legend. It was hard to think of an English captain in any sport with the intelligence and authority to lead an equivalent visit. When England's team did visit a First World War cemetery at Ypres, before the 2009 Ashes, it had the forced look of a newspaper sports page-filling exercise (in England and Australia).

Why did Waugh not visit RAF Waddington, Driffield, or Binbrook, the airfield homes of the Victory Test Australians of 1945 and their comrades? This is not to criticise Waugh. There is little to see: what was a concrete runway at Binbrook has returned to a wold farmer's field. The point: even to a man as proud of his country as Steve Waugh, the Victory Tests and the wartime cricket that led to 1945 were less known.

As so often, the reasons are practical. Post-war English cricket's two most influential broadcasters, John Arlott and EW Swanton, for different reasons were not on the scene in 1945. Gallipoli was a suitable subject for the cinema; a years-long bomber campaign in the dark is not. Nor, indeed, is cricket. In such a televisual era, a broadcaster will screen past Ashes years only if he has the rights to (colour) moving pictures. By that reckoning 2005 existed; 1981, barely; 1945 did not. Besides, the Victory Tests never became a 'proper' Ashes series, and never counted in *Wisden*. The Victory Tests and indeed the carefree summer of 1945 became cricket's Dead Sea Scrolls; the Victory series did not fit in cricket's Bible. The potential that the Victory Test spirit had to change men's thinking soon passed, if the chance was ever truly there. Perhaps it was as Don Bradman said in his 1950 book *Farewell to Cricket* – when he was careful to add the view of Bill O'Reilly, not one usually to agree with Bradman:

Tests, both men felt, especially between Australia and England, were 'not a light-hearted business'.

You did have to query the moral priorities of Bradman, O'Reilly and all the other civilians too hard-hearted, or too set in their ways, to learn from war veterans. That London and Manchester (and Darwin) had been under bombs, and Sydney and Melbourne had not, was one more difference, more room for misunderstanding, between people who happened to speak the same language and play the same games.

An Englishman simply had to show respect to a visitor risking his life to save him from Hitler. Ross Stanford told a story that must date from the North versus RAAF on Saturday, July 19, 1944. Bear in mind that George Duckworth was a tourist on the Bodyline series, a man who had seen and done everything a cricketer could:

> *We were either playing Lancashire or the North of England, and George Duckworth was the captain, and he was the wicket-keeper. And I was batting and it was one of the worst innings I ever played in my life, I think. I hadn't hit a ball in the middle of the bat, and I started complaining to myself out loud about this, and George Duckworth said to me, from behind the wicket, 'Don't get out.' Which wasn't the usual thing for an opposing skipper or anyone to say to a batsman from the opposing side. But that was the sporting attitude that was going on in the games that we played against the counties. And all the various teams that we played against. Marvellous. Absolutely marvellous.*

The typically dry *Manchester Guardian* report on the Monday said only that Stanford 'made a few lucky snicks at the start but then disclosed a nice variety of strokes'. Stanford was bowled by Constantine for 73, the RAAF's top score, another example of the form of his life in that summer of war. The Australians set the North 221 in two and a half hours. The 49-year-old Herbert Sutcliffe, opening, 'survived with incomparable dignity a suspiciously unanimous appeal for leg before wicket' according to the *Guardian* – suggesting that the umpires were trying not to give out that great retired player. Sutcliffe was leg before to Cristofani for three. Sismey kept wicket admirably to 'erratic bowling of all paces', as the *Guardian* put it, and Winston Place, Learie Constantine and above all Washbrook, with 133 not out, won, with 'one or two minutes to spare'. You could not wish for a more satisfying day's cricket.

Mercifully, as the veterans entered extreme old age, new wars (alas) threw a more forgiving light on the bomber veterans of 1939–45. In 1991, Australians and Englishmen played a 'Test' in northern Iraq, during supply of aid to Kurdish refugees. Whatever the part of the world, however wretched the time, a game of cricket made sense of things; the result hardly mattered. (Australia won.)

The last enemy, as Richard Hillary knew from his Bible, was death. The very fact that the summer of 1945 was so forgotten afterwards has left it pure. In his 1981 interview, Miller recalled that by the Australian leg of the Victory tour:

> ...*the boys were pretty fed up with cricket then and they didn't do very well and that was that ... but as far as I was concerned all of the cricket I played before and subsequently the Victory series in England was the most exciting and the best cricket I have ever played in my life, the reason being that a lot of the people were happy that the war was over, there was no money*

involved, and you just played for the sake of playing cricket.

The swift rise of the Indian Premier League threatens England and Australia's complacency that five-day games between themselves are the pinnacle of cricket. The very best cricketers of the 21st century, the Millers of their day, will see everything as a stepping stone to earning a fortune with an Indian city franchise. Yet the more the cricketers of the future are hailed as heroes, the more clothes and body spray and beer their faces, chests and voices sell, the punier they will be compared to the men of 1945.

Cricketers cannot help it, any more than the rest of us. They spoil what they achieve, thanks to some later failure, or simply the deadening crush of year on year. The name dies before the man, as Housman put it. The Victory Tests are there, if anyone ever wants to know about a summer when people embraced cricket, for itself, and because it stood for something greater: for goodwill between free people. Something greater even than the Ashes.

Pen portraits

Players

Keith Campbell: On returning to Australia in 1943, his war was not over; he flew in New Guinea, and got malaria. After playing for a Queensland country eleven against the Indian tourists in 1947, he gave up cricket for golf. In Brisbane in 2010, after his 90th birthday, he hit his first hole in one.

Keith Carmody: Named by Miller as captain of 'an eleven I'd really like to play for'. He left his native Sydney and became captain of Western Australia, winning the Sheffield Shield in 1947–8. Born 1919. *Wisden* obituary 1978.

Donald Carr: Oxford Blue 1949–51, university captain 1950. Toured India with MCC in 1951–2 and played in two Tests. Captained Derbyshire, scored over 18,000 first-class runs. A *Wisden* cricketer of the year 1960.

Learie Constantine: A *Wisden* cricketer of the year 1940. In 1945 the West Indian was passing from the first half of his life – as a well-paid, crowd-pleasing northern league cricketer – to the second half, of public service in Trinidad and England; and a peerage. The dwindling of Hammond after retirement was sad by contrast. Born 1902. *Wisden* 1972.

Hartley Craig: This Adelaide first-grade left-handed batsman was arguably the least fortunate Australian Services player; less cautious selectors may have picked him ahead of Jim Workman. Born 1917. *Wisden* 2008.

Bob Cristofani: Hardly played for New South Wales after the war. Entered Australian government service, settled and died in England. Born 1920. *Wisden* 2003.

John Dewes: Cambridge Blue 1948–50, toured Australia in 1950–1 and played there in two Tests, five in all. Went into teaching: was a master at Rugby then headmaster of a suburban Sydney private school in Hornsby, 1957–62.

Bill Edrich: A *Wisden* cricketer of the year 1940. The Norfolk farmer's boy knew, and said, that cricket had been good to him. He knew too that he had been freakishly lucky to survive as a pilot in 1941, and like Miller and other survivors lived to the full accordingly; an insight denied to – or ignored by – Bradman and the other safe-at-homes, especially once the war was over. Born 1916. *Wisden* 1987.

Reg Ellis: Hassett trusted this studious left arm leg-break bowler with most overs in the Victory Tests. Stan Sismey's death in June 2009 left him as the last Australian Victory Test survivor, living in the part of Adelaide in which he grew up.

Laurie Fishlock: An attacking left-hand batsman when England had so many bats to choose from. Two Tests before the war, two after, including one in Australia in 1947. A *Wisden* cricketer of the year 1947 (with Washbrook). Born 1907. *Wisden* 1987.

Alf Gover: This fast bowler's run to the wicket, RC Robertson-Glasgow reckoned, was 'rather as if he were exchanging insults at extreme range with the flighty conductor of an omnibus that had the legs of him by half a mile per hour'. A *Wisden* cricketer of the year 1937. Ran famous south London coaching school into old age. Born 1908. *Wisden* 2002.

Billy Griffith: A glider pilot in 1944. Played three post-war Tests overseas. Was Marylebone Cricket Club secretary from 1962 to 1974. Born 1914. *Wisden* 1994.

Walter Hammond: The greatest English bat of his time, and the cricketer Robertson-Glasgow most wanted to be, may however have meant himself when he wrote: 'I have known cricketers of perfectly equable temperaments cheerful and light-hearted when they entered the game grow morose and explosive as they got older because of the gnawing worry of what they were to do after retirement at 40 or before.' A *Wisden* cricketer of the year 1928. Born 1903. *Wisden* 1966.

Lindsay Hassett: A *Wisden* cricketer of the year 1949. It says much about the cultural backgrounds of Australians of their era that Whitington and Miller wrote: 'If Lindsay Hassett had been knocking about old London in the days of Sam Weller and David Copperfield, Charles Dickens must surely have written yet another novel.' The great novelist may indeed have been drawn to the little Australian with impish humour – and a sense of right and wrong. Born 1913. *Wisden* 1994.

Len Hutton: A *Wisden* cricketer of the year 1938. 'Yorkshire granite', according to the southerner Edrich. More insightfully Edrich called the first professional captain of England a 'private worrier' who struggled to throw off the habit of bowing to amateurs. Not a gambler, according to Godfrey Evans, 'unless there only happens to be one horse in the race'. Jack Fingleton, a fellow opener, judged him: 'Not one to underestimate the difficulties of a batsman.' Born 1916. *Wisden* 1991.

Keith Miller: Not a *Wisden* cricketer of the year until 1953. Cricket critic for the then leading London daily newspaper, the *Daily Express*, 1956–76. Bradman, like a schoolmaster marking down a gifted pupil he disliked, wrote in his *Farewell to Cricket* in 1950 of 'failure to concentrate'. The West Indian journalist CLR James, in a private letter to Jack Fingleton, called Miller's journalism 'slapdash'. That could have been James' envy of a newcomer walking into the trade at the top; two approaches to life clashing; or a truth. Born 1919. *Wisden* 2005.

Cec Pepper: Crusader, the *Brighton Evening Argus* sports reporter, in 1945 called him '16 stone of radiating happiness who always moves as if he is always engaged in a hundred yards sprint'. Arguably the typical burly loud Aussie, it spoke volumes about supposedly matey Australian society that he made his home as a league cricketer, then umpire, in England. Born 1916. *Wisden* 1994.

Jack Pettiford: Played for New South Wales after the war. Like several other Australians of his time, he sought a living from cricket in England in the 1950s; first in northern leagues, then for Kent. Born 1919. *Wisden* 1965.

Dick Pollard: Everyone agreed about this Lancashire fast-medium bowler: 'a magnificent trier'. A piano player. As with Voce, Gover and Bowes, it was not his fault he was a better bowler before wartime than after. Born 1912. *Wisden* 1986.

George Pope: Sir Michael Parkinson's affectionate obituary in 1993 spoke of 'a master of his craft' – on, and off, the field, as Parkinson made clear: including the gift of the gab with dangerous opponents, and umpires. Despite leading England's Victory Test attack, he played only one proper Test, in 1947. Born 1911. *Wisden* 1994.

Charlie Price: the Australians' 'unconscious humorist … a dreamer and roamer, to whom the ordinary things of life meant little', Whitington and Miller wrote. One of the Army reinforcements, he would not have lasted long as a bomber navigator; he left London once for Chester, and arrived at Chester-le-Street. Born 1917. *Wisden* 1998.

John Robertson: Averaged 46 in his 11 Tests after the war. Played his part in Middlesex's 1947 county championship win, and was a *Wisden* cricketer of the year 1948. Born 1917. *Wisden* 1997.

Stan Simsey: This Catalina flying boat pilot based in Scotland, who married a Scotswoman in August 1945, lost his place in the New South Wales side to Ron Saggers, himself an understudy on the 1948 Invincibles tour to Don Tallon. Born 1916. *Wisden* 2010.

Ross Stanford: Scored a record 416 as a schoolboy. He worked in the State Bank of South Australia, then went onto 25 acres of market garden with his father and brother in the Adelaide suburb of West Torrens. He played a few times for his state after the war, including against the 1946–7 England tourists. Into old age he did fund-raising work for the Leonard Cheshire Foundation. Born 1917. *Wisden* 2007.

Jack Stephenson: When serving on the Anzio beachhead in Italy in 1944, he set up cricket nets on the sand, the pitch 'rolled' twice a day, so he said, by the tide. To some, this was what made England great. Born 1907. *Wisden* 1983.

Cyril Washbrook: A 'knowledgeable cricketer as well as a magnificent batsman and he misses nothing of the game', John Arlott wrote in 1949; in 1945 he and Hutton made England's opening partnership theirs for the next few, difficult, years. Born 1914. *Wisden* 2000.

Luke White: After the third Victory Test, his first-class debut, he batted once for Middlesex in 1946 and played only a handful more first-class matches. Became Fifth Baron Annaly. Born 1927. *Wisden* 1991.

Dick Whitington: Wrote several books on Australian cricket; worked as a newspaper journalist. A man of insight and humour. Deplored South Africa's exclusion from Test cricket in the 1970s. Born 1912. *Wisden* 1985.

Graham Williams: The returned prisoner of war's walk to the wicket at Lord's during the first Victory Test, greeted by the sincere applause of tens of thousands, so moved Miller. 'A really popular bloke,' Stanford said of him in old age. 'We had some good blokes in the team.' Born 1911. *Wisden* 1980.

Jim Workman: As his surname implied, and as Wisden said of him after the 1944 season, he 'resembled WM Woodfull in his lack of strokes and abundance of determination'. Sadly, Australians have since denied their tradition of slow-scoring opening bats. Born 1917. *Wisden* 1971.

Doug Wright: A *Wisden* cricketer of the year 1940. The spin bowler was, so an anonymous Victory Test Australian said, 'too consistently good'. Was that a way of saying Eric Hollies (who got Miller out twice in a day at Blackpool in August 1945) was better? Born 1914. *Wisden* 1999.

Reporters

Bob Crisp: Former opening bowler for South Africa, won the DSO and MC in tanks in North Africa, landed on the Normandy beaches on the afternoon of D-Day. Wounded and freakishly lucky to survive. By 1945, turning 34, anything – even a staff job on the *Daily Express* – was tame by comparison. Born 1911. *Wisden* 1995.

CB Fry: Once opened the batting for England with WG Grace in the reign of Queen Victoria; a *Wisden* cricketer of the year 1895; all-round sportsman; man of affairs and writer and broadcaster until late in life. Met Hitler in 1934. In his 1939 memoir *Life Worth Living*, Charles Fry spoke of the German leader's 'innate dignity'. Born 1872. *Wisden* 1957.

RC Robertson-Glasgow: He called his reports naturalistic. 'Flippancy was never far absent,' he wrote in his memoir *46 Not Out*, 'because cricketers, especially bowlers, need flippancy to live …' He was a bowler, for Oxford University and Somerset, nicknamed Crusoe after someone mistook his surname. Yet was not the fictional Robinson Crusoe a great and honest story-teller, too? Born 1901. *Wisden* 1965.

Sir Pelham Warner: A *Wisden* cricketer of the year 1904. Like Sir Donald Bradman, he wrote long and well about cricket, which is not the same as saying he wrote frankly and all he could. To earn a knighthood takes discretion, besides achievement. Born 1873. *Wisden* 1964.

Chester Wilmot: A most able man of affairs, at home in newspapers, on radio and later the infant television. His death at 42 in a Comet jet airliner crash in 1954 denied him the legacy he deserved. Born 1911.

Characters off stage

Sir Donald Bradman: A *Wisden* cricketer of the year 1931. The most successful batsman of all time always prompted grumbles. Bill Edrich called him 'coldly efficient and practical'. Nor did that many Australian players of his generation care for him. Like Winston Churchill, thanks to his undeniable record, his sure touch, his pen, and not least his long life and influence, Bradman saw off the unimpressed like Miller and the war generation. Born 1908. *Wisden* 2002.

Neville Cardus: Having dodged the 1914–18 war in England, arguably the most famous cricket writer of his time did even better in 1940 and put *two* oceans between himself and war, in Sydney, as a newspaper's music critic. It was the act of a man blinkered to all except himself, music and cricket. Born 1890. *Wisden* 1976.

Hedley Verity: A *Wisden* cricketer of the year 1932. In his book of the 1936–7 tour of Australia, Cardus wrote of how the Yorkshire left-arm spinner read TE Lawrence's *Seven Pillars of Wisdom*, 'from beginning to end'. He died after leading men in battle in Sicily in 1943. The foreword to a post-war book of tributes was, needless to say, by Bradman. Born 1905. *Wisden* 1944.

Sources and Thanks

This book began when a 68-op bomber veteran in Adelaide called Dave Leicester drove me to Ross Stanford's house one summer November weekday in 1998. I began interviewing Australian veterans of Bomber Command in the winter of 1998 in Sydney after I watched the city Anzac Day parade pass by. I was on a day off from working as a kitchen hand at St Vincent's Hospital – I was in Australia on a one-year working holiday visa – and from seeing one of the banners carried by veterans it struck me that Australian airmen had served in Britain in the war. Ross Pearson, author of a two-volume history of the Australian air force in the 1939–45 war, was the first I spoke to. If I have written too much about Bomber Command and not enough about cricket, it's only because, for combat airmen, cricket was an after thought. In Don Charlwood's vivid metaphor, the living were the tip of the iceberg of the dead.

In Adelaide I met Bomber Command veterans and their wives – not mentioned in this book – of the generation that grew up as Bradman made his name. They, if anyone, ought to have believed, as I did naively, that Sir Donald Bradman was an undisputed great man. Instead they spoke scathingly of Bradman's war-dodging (for one thing).

In 2003 I brought out *The Luckiest Men Alive: Australians in Bomber Command in Britain in the Second World War*. I regret that I only turned to the Victory Tests in 2008. In the previous ten years, important characters – Cristofani, Keith Miller – had died. In 1998 in a flat in Kensington I shared with seven women (!) I marvelled at reading KR Miller's name and address in the Sydney telephone directory.

I had heard, third hand, how unwell he was, but something held me back from trying to meet him. Was it natural shyness, not a good trait in a journalist; a feeling that it was not for me to approach someone so famous, not a good trait either; or a sense that no good would come of it? As it turns out, Miller had already spoken and written fully about his cricket – indeed, more than some had liked at the time. But I do not believe he said all that he felt, deeply, about his war service. You can read Miller's 43-page service record online at www.naa.gov.au. The National Library of Australia in Canberra holds the transcript of its 1981 interview with Miller. Chester Wilmot's papers are there. His history of D-Day and after, *The Struggle for Europe*, a great achievement in 1952 and still fresh, is easily found second hand.

As more background reading, Roland Perry's *Keith Miller: The Life of a Great All-rounder* (2005) sensibly stresses 1945 as the making of Miller. Dick Whitington's biography of Miller, *The Golden Nugget* (1981) has the plus and minus points of a biographer having shared the life of his subject. Biographers of Bradman such as Charles Williams (1996) have, so far, left the war years alone with as straight a bat as they can. See, though, the various viewpoints in *Remembering Bradman* by Margaret Geddes (2002).

I found Donald Carr from his entry in *Who's Who*; he suggested I ask Marylebone Cricket Club to pass on a request to contact John Dewes. I thank them all. I am grateful to the library at Lord's cricket ground. I read newspapers of the day at the British Library's newspaper library at Colindale in north London; Manchester and Birmingham central libraries; Coventry History Centre; Gloucestershire record office, and libraries in Bradford, Leeds, Bristol, Northampton, Nottingham, High

Wycombe, Brighton, Eastbourne, and Hastings; and the Magic Attic archive in Swadlincote, Derbyshire.

Peter Wynne-Thomas, archivist at Nottinghamshire County Cricket Club, was kind enough to face the short-pitched ideas I threw at him. The museum at Edgbaston was an oasis on an otherwise profoundly alienating and frankly not that exciting Twenty20 finals day in August 2009. Chris Highton, the chairman of Selkirk cricket club, kindly sent me a photograph of Sismey's tree. I read Australian newspapers in the New South Wales State Library in Sydney.

At the National Archives at Kew, the squadron log books featuring Ross Stanford are AIR 27/1930 and AIR 27/1931 (467 squadron) and AIR 27/2128 (617 Squadron). For Keith Miller's two combat missions with 169 Squadron, AIR 27/1094; Reg Ellis on 463 Squadron, AIR 27/1922; Keith Carmody on 455 Squadron, AIR 27/1898; Keith Campbell and the first days of 458 Squadron in 1941-2, AIR 27/1902. The Australian War Memorial website www.awm.gov.au has many images of wartime cricket.

Besides his memoir of Bomber Command, *No Moon Tonight*, Don Charlwood returned movingly to the same subject, 'like looking back on a mountain range crossed in youth', in *Journeys Into Night* (1991). Or, see his 1986 essay in the *Journal of the Australian War Memorial*, on the AWM website, as an introduction to his unsettling and profound questioning. *Bombs Away: The Story of a Bomber Team* (1942) by John Steinbeck tells the same sort of story, only about Americans, and brings out the link between a sports team and a bomber crew. For more on 617 Squadron in Ross Stanford's day, see Andrew Boyle's 1955 biography of Leonard Cheshire, *No Passing Glory*.

You can read the Victory Test scorecards and many others from 1945 on incredibly detailed websites such as www.cricketarchive.com, or in the 1946 *Wisden*. The internet has made record books such as Whitington's *Australians Abroad* (1983) out of date, but it's worth picking up for the stories dotted around it. For numbers never tell the full story; people do. Hence the pleasures of reading around the subject; and meeting people.

For their hospitality I thank Reg Ellis and his daughter and son-in-law, Wendy and Graham Ottaway, in Adelaide; in Brisbane, Keith Campbell – I remember fondly my lamington for lunch, and the view from Mount Coot-tha; and in Mittagong, New South Wales, my old colleague William Verity and his Australian wife Caroline. An idea of William's helped me to trace Reg Ellis.

In cricket as elsewhere, many bad books are merely regurgitations of others. Not so *Gentlemen and Players: Conversations with Cricketers*, by Michael Marshall (1987), which lays out English cricket before and after 1945. *The History of Cricket from the Weald to the World*, by Peter Wynne-Thomas (1997), sets the even wider scene. So does *The Art of Captaincy* by Mike Brearley – the 1985 original hardback and the second, paperback edition with a 2001 retrospect. For photos of the Australian cricketers at Gallipoli in 1915 and 2001, see for instance *Steve Waugh*, by Peter FitzSimons (2004).

Cricket Not War is a limited-edition book on the Victory Test series from the Australian side, by Ian Woodward, published in Australia in 1994. Gerald Howat's 1975 biography of Learie Constantine explains that pioneering man; *As It Was, The Memoirs of Fred Trueman* (2004) explains that man and the England, starting afresh after 1945, into which he emerged.

Douglas Jardine's *In Quest of the Ashes* (1933) gives an understandably one-sided account of the Bodyline series, which cast long shadows; it reminds the reader also of the subtle, mixed and sometimes surprising feelings that the English and Australians can have for one another. Other contemporary books, even ones barely touching on 1945, at least give a flavour of the time. Some, in author order: *How to Watch Cricket*, by John Arlott (1949). *The Art of Cricket*, by Sir Donald Bradman (1958) and *Farewell to Cricket* (1948). *Cricketers' Cricket*, by Learie Constantine (1949). *Hedley Verity: Prince with a Piece of Leather*, by Sam Davis (1952). *Cricket Heritage*, by WJ Edrich (1948). *The Ashes Crown the Year: A Coronation Cricket Diary*, by JH Fingleton (1954). *Cricket My World*, by Walter Hammond (1958). *Cricket is my Life*, by Len Hutton (1949). *Cricket Decade: England v Australia 1946 to 1956*, by JM Kilburn (1960). *Keith Miller Companion*, by Keith Miller and RS Whitington (1955). *Cricket Crossfire*, by Keith Miller (1956). *Cricket Conquest: The Story of the 1948 Test Tour*, by WJ O'Reilly (1949). *Spinner's Yarn*, by Ian Peebles (1977). *Cricket Prints: Some batsmen and bowlers 1920–1940*, by RC Robertson-Glasgow (1943). *Lord's 1787–1945*, by Sir Pelham Warner (1946).

Richie Benaud's autobiography *Anything But* (1998) and Colin McCool's *Cricket is a Game* (1961) each give a sense of how it was to be a young Australian sportsman in those days. Sir Michael Parkinson's articles on George Pope and Keith Miller come from his 1996 paperback *Sporting Profiles: Sixty Heroes of Sport*. Trevor Bailey's 1986 memoir *Wickets, Catches and the Odd Run* is enjoyable although he could not remember any of his wartime games, 'just the fun'.

In the summer of 1945, George Orwell – a forlorn lover of cricket and AE Housman as a youth – began work on his novel *Nineteen Eighty-Four*. Early on, the hero Winston Smith tries in vain to learn from an old man in a pub about life before Big Brother. How much could be told, only has been lost! How little I recall of the cricket I have ever played! I welcome the chance to apologise to Winsley

Sources and Thanks

Cricket Club in Wiltshire, for my career highest score of 31 not out, made for them in April 1992, in 108 balls and 117 minutes. (Or was it the other way round?) It has been a comfort, reading men now dead, to feel that RC Robertson-Glasgow, for one, would have had sympathy for me.

Mark Rowe
chiprowe@hotmail.com
Burton upon Trent, Staffordshire, January–May and
August 2009; Australia, June–July 2009

INDEX

Index

Index

Index